ETHNIC

POWER

MOBILIZED

Can
South Africa
Change?

Heribert Adam and
Hermann Giliomee

ETHNIC POWER MOBILIZED
Can South Africa Change?

Ethnic Power Mobilized:
Can South Africa Change?

Heribert Adam and Hermann Giliomee

New Haven and London
Yale University Press   1979

For Francine, Adrienne, Kanya, and Maya

Published under the auspices of the
Southern African Research Program.

Designed by Thos. Whitridge
and set in VIP Palatino type.
Printed in the United States of America

Published in Great Britain, Europe, Africa (except Southern Africa), and Asia (except Japan) by Yale University Press, Ltd., London; and in Southern Africa by David Philip, Publisher (Pty) Ltd., Cape Town. Distributed in Australia and New Zealand by Book & Film Services, Artarmon, N.S.W., Australia; and in Japan by Harper & Row, Publishers, Tokyo Office.

Library of Congress Cataloging in Publication Data

Adam, Heribert.
  Ethnic power mobilized.

  Includes index.
    1. Afrikaners—South Africa—Ethnic identity.
  2. South Africa—Race relations.   3. South Africa—
  Politics and government—1961–   I. Giliomee,
  Hermann, joint author.   II. Title.
  DT888.A3 1979   301.45′19′6068   78-65492
  ISBN 0-300-02377-4
  ISBN 0-300-02378-2 pbk.

Contents

CONTENTS

Tables

Preface

This book results from a carefully coordinated division of inquiry by a historian and a sociologist. As fellows at Yale University we found ourselves working on an identical question: Can South Africa change without destroying itself in the process? We decided to pool our different disciplinary expertise without submerging our individual perspectives and styles. Therefore, each author attached his name to the pieces for which he alone bears responsibility. But we believe these chapters hang together by consistently probing a crucial argument with systematically collected evidence.

Our study concerns itself mainly with the ruling Afrikaner group. This should not imply that the dominant group has the sole initiative to determine policy. The South African government increasingly has to react to internal and external pressures alike. However, it will be argued that cleavages and currents within the ruling ethnic group—rather than the actions of the subordinates—are likely to influence South Africa's future in the short-run. It is hoped that a planned analysis of black politics by one author (H.A.) will adequately complement this investigation.

The book examines interrelated aspects of white hegemony. With an emphasis on historical process, chapters 4, 6, and 7 discuss the evolving self-concept of the Afrikaners and their economic advance, highlighting the extent to which specific interests rather than an immutable ideology condition Afrikaner strategies. Chapter 8 describes the political structures of the ruling National Party and the processes of decision making and legitimation. Chapter 2 critically evaluates the diverse perspectives in the vast literature on South Africa. The concept of ethnic mobilization (chapter 3) is explored in order to understand the present ideological redefinition (chapter 5). Finally, the failure of political liberalism (chapter 9) is analyzed in conjunction with the current debate on political alternatives (chapter 10) in South Africa.

We share the dissatisfaction with many of the approaches and focuses in the dominant literature on South Africa, particularly the emphasis on racism and prejudice. The perspective of political economy, on the other hand, clearly explains more than attitude surveys. However, mere class analysis frequently is too dogmatic to come to terms with ethnic ideologies. A key lies in viewing ethnicity, as anthropologist Abner Cohen rightly stresses, as basically a political and not a cultural phenomenon.[1] But labor, capital, and markets, while never sufficient as monocausal explanations, do determine the organizational needs from which ethnic ideologies emanate and with which they dialectically interact.

The empirical data for this study derive essentially from three sources: (1) a comprehensive review of the recent academic and nonacademic literature on South Africa in three languages (English, Afrikaans, and German). This includes all available opinion surveys and relevant statistics, many journalistic accounts, particularly the systematic content analysis of editorials in the Afrikaans press as well as the current affairs comments of the South African Broadcasting Corporation. Another part of the reviewed data consists of numerous special reports by government agencies and international institutions as well as the literature of most opposition groups, from street leaflets of protest groups in Cape Town to the pamphlets of the Black Consciousness Movement and exile movements. (2) Almost more valuable then the written testimonies were the informal talks with key political actors and experts at about two dozen international conferences on South Africa in which one or both of us actively participated during the past five years. These gatherings—an increasingly thriving business of its own for special reasons—form, never-

1. Abner Cohen (ed.), *Urban Ethnicity* (London: Tavistock, 1974), "Introduction: The Lesson of Ethnicity."

theless, a crucial source of information. The nuances of direct discourse, particularly when the arguments represent the full spectrum of political views, such as during several Mount Kisco sessions and the unique Freiburg conference, add an important dimension to the more considered public statements. (3) Finally, our third source of data emanates from conventional interviews with selected policymakers in South Africa during July and August 1978.

The study owes its very conception to the generous support of the Southern African Research Program at Yale University, funded by the National Endowment for the Humanities and the Ford Foundation. By inviting us to a year's residence at Yale as fellows with few commitments or strings attached, the program's directors—Leonard Thompson, William Foltz, and Stanley Greenberg—provided the structural framework for an ideal intellectual exercise. There must be few places where academics have so genuinely and enthusiastically shared their resources and disciplinary interests in the same problem. We remember the weekly seminars and rotating Thursday evening discussions as stimulating highlights of intense, uninterrupted reading periods. During these sessions part of this book in the form of first drafts has been exposed to the trained skepticism of our Yale colleagues and also to our cofellows Richard Ralston and Newell Stultz. Despite our candid mutual criticism, all of us remained friends.

The insights of André du Toit, who joined the group in its last three months, further challenged us to clarify contradictions. To J. L. Sadie and S. J. Terreblanche we are very much indebted for providing detailed socioeconomic statistics on the Afrikaner economic position. With Anthony Delius, F. van Zyl Slabbert, and Lawrence Schlemmer we shared memorable discussions on various occasions.

In addition to these common influences on our work we have accumulated intellectual debts individually. Heribert Adam would like to single out his wife Kogila as his foremost critic. Her unique experiences at the receiving end of the South African system frequently raised doubts about attempts at dispassionate scholarship on such a trying subject. It was always a joy to argue about South Africa comparatively with such seasoned observers as Hamish Dickie-Clark, Pierre van den Berghe, and Theo Hanf.

Hermann Giliomee owes valuable criticism and help to many friends and colleagues in South Africa. In alphabetical order they are: Piet Cillié, René de Villiers, Dian Joubert, Bernard Lategan, Jeffrey Lever, Andrew Nash, Lourens Pretorius, Gerald Shaw, Nico Smith, and Marinus Wiechers. Without the understanding of his wife, Annette, the chapters would not have been completed in time and writing would have been an even lonelier business.

Those public figures in the cabinet and Pretoria administration whom we interviewed individually we thank best by leaving unnamed. Thus they cannot be embarrassed by possible accusations that they might have contributed to our heresies, for which of course we alone are responsible.

First drafts of several chapters were also presented to different public audiences by the respective authors: Chapter 2 to a conference on Canadian and Scandinavian policy alternatives toward Southern Africa at Carleton University in Ottawa in February 1978, and subsequently at Brown University; parts of chapters 8 and 9 to the Institute of International Affairs at the University of California, Berkeley in March and April 1978; and the Introduction and Chapter 4 to the "Road Ahead" Conference of the 1820 Settler Monument in Grahamstown, South Africa in July 1978.

We owe thanks to the comments of these audiences as well as to the searching questions of our students with whom we discussed most of these issues in the classroom. It is to our youngest students—our children—that this book is dedicated in the hope that they may be able to live and play together in a more just, new South Africa.

Heribert Adam
Hermann Giliomee

January 1979

1 Introduction Heribert Adam

The vast critical literature on South Africa almost unanimously emphasizes the *benefits* of black exclusion for the ruling white group. Perhaps the time has come to examine the rising *costs* of this privilege maintenance. Costs must not be calculated only in narrow financial terms. In a wider sense, costs result from threats and the precautionary defense of a system. Negative changes in the quality of life, even missed opportunities for human enrichment, may be part of "social costs." Cost assessments are relative, dependent on who makes the calculation. Three main interest groups stand out: (1) the Western powers, (2) the blacks in South Africa, (3) the South African government, that is, Nationalist Afrikanerdom, which holds the key to the cost-benefit ratio.

From the perspective of Western policymakers, the internationalization of the Southern African conflict since the collapse of the Portuguese colonial empire in 1974 has meant a threatening direct East-West competition for regional hegemony. Legalized racial exclusion of a black majority by a white minority is increasingly seen as a costly liability. Relics of colonialism, with which international capital is portrayed as closely intertwined, have become a safe recipe for antiWestern sentiment. An American report ponders: "What juicier example could Communist propaganda ask to depict the alleged decadence and racism of the capitalist system?"[1]

1. Bruce Oudes, *Report on a Symposium on South Africa: Issues and Policy Implications for the United States* (Mount Kisco, N.Y.: Seven Springs Center, 1978), p. 19. The report also asks: "Why should the Soviets stress an early military solution in South Africa when, at no cost in hardware, it can watch the West squirm as Moscow modestly supports in Southern Africa an ideological struggle?"

1

The risks of having to bail out a stubborn ally, therefore, are contemplated with unease among affected Wall Street bankers and British Tories alike. Above all, corporate investment policy requires *predictability*. This presupposes long-term *stability*. Multinationals prefer dealing with reliable Communist foes rather than with unstable ideological friends. In terms of image-making, too visible an association with white South Africa can be disadvantageous, particularly for vote-seeking politicians. The ceaseless rhetoric against South Africa, couched as moral indignation, now reflects a shrewd disassociation from a leper among nations. A more credible image of cleaner hands is sought, particularly for the increasingly important dealings with black Africa. More direct involvement of the West in bolstering bankrupt African regimes against Cuban/Russian imperialism may well necessitate greater demonstrations of moral purity toward South Africa.

From the South African domestic perspective these outside signals are registered with fury. The manifest anti-American sentiment of Pretoria not only aims at rallying the doubtful behind the leadership in the name of patriotism but also reflects frustration over the dependency on the West for capital, expertise, markets, and diplomatic support. Pretoria's defiant postures indicate the anger with which Afrikanerdom is being forced to react to external and internal pressure alike. While white South Africa would like "to go it alone," it cannot afford to adopt an isolationist stance. The initiative to shape policy no longer rests with Pretoria alone.

On the other hand, more vociferous outside rejection does not mean greater vulnerability of South Africa. On the contrary, threatened sanctions and isolation may well strengthen domestic productive diversification and thereby reduce outside dependency. Through economic and military collaboration with other condemned pariah nations, particularly Israel, Pretoria substitutes for the few items not available locally.[2]

2. In the view of Afrikanerdom, there is room and need for a closer alliance of pariah nations: "Apart from South Africa's value as a trustworthy source of raw materials, there is for Israel the added element that it is also beginning to feel the weight of the West's caprices in its own person. This not only

The immense wealth in scarce minerals and long-established trade links make countries such as Britain more dependent on South Africa than vice versa.[3] Powerful interests in most Western states could successfully intervene if the anti-South African rhetoric was carried so far that it affected crucial business. The genuine liberal repulsion against a defiant racial oligarchy is always balanced by pro-South African interests. The factions frequently veto and paralyze each other. Besides, there exists in the West a basic racial solidarity with white South Africa. Widespread resentments against minorities at home and suspicions arising from repeated African atrocities elsewhere merge with sentiments for the whites, who are portrayed as the vulnerable underdog.

Outside pressures, whether real or fictitious, may have little more than symbolic effects on Pretoria's overall defensive capacity in the short run. But they operate in conjunction with the crucial internal events. African morale draws partly from the international constellation. Black perceptions in turn affect forms and frequency of resistance as highlighted in the township upheavals of 1976 or the ever threatening strikes of unorganized frustration. Spontaneous outbreaks of anger are far more difficult to contain and have wider implications than institutionalized conflict regulation based on mutually agreed upon rules. Prudent counsel, therefore, favors recognized, representative African unions with genuine bargaining power in place of disgruntled, unmotivated, and unproductive labor.

----

makes South Africa and Israel brothers in oppression, but also gives them a common interest. There must easily be a dozen other countries which are basically in the same position. To us it seems only sensible, despite problems of policy and other things, that these countries should draw closer to one another." (*Beeld,* February 14, 1978).

3. South Africa controls 80 percent of the Western world's chrome reserves, 89 percent of platinum, 75 percent of gold, 48 percent of vanadium, 60 percent of manganese, 50 percent of titanium, and 25 percent of uranium of known world reserves. The country has the potential to develop a ferroalloys and special steels industry that could rival precious metals and minerals as a foreign exchange earner. Also copper, lead, and zinc production is expected to increase dramatically.

In the absence of minimal consensus about a mutually acceptable conflict solution, the costs of maintaining white domination increase. To be sure, blacks bear most of it in the form of unequal wages, deprived opportunities, and denied life-chances. There also does not exist a zero sum relation: if costs are rising for the ruling group, it does not mean that they diminish for the subordinates, whose militancy may well bring its own costs. And yet the rulers also are affected by the rising cost spiral, although the benefits are still huge for those on the right side of the color/class line. However, with rising opposition these benefits decrease. If the trend continues, there will presumably be a point where the costs for whites outweigh the benefits: (1) Is such a trend discernible? If so, can this threshold be calculated, taking into account the perceptions of the Nationalist Afrikaners? (2) Above all, what strategies are open for the key Afrikaner group in the power structure to counteract escalating costs of its rule?

In one of the few attempts at assessing the direct costs of apartheid implementation in policing pass laws, doubling public facilities, and reshuffling population groups, Michael Savage has calculated that with a fraction of these costs an immediate and dramatic change in the quality of life in Soweto could have been financed.[4] However, such moral appeals overlook the various losses for white South Africa if apartheid were to be abolished. So far, it is still cheaper to manage with traditional policy. For the future this becomes increasingly doubtful. The rising costs of the defense budget comprise only the most visible aspect. Additional inflation brought about by undertrained, underutilized black labor and overpriced white workers add to the hidden costs. Above all, the likelihood of urban guerrilla warfare, although nowhere in a position to overthrow a determined government, has a magnified impact on the economic climate in South Africa.[5]

The future costs are difficult to control if newspaper reports

4. Michael Savage, "Costs of Enforcing Apartheid and Problems of Change," *African Affairs* 76, no. 304 (July 1977), 287–302.

5. Among the substantial evidence for the changed "risk assessment" of South Africa, statements by Gabriel Hauge, chairman of the Manufacturers

are correct that 25,000 young blacks have left the country as a result of the 1976–77 unrest. The belated insight of an Afrikaans paper illustrates the predicament: "This is the kind of investment we cannot afford. For it is an investment in hate and violence. There is a good chance that when South Africa again sees these young blacks it will be over the barrel of a gun."[6] When substantial numbers of people feel that they can no longer live in a political system and instead accept statelessness and the exigencies of exile, and moreover, when they are prepared to risk their lives for a political cause, then a true legitimation crisis of such a system has arisen. While the overwhelming majority of urban blacks still seek accommodation within the limited opportunities, though by no means as a matter of choice and voluntary consent, many politicized youngsters are impatiently searching for alternatives. Some may be ready to die if not yet to murder. But in an interdependent, vulnerable urban complex it takes only a few desperados to change a comfortable life drastically overnight. If urban terror in Western Europe has taught one lesson, it is that the most efficient police methods remain inadequate to deal with this threat unless accompanied by serious attempts to limit and eliminate the causes of such ultimate political alienation. If this represents the state of affairs in democracies with a population overwhelmingly content with its political arrangements, how much more do such lessons apply to a society with a government confronted with popular rejection and internationally castigated as the outcast of the world?

Some English-speaking whites with options abroad already confirm through emigration this skeptical assessment of the

Hanover Corporation are most informative. In explaining why the lending to South Africa of his Trust Company, one of the largest U.S. banks, was now inactive, Hauge stressed "because national, social and political issues are closely related to a country's economy and therefore have a bearing on its ability to repay its debt." Similar concern was expressed by Citicorps, New York's largest banking company, which regards "tangible progress away from apartheid as a positive factor in its risk-evaluation process." (*New York Times*, April 22, 1978), p. 25. In short, it is "impaired credit rating," not moral concern, that contributed to the policy change. However such an evaluation can also change quickly once coercive stability is restored.

6. *Die Vaderland*, November 21, 1977.

future.[7] The declining immigration rates also testify to the spreading pessimism. Representative opinion surveys show that anxiety about the future has increased dramatically between 1974 and 1977 among English and Afrikaners alike.[8] For the first time in a long period, domestic savings exceed investments, reflecting uncertainty. Two-thirds of the white electorate expect a lower living standard for their children, as well as black upheavals. To be sure, there is also a 75 percent declared readiness to fight rather than make concessions among Afrikaners, particularly among the less educated. But the enthusiasm for war instead of accommodation is markedly lower among the Anglo-whites, especially among the 16–24 year old group where only a third opt for war.[9] These results suggest that any drawn out conflict would see many more defectors, not just a few valuable professionals as at present. A government may delude itself by legislating against money transfers abroad. It is even less likely to succeed in ordering fighting spirit.

These prospects also signal heightened psychological costs of maintaining privilege. The many insecure who seek security in handguns hardly link their habitual anxiety to a destruction of African family life by the pass laws or the hopelessness of unemployed youngsters. Grossly unequal life-chances impoverish and brutalize both adversaries. In addition, whites as an affluent group pay with a fast growing black birthrate for continuing mass poverty and hopelessness.[10] The rapid population growth will not only undermine

7. South African papers report the drop from 41,000 immigrants in 1976 to 21,000 in 1977 and the simultaneous rise of declared emigrants from 12,000 to 23,000 as "immigration was overtaken by desertion" (*The Star*, December 21, 1977).

8. Theodor Hanf, Heribert Weiland, Gerda Vierdag, *Südafrika: Friedlicher Wandel?* (Munich: Kaiser, 1978), p. 218.

9. Ibid., p. 222.

10. The white birthrate approaches the zero population growth figure. Various projections indicate a decline of the white percentage in the total population from the present 17 percent to 13 percent in 2000. The implications of this trend for the labor market remain uncertain, but it certainly indicates a long-term undermining of traditional racial domination.

the quality of life for all groups but also will hamper the task of uplifting living standards for any South African government in power in the twenty-first century. The self-comforting finger pointing at New York, Rio, or Lagos as hardly more livable places ignores the fact that there it is mainly poverty, whereas in South Africa it is race without exception, that defines the ghetto. It is because there is by legal definition no individual escape from the stigmatizing poverty that race becomes such an offensive criterion of social stratification. Even if the rulers, as some more enlightened ones now argue, were to increase dramatically the living standards of subordinates, it would not take out the sting of official racial classifications.

The most common behavior of political elites in such a crisis situation is only to react: they seldom anticipate costs. However, there is no longer a possibility of avoiding risks and potential costs by sitting tight. Any indecision or more support of the status quo is in itself costly. Afrikaner leaders are therefore forced to make a choice either by enduring escalating costs through indecision or by attempting to reverse these trends by new policies. If the leadership should decide for whatever reason not to pursue new alternatives or only to dabble in insufficient modifications of existing policy, there are only two outcomes, either (1) it will be progressively weakened by rising costs, or, more likely, (2) sections within the ruling group who are most affected (either by being directly hurt or by losing potential opportunities) will press for a different course, and if unsuccessful, split and seek new alliances. It seems impossible to predict with any certainty the threshold above which either of the two reactions will occur. It would depend on the issues that could change or split Afrikanerdom.

There exists the powerful imagery, fostered by Afrikaner ideologues as well as by their liberal critics, of the rugged rifleman of the Boer War who still places his beliefs before his pocketbook. To what extent does such principled behavior apply to an Afrikaner elite behind BMW and Mercedes steering wheels? What other options does an ethnic oligarchy have in the specific historical circumstances of the domestic and international context of South Africa at present and in the foreseeable future?

Faced with an escalating cost crisis, a regime can essentially adopt three courses of action apart from indecision: (1) it can give in and sooner or later abdicate, (2) it can attempt to repress the causes of its crises, and (3) it can try to manipulate the challenges by policy changes and cut the costs. One may call these three different policies the strategies of *abdication, coercion,* and *co-optation.* They correspond to the tactics of *succumbing, fighting off,* and *compromising.* The latter two strategies are often exercised simultaneously. Which course of action is open to Afrikanerdom?

Abdication

The possibility of voluntary abdication of Afrikaner power in favor of majority rule is almost unanimously ruled out in the literature on South Africa. No ruling group has ever surrendered its vast privileges because of moral pleas to its conscience. Nor is there the option of departure. Although emigration of whites has been suggested as "the most desirable and humane solution to the Southern African problem,"[11] this alternative remains open to selected individuals only; it does not square with the reality of Afrikaner perceptions of home and motherland. Abdication of Afrikaner power can, therefore, be conceived only as defeat. More sober analysts of existing power relations and attitudes expect such a defeat only as the final result of direct superpower intervention. With large Cuban expeditionary forces employed throughout Africa and perhaps other foreign units moving in, a full-scale conventional military confrontation can no longer be ruled out in Southern Africa, particularly with an unsettled Namibia and Zimbabwe providing suitable entrées in terms of international legitimacy. South Africa could not afford to

11. Pierre L. van den Berghe, "The Impossibility of a Liberal Solution in South Africa," manuscript, 1977.

stay on the sidelines. In such an event, much would depend on U.S./Western European moves against such an Eastern backed initiative. While Western intervention would be severely handicapped and discredited, not least by the nature of the South African regime, it would certainly have to protect its own interests, but most likely at the expense of and not in support of Afrikaner power.

In short, while wars of attrition in various forms could substantially raise the cost of white privileges, including a lowering of morale among many, they will fall short of leading to a defeat of Afrikanerdom in the present international power constellation. With the possession of advanced weapons on both sides, with the likely inclusion of nuclear devices, a costly stalemate similar to the East-West or Israeli-Arab conflict must be envisaged. Mutually devastating new weaponry cautions against applying the concepts of winners or losers in any conflict in which the very existence of the controller of such weaponry is at stake.

Coercion

Afrikanerdom has certainly not shied away from using coercion to the fullest against its serious challengers. South Africa is surpassed by few countries in watertight legislation against political dissenters outside the approved framework, though by many more in scope and ruthlessness of political oppression. Nevertheless, the authoritarianism of a minority in power also operates under various constraints. The least, but frequently crucial, constraining factor is the need to maintain white unity. Among Afrikaners in particular there still exists a remarkable concern that their rule should be perceived as just in terms of group morality and legitimacy. The debate about Biko's death has also revealed other than "leaves me cold" attitudes.

Radically extended repression would presuppose a one-party state and/or military rule that would severely tax the cohesiveness of the white camp with its wide tactical cleavages, interest constellations, and international dependency. It would invite costly repercussions of various kinds. Technocratically ruthless repression would defeat its purpose in an integrated, interdependent, industrialized economy where blacks constitute 80 percent of the labor force. But above all, the regime has too weak a political and demographic base to allow for such unlimited ruthlessness. Its most crucial restraint is the need to cultivate allies across the color line, both in the form of an acquiescent apathy on the part of the black proletariat and in the form of active collaboration on the part of an emerging African middle-class and bureaucratic bourgeoisie. White South Africa simply lacks the manpower to staff the garrison itself and increasingly needs to rely on African self-administration, self-policing, and self-motivation for a guarantee of minimal stability. Despite all the rhetoric and continuing practice of *kragdadigheid*, Afrikanerdom can no longer afford to alienate all black strata and leaders equally.

Co-optation

Such considerations illustrate the simultaneous strategy of co-optation by manipulating and, above all, fragmenting the challenge. Critics who constantly ridicule the Bantustans as economically unviable and internationally unrecognized fictions of dreaming Afrikaner minds ignore the success of the policy in the form of retribalized nationalisms with vested interests of a growing administrative class of civil servants, professionals, petty traders, and market-producing peasants. This middle group might ultimately come into direct conflict with its foster parents and an impoverished migrant population alike; but in the meantime Matanzima claims liberation. With the symbols of nationalism in his hands, he splits the common threat to white rule despite the militant rhetoric. For Pretoria it is well worth financing 75 percent of the budget of an independent Transkei and various other developments in the other black hinterlands. If a similar social stratification in the urban areas could be translated into legitimate political structures—which is the major aim of "normalised plural relations"—would then a heavy burden have been shed and an uncontrollable realm suitably stabilized? An answer depends on the as yet unproved seriousness of government promises to abolish racialism and to work for a mutually acceptable accommodation of all population groups.

Will the ruling group adopt such pragmatic policies of deracialization? If so, how soon and how far? Again, an answer depends on who precisely the ruling group is, which interests are represented or underrepresented in the government, and what other considerations enter the cost assessment of traditional domination.

This analysis argues that it is ethnicity in conjunction with intraethnic class stratification that holds the key to understanding present South African government policy. The emphasis throughout this study lies on Afrikanerdom because it constitutes the most relevant part of the superordinate group. Moreover, despite continuing inequities between Afrikaner and English sections in income and education, the most significant development of the past two decades represents (1) the emergence of the Afrikaner industrial and bureaucratic bourgeoisie as the dominant part of the South African state and (2) the linkage and interpenetration of both English and Afrikaner capital. Foreign as well as state (Afrikaner-controlled) capital are now frequently interlocked in common projects under state direction.

But such "merger" does not mean that the historically mobilized ethnic group perceptions and rivalries have disappeared into a common white South Africanism. As all opinion surveys show, language (that is, Afrikaner or English upbringing) remains the most discernible factor, correlating with substantial differences in world views—from detention without trial to reading habits, conversation topics, and leisure behavior. It is within these intensely held particularistic heritages that political decisions are shaped and carried out. This analysis attempts to show when, why, and how such differences emerged, what political implications they hold, and whether they are likely to hold sway. In this respect, this study departs from much of the Marxist literature on South Africa, which gives little or no recognition to ethnic belief

11

systems. Instead of ignoring this important subjective reality, its origin and interaction with class forces will be traced.

This perspective will focus particularly on the new role of the state with its unique steering problems in South Africa. The new role of the state may best be labeled "crisis management." Traditional Marxist theory considers the state merely as the coercive wing of capital to ensure its spread and protection. With the growth of the Afrikaner-controlled state-capitalism and its role in the crisis management, the South African state frequently conflicts with private interests and has been able to impose its blueprints on private capital. Therefore much of South Africa's recent economic history appears as the subjugation of laissez-faire economic policies to ideological designs of Afrikanerdom, from which private capital on the whole nevertheless benefited immensely. This, however, did not occur without intense conflicts. What then constitute core questions of this study are how different interests emerged historically, how they articulated themselves at particular junctures of their competition, and how these interests are now mediated by a state bureaucracy as well as translated by professional ideologues in the church, press, and universities. Their influence will be weighed and relative strengths assessed.

This study will, therefore, explore whether there is a differential assessment of the apartheid costs by different sections of Afrikanerdom based on the fact that the costs are borne unevenly, reflecting the social stratification of the ruling group. Afrikaner capital with international interests will presumably pay a higher price for escalating instability than isolated farmers or civil servants with mere promotion anxieties and fixed pensions. Different placement in the occupational hierarchy naturally leads to divergent conclusions about accommodation or intransigence. A demand such as the scrapping of Afrikaans in the African curriculum may be unacceptable to a politician whose career is dependent on not being perceived as weak by his rural constituency. An Afrikaner industrialist on the other hand will view the abolition of hated racial symbols as the easiest gesture to restore calm.

Both contradictory policy conclusions are based on rational perceptions of particular interests.

Which view will prevail? Will those who advocate African unions as suitable instruments for bringing a restless labor force in line eventually win out over their opponents who consider European type unions as the greatest political threat to the system? Is the fostering of a collaborating black middle class the way to strengthen a weak oligarchy in search of allies; which lobby within the dominant group will press for this strategy and who will oppose it? Again, the answers to such fundamental decisions depend on a variety of calculations. Their outcome is likely to be contradictory because they are made on the basis of different assumptions by differently placed actors. Which interests will finally prevail, however, may be gauged by comparing the strength of the competing groups and by analyzing the nature of the decision-making process and the past record of similar controversies.

In this endeavor Afrikaner politics of privilege maintenance is viewed as comparable with similar situations of conflict elsewhere. The commonly held assumption that there is an apparently unbridgeable species difference between Western pragmatists on the one side and Calvinist ideologues on the other is doubted. One view maintains that "They are different political animals,"[12] while our approach tends to consider all the actors as rational within the confines of their special interests.

In order to substantiate such crucial assumptions, a critical survey of the social science literature on South Africa is helpful. If analyzed in the wider context of insights into comparative ethnic relations, the South African conflict can be understood in both its unique as well as its general features. Above all, a critical survey of the vast literature may provide clues to the central question: How does a ruling group perceive of and face an objectively escalating cost crisis?

Few academic analysts of revolution have stressed fissure of the ruling group as the decisive precondition for a success-

12. Stanley Uys, quoted in *Race Relations News* (November 1977).

ful change.[13] In the tradition of Pareto's fatigue of the bourgeoisie, loss of élan and morale needed to rule, if only in the most ruthless fashion possible, amounts to the final submission to the revolutionary challenge. Under what conditions, if any, can such a failure of nerve be expected from Afrikanerdom? If not ethnic abdication, is disunity of the white camp conceivable where sections of the ruling group turn on each other rather than unite in a monolithic bloc against their common adversary? What has to happen that not only neutralizes or isolates ruling factions from a confrontation but that makes them ally with the progressive forces? If there is to be any change in the protracted stalemate of two polarized camps, a breakdown of white cohesion, particularly of Afrikanerdom, with subsequent policy changes and realignments across the color line, would almost seem to be a precondition at present. This makes it necessary to explore the ideologies and organizational mechanisms that Afrikanerdom has deployed to maintain its crucial unity. A detailed assessment is provided of the inner-working and changing role of (1) the Nationalist Party, (2) the Broederbond, (3) the press, (4) the church, (5) the apartheid bureaucracy, and (6) the security apparatus. What led to the failure of political liberalism compared with the success of ethnic appeals? What constitutional alternatives appear on the horizon when the present political dispensation finally breaks down?

It is standard wisdom that groups under threat close ranks or that group integration increases during a crisis caused by an outside enemy. Such popular stereotypes have given rise

13. In the tradition of Marx's discussion of Bonapartism in the 18th Brumaire, earlier revolutionaries, such as Lenin and Trotsky, focused frequently on the vital strategic questions of their success. Trotsky, for example, wrote at length about the wavering military in the St. Petersburg clashes. However, as even radical sociologist John Leggett admitted, commenting generally on the contemporary conflicts: "The origins of elite disunity are often neglected by armchair Marxists, as they do spend entirely too much time on the falling rate of profit, rates of exploitation, the organic composition of capital and like considerations to the exclusion of elite failure of nerve." (*Contemporary Sociology*, November 1977), p. 699.

to the notion of "siege-culture" in South Africa.[14] Even such a sober analyst as R. W. Johnson talks about "the formation of a white political bloc of monolithic proportions, with hitherto existing social divisions within the white community simply submerged." The important result of such a process is said to be that "it robs the established economic and political elites of any possibility of independent room for manoeuver."[15] However, it seems doubtful that such popular psychology is empirically correct.

Ruling groups, composed of divergent interests, might well split over strategies and tactics as how best to preserve their threatened privilege. In laboratory experiments, researchers found that the Durkheim thesis of group integration during a crisis is true only "if a likely cooperative solution to the crisis problem is present."[16] In situations in which no solution is possible, psychologists found a disintegration in the group. South Africa does not constitute a clear-cut laboratory. To wait for the real test represents little comfort either. But if the situations in Rhodesia and Namibia are at all comparable, the assumption of a likely split in the ruling group in a crunch situation in South Africa does not seem farfetched. In both Zimbabwe and Namibia the ruling party split because substantial sections could not reconcile their notions of how to save their skins in case of an imminent showdown. Unlike the colonial situation in Rhodesia and Namibia, however, the sovereign ruling oligarchy in South Africa at present need not enter into negotiations for capitulation, perhaps not even power-sharing, with the unrepresented black majority. This necessity for future coexistence rather than European surrender and departure gives the polarizing conflict in South Africa its unique dimension, incomparable with processes of decolonization elsewhere.

14. Donald Baker, "Race, Power and White Siege Culture," *Social Dynamics* 1, no. 2 (1975), 143–57.

15. R. W. Johnson, *How Long Will South Africa Survive?* (London: Macmillan, 1978), p. 304.

16. R. L. Hamblin, "Group Integration During a Crisis," *Human Relations* 11 (1958), 67–76.

2 Perspectives in the Literature: A Critical Evaluation Heribert Adam

This chapter attempts an impossible task: to introduce briefly the major approaches and theoretical concepts in the vast social science literature on South Africa, ethnicity, and race relations in general. It aims essentially at the reader unfamiliar with this literature. At the same time the discussion is addressed to professional experts by pointing to the shortcomings and merits of their perspectives. Such critical evaluation cannot be expected to begin to do justice to the sophisticated elaborations in this burgeoning field. Yet the simplified assessment and deliberately provocative review of six artificially separated approaches should be useful for clarifying the theoretical framework of our own focus in comparison with rival interpretations of South Africa. It delineates an empirical area in which literally hundreds of professionally qualified writers come to dozens of contradictory conclusions. It is up to the reader to decide which theoretical concepts have greater explanatory value in light of the empirical evidence presented in later chapters. Our favored method attempts to utilize insights from various perspectives without elevating a particular approach to the sole truth. This will be outlined in chapter 3 after an evaluation of (1) the focus on Calvinism, (2) the fascist analogy, (3) the focus on racism, (4) the concept of pluralism, (5) the focus on class formation, and (6) the colonial analogy.

THE FOCUS ON CALVINISM
AND RELIGIOUSLY INDUCED PREJUDICE

*Yes, I believe profoundly, as always, that we have been ap-
pointed by Providence to play a role here and that we have the
human material to play that role*—B. J. Vorster, as quoted in
Beeld, April 21, 1977

One of the most recurrent perspectives used to explain apartheid policies stresses the primitive Calvinism of backward
Boers who, in an isolated corner of the world, missed the
Enlightenment by being exposed only to the Old Testament
rather than Voltaire. In their harsh frontier existence, it is
said, Afrikaners developed Israeli-like visions of a civilizing
mission by a chosen people with a destiny in a sea of primitive heathen natives. Such ideological fixations are frequently
detected in contemporary policies which in this view render
Afrikaners psychologically incapable of adapting to a post-
colonial reality.

In this vein, Jan J. Loubser focuses on the rigid "fundamen-
talistic faith system" that Afrikaners developed as relief from
"existential anxiety" caused by a large, threatening indigenous population.[1] A less dissident Afrikaner, W. A. de Klerk
bases his popular book *The Puritans in Africa* on the premise
that "the key to the Afrikaners is Calvinism." De Klerk casti-
gates the outside critics for failing to understand that in the
Afrikaner perception apartheid is less of an oppressive
tyranny than the necessary result of the divine task "to re-
structure the world according to a vision of justice," the vocation of "a separate nation called by God to create a new humanity."[2] Visitors from abroad have readily accepted such
familiar reasoning, obfuscating even the profit motive behind
the forced labor system since it is "religion which has pro-

1. Jan J. Loubser, "Calvinism, Equality, and Inclusion: The Case of Afrikaner Calvinism," in *The Protestant Ethic and Modernization*, ed., S. N.
Eisenstadt (New York: Basic Books, 1968), pp. 379–80.
2. W. A. de Klerk, *The Puritans in Africa* (Harmondsworth: Penguin, 1975),
pp. xiv, 233, 241.

17

vided [the Afrikaner] with a necessary vision of the black man as fit only for labour."[3]

Afrikaner religion was undoubtedly shaped and reinforced by the harsh conditions of a dangerous frontier life, engendering heightened "existential anxiety" that demanded meaning. In the most comprehensive study of this question, Gerhard Becker concludes that the frontier isolation with its individual bible interpretation fostered unique race attitudes in a way similar to how Calvinism facilitated industrial capitalism by encouraging thrift and asceticism.[4]

From a sociological point of view, this expansion of the Weberian thesis, however, faces the same question as *The Protestant Ethic and the Spirit of Calvinism*. Which historical circumstances made people embrace the Calvinist belief system over rival interpretations of the world? It makes sense to view the rise of a successful religious Weltanschauung as a more appropriate collective response to changing socioeconomic conditions. The new ideological paradigm represents the superior group adaptation to new exigencies and opportunities. Once institutionalized, the new religion shapes its environment in turn. In this respect, an ideology once entrenched must be considered an independent force, generating its own dynamism and motivations beyond a mere reflection of narrow group interests. If one accepts this dialectical interaction of structure and superstructure, one must also concede that even the most rigid belief systems undergo changes if new circumstances of group survival so require. To assert otherwise would assume a static society in which belief systems remain frozen regardless of surrounding fundamental changes whose interpretation they could no longer deliver. To be sure, discrepancies, or so-called cultural lags, regularly occur between advanced conditions on the one side and an outdated collective consciousness or institutional

3. Jim Hoagland, *South Africa: Civilizations in Conflict* (Boston: Houghton Mifflin, 1972), p. 20.

4. Gerhard Becker, *Religiöse Faktoren in der Entwicklung der Südafrikanischen Rassenfrage. Ein Beitrag zur Rolle des Kalvinismus in Kolonialen Situationen* (Munich: Wilhelm Fink, 1969).

practices on the other. But a religion or attitudes suitable to a frontier existence cannot be easily transplanted unchanged into an industrial, bureaucratic city life without creating unbearable strains. Such contradictions are lessened by an ongoing reinterpretation of traditional parameters. In this process different sections embrace new outlooks at differing paces and a variety of competing definitions exist side-by-side or may even overlap.

It would seem decisive that the pace as well as the extent of change in official doctrine hardly depends on the intrinsic content of the religion, that is, its openness or closedness for incorporating new challenges. What proves to be much more crucial in such a situation is the role of the designated interpreters, in other words, the specific organizational form of religious praxis, particularly the degree of centralization. One would expect that a relatively decentralized organization with a high degree of lay participation, such as Calvinist churches, would prove more responsive to new needs than highly centralized churches, such as the Roman Catholic church. But even such rigid organizational structures as Catholicism have lately shown a remarkable capacity for transforming liturgy and relaxing sacred rules in light of new circumstances. A similar flexibility can be ascertained, for example, in Islamic attitudes toward the role of women or in Hindu perspectives on the caste system. The schisms and rise of sectarian movements in the Protestant tradition constitute a reminder of an ongoing adaptation process according to new needs. There is nothing in the creed or organizational structure of Calvinism that would immunize this religion from such worldwide processes. Seasoned observers of Afrikanerdom recognized this predicament long ago. O. D. Wollheim aptly comments on the implications: "The problem of the Afrikaner leaders today is that this religion has become irrelevant and impracticable in our present circumstances and they are left with nothing to provide further fuel to hold the group together."[5]

5. O. D. Wollheim, *Race Relations News*, April 1976.

However, the literature on the irrationality and impermeability of Afrikanerdom does not evoke only the Calvinist two-class distinction of the elect and the damned, which supposedly provided the justification for the exclusion of the children of Ham. Rigid racial outlooks are said to be transmitted and reinforced by a religiously justified patriarchal family system. Conformity pressure of authoritarian socialization is said to account for the fact that "repressed aggressiveness to the strong Afrikaner authority figures could be displaced and projected on the African."[6] According to Loubser, the Afrikaners' "high level of anxiety about guilt, their consequent strong sense of mission and political destiny ... provides a more plausible interpretation of the nonrationality of their political action."[7] In this version, the alleged uniqueness of Afrikanerdom stands in a long tradition of social-psychological studies on prejudice in the literature on minority discrimination. These studies are characterized by a tendency to psychologize group relations into personality processes.[8]

The focus of these studies on prejudice monopolizes attention to the neglect of social and structural conditions. A tendency to start at the individual level and project attitudes of single persons into national politics and large-scale social effects is evident, so that prejudice appears to be a prime mover in racial and ethnic problems. However, if subsequent research has confirmed anything, it is that prejudice is a product of situations—historic, economic, and political, "it is not a demon which emerges in people simply because they are depraved."[9] This is not to deny the importance of prejudice, but to show that it is not central to the explanation of race and ethnic relations. At best, it can perhaps be useful as a dependent or intervening variable.

6. Loubser, "Calvinism, Equality, and Inclusion," p. 374.

7. Ibid., p. 375.

8. George Simpson and J. Milton Yinger, *Racial and Cultural Minorities: An Analysis of Prejudice and Discrimination*, 3rd ed. (New York: Harper & Row, 1965).

9. R. A. Schermerhorn, *Comparative Ethnic Relations: A Framework for Theory and Research* (New York: Random House, 1970), p. 6

While social psychological theories alone therefore can hardly explain the rise of ethnic antagonism in situations determined by historical-structural conditions, these perspectives do give insights into the specific content of hostile attitudes and the varying degree of intensity with which they are held. Social psychological theories, particularly in the Freudian tradition, shed light as to why certain people are susceptible to hate and others in the same group resist such mobilization. For example, Sumner's concept of ethnocentrism—the glorification of one's own group—can be fruitfully utilized to analyze in-group-out-group relationships.[10] Freud regarded ethnocentrism as narcissism at the group level. In *Civilization and Its Discontents* he saw the social function of group narcissism facilitating the displacement of aggression from in-group to out-group.

John Dollard and his associates assumed an innate potential of aggression resulting from the frustrations of constraining socialization in all human beings; the displacement of such aggressiveness away from the source onto some other object was seen as decisive.[11] The concept of projection—the attribution to others of unacceptable impulses within one's self—lends itself to convincing explanations of aversion, particularly when the outgroup is no real threat.

The research on the authoritarian personality revealed the background of the stereotypes in which the "strangers" are portrayed.[12] By focusing on different child-rearing practices and the severity of socialization, the work of Adorno and his colleagues engendered a rich literature of cross-cultural studies of ethnic antagonism. The research was originally motivated by the virulent anti-Semitism that had become a gruesome state doctrine in Germany but that was also prevalent in anti-fascist Western countries. It soon became evident

10. William Graham Sumner, *Folkways: A Study of the Sociological Importance of Usages, Manner, Customs, Mores and Morals* (New York: Ginn, 1906).

11. John Dollard et al., *Frustration and Aggression* (New Haven: Yale University Press, 1939).

12. T. Adorno et al., *The Authoritarian Personality* (New York: Harper, 1950).

that the syndrome of scapegoating had little to do with the behavior of Jews. What emerges from Adorno's work is that the victims of collective aggression are interchangeable and can be redefined according to social needs and the historical constellation. It is this sociohistorical context that seems neglected in the prejudice studies. As Thomas F. Pettigrew has shown for the South African case, it is conformity pressure rather than mere authoritarian upbringing that accounts for the adherence to racial doctrines.[13] Furthermore, the debate on the basic aggressiveness of all humans is far from being conclusive as yet. On this point, the New Haven experiments by Stanley Milgram are directly relevant to South Africa.[14] Milgram found a remarkable willingness among ordinary persons to administer alleged painful electric shock treatment if ordered to do so. But Milgram's experiments also proved that such potential aggressiveness had to be motivated. It immediately dropped when the coercion in the form of legitimate authority disappeared.

If some generalized conclusions for South Africa can be drawn from this literature it would appear that the perceived Afrikaner minority position results in a high level of anxiety among the white population. This and the privileges of Afrikaner unity make for an intense need for identification or conformity with groups or leaders offering security. This relief from anxiety and awareness of privilege maintenance, bought by group allegiance, occurs at the individual level largely irrespective of the specific policy of the group leadership. Therefore if the group leadership changes or decides to switch policy for whatever reason, comparatively ready compliance among the followers can be expected.[15] Such a situation of psychological group "bondedness" must be distin-

13. Thomas F. Pettigrew, "Personality and Sociocultural Factors in Intergroup Attitudes: A Cross-national Comparison," *Journal of Conflict Resolution* 2, no. 1 (March 1958), 29–42.

14. Stanley Milgram, *Obedience to Authority: An Experimental View* (New York: Harper & Row, 1974).

15. This is one of the main results of the "Freiburg Study," See Theodor Hanf et al., *Südafrika: Friedlicher Wandel?* (Munich: Kaiser, 1978).

guished from an irrational response to feelings of frustration, resulting from an individual life history. The advantages of conformity and the severity of sanctions for defiance among Afrikaners, not personality characteristics of a heightened individual authoritarianism, account for the relative cohesion of a minority in power. The crucial question remains: Under what conditions can such cohesion be expected to erode?

The Calvinist doctrine among some segments of Afrikanerdom does not manifest itself only on the race issue. Racial prejudice is but a facet of a bigot syndrome that includes other outgroups. In this vein, Dutch Reformed Church circles still refer to the Catholic Church as the "*Roomse gevaar*" (Roman menace). Synods regularly express alarm over statistics that the Catholic Church, comprising presently approximately 6 percent of the population, could become stronger through Southern European immigrants. In 1975, the Cape Synod without dissent adopted a motion making an "urgent call" on its members to have more children as a means of "combating the growth of the Catholic Church."[16] Church members are urged not to frequent Catholic institutions, such as hospitals, in order to keep uninfected. Women's rights and feminist emancipation, let alone other stigmatized groups, have not even become issues of synodal pronouncements, which are still concerned with such topics as gambling or sports on Sundays.

But the assessment of Afrikanerdom mainly in terms of religious stubbornness leads to policy implications that stress "change of heart," reeducation, and exposure to more congenial doctrine. An amusing example of such naiveté was described by a U.S. foreign service official:

As the desk officer responsible for South African Affairs in the State Department 25 years ago, I promoted a government-sponsored visit to South Africa by a leading theologian of the American Dutch Reformed Church. The object was to improve communication, to reduce the in-

16. Quoted in the *Star Weekly*, November 1, 1975.

tellectual and religious isolation of the Afrikaners. Perhaps no foreign churchman could really succeed in breaking down the dogmatism that led these hard-shell Calvinists to find scriptural sanction for their apartheid doctrine. But if anyone could dent their armor of self-righteousness it would be a theologian trained in their own tradition but whose interpretation of Christianity led him to quite different conclusions on race relations.[17]

As could be expected, the money of the American taxpayer was wasted since even in the official's view, "this particular seed fell on stony ground."

The religious explanation reveals its weakness by a casual glance at an almost identical English segregationist practice in Natal, which preceded apartheid in all but its codified and legalistic features. Therefore, the policy needs structural, not merely cultural, explanations. Additional historical differences and changes in contemporary secularized ideology add to these questions. Contrary to comparisons with the Puritans of New England, most early settlers in South Africa (with the exception of the small Huguenot community) arrived as individual company employees, many of them adventurers, usually representing the very opposite attitudes of those found in a cohesive persecuted religious community. What later evolved as the Afrikaner "civil religion" resulted from the nineteenth-century fundamentalist imports, expressed mainly through one of the three smaller Dutch Reformed Churches in Potchefstroom.[18] Furthermore, as will be explicated in subsequent chapters, official ideology in con-

17. A. M. Lee, letter to editor, *Foreign Affairs*, April 1978, p. 648.

18. Dunbar Moodie, *The Rise of Afrikanerdom: Power, Apartheid, and the Afrikaner Civil Religion* (Berkeley: University of California Press, 1975). See also Irving Hexham, "Dutch Calvinism and the Development of Afrikaner Nationalism," unpublished paper, University of York, Centre for Southern African Studies, 1974. A comprehensive general overview is Daniel Walker Howe, "The Decline of Calvinism: An Approach to Its Study," *Comparative Studies of Society and History* (June 1972), pp. 306–27. See also Randall K. Stokes, "Afrikaner Calvinism and Economic Action," *American Journal of Sociology*, 81, no. 1 (1975), 62–81.

temporary South Africa justifies white supremacy with technocratic law-and-order arguments, no longer with any sacred mission. To be sure, the will of the Almighty is called upon on New Year's Eve or on the cherished Day of the Covenant but more as a ritualistic assertion of group solidarity than as a guide to policy, despite high degrees of church attendance and Vorster's assurance that he reads the Bible daily.

THE FASCIST ANALOGY
AND FOCUS ON POLICE STATE METHODS

> *The depressing thing about the election results is the fact that . . . in spite of the uncontested evidence in the Biko Inquest that we have now bred our own version of the Gestapo here, many people who were prepared to die to oppose Hitler now seem to be getting redy to die to defend a system which, to survive as it now is, will have to depend more and more on Hitler's methods.* Reality, A South African Journal of Liberal and Radical Opinion, January 1978

There is no doubt that the emphasis on police state methods and associations of facism, which dominate the critical literature on South Africa, express deep concern about violations of civil liberties in the only contemporary society with legalized racial distinctions. The structural violence of such a system, the deprivation of life-chances, the sheer brutality of social relations forced upon human objects of exploitation within an unparalleled network of restrictive laws have all been amply documented and need not be repeated here.

And yet it can be shown that contemporary South Africa hardly resembles fascist Germany, that the differences outweigh the similarities, and that the fascist analogy obscures a proper understanding of the South African system. No amount of indignant labeling achieves better insights, particularly when the labels are based on ignorance or political dogmatism. Thus, Ann and Neva Seidman begin a chapter on South African fascism with the statement: "Over time, the white settlers in South Africa, particularly the more wealthy and powerful Afrikaner elements, succeeded in welding the majority of whites behind a powerful political movement built around the chauvinist ideology of white supremacy and centered in the Nationalist Party."[19] Through the use of state capitalism without welfare pretenses, "the resulting system constituted fascism of a classic type." Because of the "inextricably linked" state and mining capital, the authors conclude: "as an 'open terrorist dictatorship' South Africa is unsurpassed."[20] In this paragraph alone, typical of this brand of literature, at least two empirical errors can be marked: (1) there are indeed "welfare pretenses," though totally inadequate, in the form of some black minimum wages and other ameliorating labor legislation, (2) in the application of open and large-scale terror methods, South Africa is presently widely surpassed by several dozen other countries. The important task would be to pinpoint the unique forms of South African domination compared with other autocracies rather than lumping them all together under the meaningless label, fascism. Three differences stand out as far as contemporary Afrikanerdom is concerned: (1) the ideological slack, (2) the greater rationality of a group dictatorship compared to one individual leader, and (3) the restraints on the use of coercion.

The absence of an eschatology in apartheid distinguishes South African authoritarianism from both fascism and Stalinism. Moral mobilization is confined to the Afrikaner in-group. The millennium lies in the past, in the desperate attempt to arrest the inevitable institutional changes of the industrial revolution and yet benefit from it materially. Unlike fascism or Stalinism, apartheid blueprints do not aim at remoulding traditional institutions in the image of a glorified utopia, be it the world domination of a master race or the

19. Ann and Neva Seidman, *South Africa and the U.S. Multinational Corporations* (Westport, Conn.: Lawrence Hill, 1978), p. 56.
20. Ibid., p. 69.

classless society. By not pursuing virtue, acquiescence of the subject population, not its ideological mobilization, remains the overall goal. This makes South African style supremacy comparatively less totalitarian. The political persecution of the system is directed against those who challenge it, not those who merely abstain. No commitment is demanded from the dominated intelligentsia, since there is nothing to dream about, no sacred doctrine which would call for sacrifice from the total population. In other words, apartheid represents a holding operation rather than a vision of a better future.[21] Relative pragmatism gives the system flexibility in reacting to pressure, compared to blindly enforcing doctrine. This represents in essence the survival politics of an entrenched oligarchy.

This group dictatorship can be expected to pursue on the whole more rational policies of privilege maintenance, compared with the emotional and frequently irrational dictates of a charismatic fascist leader. A democratically organized oligarchy constrains itself from impulsive, fatal policy changes (such as Hitler's decision to attack Russia) since it does not recognize the infallibility of individuals but acts according to a broad consensus. The pragmatic argument is at least aired and taken into account, although frequently stalled by the consensus mechanism. In contrast, the true believers of the Nazi, Stalinist, or other tyrannical creeds were blind to contradictory evidence against their strength. Individual despots or small ruling cliques are usually sufficiently isolated from reality and hence unable to read danger signals to their rule. Accordingly, when Vorster became Prime Minister he was quoted as having said he had learned three great truths about life. "The first is never to underestimate an opponent, the second is never to overestimate my own abilities, and the third is not to hesitate to abandon a philosophical idea if circumstances so dictate." On all three accounts, Hitler frequently stated the exact opposite, particularly that he was

21. For further elaboration see Heribert Adam, "Ideologies of Dedication vs. Blueprints of Expedience," *Social Dynamics* 2, no. 2 (1976), 83–91.

proud about never having compromised his original Weltanschauung. If the Nationalists so far have not fundamentally altered their race policy it might not be due to intransigence but to circumstances that have not developed sufficient force to dictate an abandonment of apartheid principles. After all, when in history has an oligarchy voluntarily surrendered its position because of moral condemnation?

In short, while a strong ideological affinity existed between National Socialism and influential sections of Afrikanerdom during the war years, culminating in the terrorist activities of Ossewa-Brandwag in which many present Afrikaner leaders (including Vorster and van den Bergh) participated actively, the collapse and exposure of fascism has discredited its ideas and praxis sufficiently, that only lunatic fringe groups can now afford to adhere to fascist ideologies.

This awareness begins now also to extend to the violation of civil liberties of political opponents. There is a widespread realization that the international dependency of the country puts restraints on internal coercion. In the words of the President of the South Africa Foundation, Basil Hersov: South Africa "simply cannot allow individuals—be they members of the security police, the police, government officers or private individuals—to damage South Africa in the way the Biko affair and other events have done."[22] The Biko case marked the watershed for the hitherto claimed innocence of Afrikaner rule. No longer could the Afrikaans press, for example, maintain its previous unity by first giving credit to the police whenever their conduct was questioned. Thus *Rapport* comments: "The most shocking thing is that no official disapproval of that treatment has yet been expressed." In light of the gruesome details which the inquest revealed, the Afrikaner sections, still valuing legitimacy of white power, had to reassure themselves that "it is necessary to prove that the treatment Biko received is not general practice and never will be."[23] The very fact that such questions are publicly aired

22. *South African Digest*, March 24, 1978.
23. *Rapport*, December 11, 1977.

points to the crucial difference between fascism or Stalinism where many disappeared for merely expressing doubts.

In contrast, Afrikaner repression needs internal justifications. Too ruthless a police autocracy deprives the ideologues of their rationale. The Biko case opened such splits within Nationalist Afrikanerdom, not to speak of the international repercussions of concern to the pragmatists. Hence, the soul-searching in sections of the Afrikaans press and the unpublicized but widespread blame of the minister in charge (Kruger), said to be retained only because of the personal loyalty of Vorster.

Three distinct reactions to the Biko affair could be discerned: (1) uncritical support of the police as always in the past, (2) strong critique of the police for bungling, damaging the reputation of South Africa, and other considerations of expediency, and (3) hitherto unheard critique of the police for moral reasons, flamed by the widely publicized details of Biko's death. "It is not only opponents of the Government who have grave misgivings about detention without trial and the dimensions it has assumed," editorialized *Rapport*, "it is obvious that one cannot keep on locking up people one after the other."[24]

Such considerations demarcate the present limits of political suppression in South Africa. This is due in part to the regime's physical incapacity to extend the repressive machinery but more so to its need for legitimacy within the ruling group. A mere cynical use of power without the perceptions of a just cause would alienate important sections of Afrikanerdom from the technocrats and ultimately destroy the delicate unity. In this respect, the historical allegiance to a moral heritage of Western values acts as a brake on the unrestrained exercise of coercion in the most ruthless manner. The relics of Calvinism in part of the *volk* together with the cherished memory of British barbarism during the Boer War do not only represent quaint stumbling blocks for a more cosmopolitan and secularized outlook. At the same time they

24. *Rapport*, February 5, 1978.

immunize against too naked a brutality. This explains the paradoxical need to apply coercion according to proper procedures, the maintenance of some semblance of an independent judiciary,[25] and the concern for the conduct of oppression according to internationally practiced standards. The often asked question, why the embarrassing public Biko inquest was held in the first place must be answered in this light. A possible *in camera* trial or a simple cover-up, as for the death in detention by lesser public figures, would have amounted to an official admission that the quest for internal legitimacy had been replaced by unjustifiable actions.

The white power structure is simply too weak to be able to rely on coercion alone. It needs to solicit the voluntary cooperation or at least acquiescence of the subordinates. The Potchefstroom academic Johan van der Vyver makes the interesting point that "political control of a minority by the majority can lead to more ghastly consequences than if a minority dominates the majority. With minority rule, the numbers of the subjected group restrain the exercise of arbitrary powers."[26] The history of genocide and other atrocities would not seem always to support such a generalized statement. The ruling Tutsi minority of Burundi, for example, was hardly restrained in its elimination of the entire educated strata of the Hutu majority in 1972. Because the majority constitutes a greater threat to minority rule, it could also trigger greater ruthlessness. Minority action is more determined by the dependence on the majority as well as the various costs

25. On the role of the South African judiciary and its controversial independence see the two assessments by Martin Garbus, "South Africa: The Death of Justice," and "South African Justice," *New York Review of Books,* August 4, 1977, pp. 41–42 and September 15, 1977, p. 46. For a concerned but optimistic view see the authoritative work by A. S. Mathews, *Law Order and Liberty in South Africa* (Wynberg: Juta, 1971). The most recent distinguished treatment of the topic by a liberal South African academic is John Dugard, *Human Rights and the South African Legal Order* (Princeton, N.J.: Princeton University Press, 1978).

26. Johan van der Vyver, interview, *Financial Mail,* February 24, 1978, p. 568.

(outside interference, internal conflict) that arbitrary use of power is likely to cause in the perception of those threatened. Such structural constraints do not allow total control, let alone ideological regimentation. The Hungarian writer George Konrád has pointed out that "the true symbol of the totalitarian state is not the executioner but the exemplary bureaucrat who proves to be more loyal to the state than to his friend."[27] The difference between South Africa and the European totalitarian examples lies of course in the fact that for the Afrikaner civil servant, state and society appear identical, that he has no friends outside his ethnic unit to be loyal to, merely objects to administer. The Afrikaner policeman only fulfills his unquestioned duty to his people by roughing up those who appear "cheeky" in his world view. He is not a villain who has made an evil choice but merely a product of a system that predetermines his roles and attitudes. For the victim, his viciousness lies in his normalcy.

However, because of the nonideological nature of the conflict, active individual challengers to the power center are not annihilated and simultaneously purged from the history books. Nor need successful ethnic revolutionaries display the venom against foes, as characteristic of Nazism. On occasion, such as the death of leading African nationalists, even reluctant respect for the stature of the opponent emerges. Vorster called Robert Sobukwe, the persecuted leader of the Pan Africanist Congress, a man of magnetic personality. The Afrikaner press came close to conventional eulogies at his death from cancer in 1978: "Here was a black man who represented facets of black nationalism which can be especially appreciated by nationalists who have fought their own battle for freedom, but at the same time unfortunately represented dangerous facets of that same black nationalism which necessarily had to lead to a collision."[28] Other papers deplore the

27. George Konrád, "The Long Work of Liberty," *The New York Review of Books*, January 26, 1978, p. 28.
28. *Beeld*, February 28, 1978.

failure of co-optation and view it as "tragic that a black leader like Robert Sobukwe saw no prospect of playing the leadership role within this [apartheid] framework for which he would have been so eminently fitted."[29]

It would seem important to grasp these subtle differences for assessing the chances of South African liberalization rather than blocking such inquiries by false analogies with fascism.[30]

THE FOCUS ON RACISM

The Coloured man is not by nature a revolutionary—Die Vaderland, January 6, 1977.

How much the accumulated racism presents a stumbling block for the pragmatic pursuit of group interest remains a decisive question. If reified racism has indeed developed a dynamic of its own, there is little hope for a pragmatic policy as distinct from fanatic allegiance to a sacred creed. An obvious institutionalized racialism, which leads to unequal distribution of opportunities and life-chances according to skin pigmentation, pervades every corner of South African society. However, the very structural entrenchment of racial segregation in conjunction with the Afrikaner ascendancy to political power in 1948 has changed the expression of this racist reality as well as its impact on intergroup relations. In order to explore this crucial aspect in more depth it is necessary to review the general literature on racial antagonism and place South Africa in comparative perspective.

In our view, racial conflicts represent only one, though the

29. *Die Transvaler,* March 1, 1978.

30. In the vast literature on German fascism from which the outlined distinctions are derived, one author stands out: Barrington Moore combines comparative and truly interdisciplinary approaches with rich insights from a lifelong study of the pertinent questions in political sociology. His most recent book, *Injustice. The Social Bases of Obedience and Revolt* (White Plains, N.Y.: M. E. Sharpe, 1978), makes fascinating reading not just on fascism but on most crucial issues in the social sciences in general.

most salient and impenetrable, variant of ethnic inequality. Whether an ethnic system of stratification is based on linguistic, religious, sexist, regional, or racist criteria for differential distribution of political power, wealth, and status is of minor theoretical significance. What is unique about race is its visibility and impermeability, whereas communal mobilization on language or religious lines may allow for individual "passing" in rare cases of acculturation and conversion. Furthermore for the victims, racial discrimination has nowadays become more offensive and, therefore, is frequently rationalized with cultural differences. In this respect, ethnicity can easily serve as an obfuscating euphemism for old practices of racialism. But on whatever criteria communal groups are mobilized or excluded, this does not amount to a qualitative difference for group relations from a sociological perspective. The Ulsterman is convinced that he can smell a Catholic fellow Irishman. The British in South Africa for a long time referred to the Afrikaner as an inferior race. Perhaps all communal exclusion needs the certainty of supposed inherited biological characteristics of the out-group, at least at the level of folk wisdom. For the actors in the concrete social reality of communal conflicts such fine distinctions between themselves and "strangers" overlap and remain academic. Why, therefore, should they be so crucial to the academics?

There is no paucity of theories of racial antagonism in the social science literature. The theories range from color as an independent cause[31] to the Marxist explanation of racism as a manipulative device to fragment international working-class solidarity and to justify imperialist expansion.[32] A recent perceptive study of the emotional barrier to an integrated society in the United States concludes that a "fear of sexual loss" must lie at the root of racial hostility. It attempts to explain why the white male might be sexually threatened by extending equality to the black.[33]

31. Kenneth J. Gergen, "The Significance of Skin Color in Human Relations," *Daedalus* (Spring 1967), pp. 390–406.

32. The classic in this respect is O. C. Cox, *Class, Caste, and Race* (New York: Monthly Review Press, 1959).

33. Charles Herbert Stember, *Sexual Racism* (New York: Elsevier, 1976).

33

Among undogmatic observers there can be little doubt that the Marxist and liberal hopes of increasingly color-blind societies, with autonomous individuals relating to each other on the basis of common class interests rather than ascriptive characteristics, falls far short of reality everywhere. In fact, a revival of nationalist, racial, and sectarian appeals has been authoritatively diagnosed as a global tendency, despite increasing economic interdependence, better education, and contact of formerly isolated groups. Ethnicity is considered to be "a new social category as significant for the understanding of the present day world as that of social class itself."[34] The paradox has been recognized that despite "modernization" in all its forms, communal attachments do not automatically wither away but in fact heightened ethnic attachments might be a reaction against modernity. Ethnic rivalry is found greatest not among culturally isolated peasants but among urbanized elites who have the most contact with each other and who were educated in the same tradition of non-parochialism and, often, bilingualism. A growing number of sociologists, therefore, account for racial and ethnic antagonism in terms of group competition for scarce resources. Prejudice toward out-groups is no longer viewed as a fundamentally irrational fear of the stranger but as a social construction of reality on both sides, corresponding to perceived group needs, threats to a traditional status, or strife for a better one in the continuing battle for security and equality.

34. Nathan Glazer and Daniel P. Moynihan, *Ethnicity, Theory and Experience* (Cambridge, Mass.: Harvard University Press, 1975), p. 3. See also Crawford Young, *The Politics of Cultural Pluralism* (Madison: The University of Wisconsin Press, 1976). A rather unsatisfactory study despite its high praise as the last word on the subject is E. K. Francis, *Interethnic Relations* (New York: Elsevier, 1976). I found John Stone (ed.), *Race, Ethnicity and Social Change* (North Sciuate, Mass.: Duxbury Press, 1977), the most useful general reader available at present. For sociological insights the work of John Rex and Pierre van den Berghe remains unsurpassed while Michael Banton's, *Race Relations* (London: Tavistock, 1967), still provides a generally useful overview of early research results. A stimulating attempt of hypothesis construction with a focus on anthropological research is Robert A. LeVine and Donald T. Campbell, *Ethnocentrism. Theories of Conflict, Ethnic Attitudes, and Group Behavior* (New York: Wiley, 1972).

Particularly, insightful recent analyses by Edna Bonacich have isolated a split labor market as a cause of ethnic antagonism.[35] Central to her scheme of the split labor market is the conflict between three key classes: business, higher-paid labor, and cheap labor. Factors affecting the dynamics of such constellations are carefully scrutinized. Ethnic antagonism is said to germinate first in a labor market in which immigrant workers are introduced at a lower wage level. Two groups of workers are differentially remunerated for the same work. Factors that determine the price of migrant or immigrant labor are (1) level of living or economic resources, (2) information on which immigrants base their expectations—the best example of this being the case of indentured laborers who accept conditions of employment in the home country before they have seen the host country, (3) political resources, namely the group's organizational skills and the extent to which they can bring pressure to bear from their home areas, (4) motives for working permanently or temporarily and their influence on likely labor disputes, and finally, (5) differences in skill.

Ethnic antagonism is presented as taking two antithetical forms: exclusion movements, such as the former policy adopted by Australia toward Asian immigrants, and caste-like systems, such as South African apartheid. "Caste is essentially an aristocracy of labor in which higher paid labor deals with the undercutting potential of cheaper labor by excluding them from certain types of work."[36] This is illustrated in the South African case with special reference to the mining industry. In this instance, despite the availability of cheaper African labor, mine owners have had to take account of the political strength of the white workers in defending their positions. Whereas exclusion movements serve the interests of higher-paid labor and deprive the entrepreneurs of cheap labor, caste arrangements are based on exclusiveness rather than exclusion. Both protect higher-paid labor

35. Edna Bonacich, "A Theory of Ethnic Antagonism: The Split Labor Market," *American Sociological Review* 37 (October 1972), 547–59.

36. Ibid., p. 555.

from being undercut. It was the entrenchment of Afrikaner-dom as a *political* class, encompassing all *economic* classes of the ethnic group, that made possible an ethnic revolution through the capture of state power. Theories of middlemen minorities have been constructed to explain the almost universal hostility against the "marginal outsiders" in between.[37] Other studies have analyzed secessionist ethnic movements as resistance by a neglected periphery against an encroaching centralization, which was supposed to decrease parochial sentiments.

Without paying attention to the important different historical origins of culturally heterogeneous population groups in contemporary nation states (migration, conquest, slavery), it is useful to delineate three structurally different situations of apparent ethnic/racial conflict in order to view South Africa in comparative perspective. These three contexts are (a) state violence against a scapegoat minority, (b) colonial labor exploitation, and (c) ethnic group competition.

State Violence against a Scapegoat Minority

The obvious example of an extreme case of racial violence was the institutionalized aggression of Nazi Germany against Jews and other stigmatized minorities. Neither minority was objectively a threat to the dominant group. Most German Jews were fully integrated economically and socially and were secularized and culturally German. They could not even be visibly distinguished from the host society. The victims were set up as villains, independent of their behavior but in accordance with a convenient tradition of historical anti-Semitism. Their fate has to be explained in conjunction with a social movement in which the scapegoat minority fulfilled the indispensable function of welding together the heterogeneous elements through a common cause. In order to achieve the total mobilization, an enemy had to be overcome, a

37. See the classic study by E. V. Stonequist, *The Marginal Man* (New York: Scribner, 1937), and its theoretical elaboration by H. F. Dickie-Clark, *The Marginal Situation* (London: Routledge & Kegan Paul, 1966), with a case study of the Durban "coloured" community.

morale and esprit de corps created. The agitator pointed out the obstacle in the path of the chosen goals as formidable and dangerous but yet weak and vulnerable with proper determination. The metaphor of Jews as vermin and parasites satisfied both requirements.[38]

The Nazi deeds cannot, however, be explained by the exigencies of war. While the Nazi crimes were committed during the war, they were not directly related to the war. The unique aspect of Hitler's murdering consisted in its senselessness: the *raison d'état* did not provide any reason or even pretense for the genocide. In this respect Hitler differed from other criminals. Analogies with Hiroshima, Dresden, or Vietnam do not fit. The Nazi machinery had set out to eliminate selected groups (not only Jews, but also gypsies, Russian prisoners of war, the mentally retarded, the Polish intelligentsia) regardless of their role in the war.

What has to be explained, above all, is not the ultimate genocide that was already inherent in the early propaganda, and incidental to the victims' role, but why so many were susceptible to the tunes of the agitator. Widespread psychological predispositions which were nonetheless socially produced would seem to have been obviously exploited. The earlier mentioned classic study *The Authoritarian Personality*, despite its methodological deficiencies[39] and its political bias,[40] still provides the most penetrating insight into a character syndrome in need of identification with strong leaders and victorious groups. However, the socialization of ego-weak personalities takes place under different cultural circumstances and the underlying anxieties assume a continuously changing content. While Nazi fascism was certainly not a unique historical accident or an exclusively German phenomenon, its potential reappearance in other situations

38. Leo Lowenthal and Norbert Guterman, *Prophets of Deceit*, 2nd ed. (Palo Alto, Calif.: Pacific Books, 1970).

39. Richard Christie and Marie Jahoda (eds.), *Studies in the Scope and Method of "The Authoritarian Personality"* (Glencoe, Ill.: Free Press, 1954).

40. Milton Rokeach, *The Open and the Closed Mind* (New York: Basic Books, 1960).

could occur in quite different guises. From a sociological viewpoint what is decisive are the specific historical sociopolitical conditions that allowed the fascist movement to sweep into power and then use, unhindered, the state machinery of coercion for the extermination of a scapegoat minority.

To explain the political rise of such extremism as a result of capitalism in crisis, as some Marxists stress, does not answer the questions why equally depressed capitalist economies turned to "New Deals" and other social welfare measures instead of to authoritarian despotism. Historical differences in the democratic tradition and political culture of Western societies together with a differential state of competition for colonial hegemony among imperialist rivals account for such decisive different developments. In a similar vein, differences in the treatment of guest workers in Western Europe, policy changes regarding colored immigrants in Britain, civil rights measures and affirmative action in the United States, or discriminatory measures against politically powerless cultural minorities in many Third World countries can largely be explained in terms of different political cultures rather than pure economic reasons.

Colonial Labor Exploitation

Race relations in colonial situations or in feudal slave societies are fundamentally different from the state-directed violence against a scapegoat minority, although the term fascism is frequently applied to these forms of tyranny by the few over the many. However, labor exploitation by an upper caste in a feudal or colonial setting exhibits, above all, benevolent despotism or what van den Berghe has called paternalistic race relations.[41] The status differences between the rigidly stratified two casts are clear and the social distances between

41. Pierre van den Berghe, *Race and Racism* (New York: Wiley, 1967), pp. 22–29. See also the perceptive revision of paternalism in Eugene Genovese, *Roll, Jordan, Roll* (New York: Vintage Books, 1972), pp. 3–7. The burgeoning research on slavery, particularly the work of C. Vann Woodward and David Brion Davis, is very useful for understanding the South African differences.

unequal roles can therefore go together with great intimacy in the common household or work place between master and servant.

The assumed childlike inferiority of the dependents has frequently been internalized by the subordinate group and there is, therefore, no personality need for demonstrations of hostility. On the contrary, rather than hate, protective love and "pseudo-tolerance" for those who "know their place" is common. Those individuals who are perceived as "stepping out of line" are targets of swift retaliations in lynchings or in other punishment. Mass violence, however, originates from the subordinates in rare rebellions that are brutally squashed. But short of insurrection, the terror of the rulers is seldom directed indiscriminately against all members of the subordinate group. In fact colonial labor exploitation has a direct interest in the basic loyalty of its subject class, not its persecution. Acquiescence is required from the colonial population, who are legally excluded from all political or socioeconomic activity (trade unions) that could threaten the vast privileges of the ruling caste. Given the numerical majority status of the surbordinates, their ultimate aim is the capture and reversal of state power. The extent of racial violence depends on the degree of politicization of the colonized and the degree of resilience, manpower, and resources of the ruling caste. South Africa, like many former feudal societies, is growing out of the period of colonial labor exploitation into a different stage of conflict.

Ethnic Group Competition

Different from state violence against insignificant minorities or colonial labor exploitation is ethnic group competition. What is in dispute is access to political power and its spoils.

As current examples in Northern Ireland, Lebanon, and Cyprus have so vividly demonstrated, precipitants for ethnic mass violence exist when sizable ethnically organized groups with different cultural traditions compete in the same state for greater equality under unequal institutional conditions. What these situations have in common is that (1) the dominant

39

group has restricted institutionalized competition in its monopoly over state power and so reduced the subordinate group to second class citizenship, (2) as legitimation the dominant group has translated its culture into national values that it is said would be threatened by the ascendancy of the excluded group, (3) the competing groups foster the allegiance of their members through separate institutions, particularly education, and frown on intergroup links of individuals as traitorous.

Almost invariably, the mutual group perceptions draw their militant sentiments and symbolisms from previous historical conflicts as well as wider external forces. These have often adopted respective clients who receive essential support from outside interests. Frequent cases of such interethnic warfare have emerged in the so-called plural societies of the Third World (Biafra, Sudan, Ethiopia, Bangladesh, Kurdistan) where the former colonial powers are responsible for national boundaries that coincided with their administrative and strategic blueprints but rarely with the ethnic composition of the inhabitants. Weak identification with the national center, whose rewards and resources (particularly civil service positions) were dominated by one ethnic group at the expense of others, has led to feelings of "relative deprivation" among disadvantaged elites, culminating in counterethnic mobilization for rebellion or secession.

After a spectacular atrocity, civil war usually starts with the disintegration of the national army and police force which openly switch their allegiance to their respective community leadership. In cases where the regime's forces already consist of members of the ruling group, increased repression of dissident demonstrations lead to territorial fortification (barricades on the Bogside, Christian and Moslem enclaves in Lebanon, Greek and Turkish sectors in Cyprus) and the emergence of counter defense groups in two virtually separate states, according to existing residential patterns. The outcome of the contest depends on the resources, particularly military hardware and trained activists, each side can muster, but above all, whether, when, and on whose side a third party intervenes to constrain both contestants and to impose a truce (Syria in Lebanon, the United Kingdom in Northern Ireland, U.N. peacekeeping forces in Cyprus and the Middle East).

Compared with the outlined situations of ethnic group mobilization, South Africa represents a unique case in two respects: (1) in the explicit legalization and institutionalization of racial criteria for exclusion, although the competing elites have frequently identical or similar backgrounds in terms of language, religion, and political orientation, and (2) in the fact that because of the numerical weakness of the ruling Afrikaner group and its intention to forestall a threatening confrontation as just described, the government itself has adopted a policy of dismantling the nation through the creation of self-governing ethnic units, which nonetheless remain in a client relationship to the center because of their economic interdependence.

Such a policy however represented only the final outcome of Afrikaner entrenchment and unification. As is shown in subsequent chapters, the enactment of racial laws (social apartheid, prohibition of interracial sex, residential and education segregation) in the first decade of Nationalist rule was as much directed at fostering Afrikaner unity in light of its internal stratification as it aimed at holding the "black threat" at bay. The petty apartheid laws placated the poor Afrikaners with status symbols but also ensured their proper behavior. At the same time Afrikaner unity, the prerequisite of its political power, introduced exclusive Afrikaner education or, better still, Christian-National indoctrination. Afrikaner exclusivism insisted on the prohibition of white immigration since the mainly British newcomers were viewed as unassimilable with the *volk* but as likely additions to the English out-group. These policies indicate that not only an antiblack racism but a comparably strong antiforeigner sentiment accompanied the evolution of Afrikaner power. Had antiblack racism been the main mobilizing force, European immigrants would surely have been welcomed as staunch supporters of a white minority, as they became in the early 1960s.

41

The initial biological racism shifted to an ideology of cultural differences with the development of Verwoerd's grand apartheid designs. No longer were blacks officially considered to be inferior but as being capable of similar potential, given the same opportunities. Under Vorster then, it became increasingly clear to Afrikaner ideologues that apartheid blueprints, unless substantially modified, could not provide the conditions for lasting racial stability in the country. Above all, the social racism of petty apartheid was no longer necessary and had even become an embarrassment, since Afrikaner power was firmly in the saddle. Ideologically, and in institutional practice, the regime now moved to favor crosscutting political links with a coloured and Indian bourgeoisie confined to but also profiting in status and power from their separate semi-autonomous realms. Black client bureaucracies in independent Bantustans took care of the rural part of the numerical "black menace" and provided, for the time being at least, the legal device for depriving urban Africans of their citizenship.

This scenario would seem to demonstrate that the liberal focus on traditional racism, particularly in its attitudinal aspects of prejudice and irrational hate or rejection of other race groups, becomes increasingly insufficient for grasping the intricate group interaction in South Africa. Government policy in South Africa can be much better understood in terms of the consolidation, defense, and expansion of Afrikaner power. In this respect, Afrikaner policy differs only in its methods but hardly in its moral cause from similar exclusivist ethnic groups in power, be it the Protestants in Ulster or the Tutsis in Burundi.

THE CONCEPT OF PLURAL SOCIETIES

It has become fashionable among both supporters and opponents of the South African government to describe situations of ethnic dominance as intrinsic problems of plural socie-

ties.[42] John Rex, in rejecting the usefulness of the stratification approach to race relations, points to the absence
of "universal" societal standards.[43] Instead he refers to the
existence of internal standards of various ethnic groups. This
is considered prevalent in colonial societies where the absence of shared values among the constituent segments is
most noticeable.

The theory of the plural society, with its focus on cultural
and institutional variation as the major force determining social organization and social change, was initially proposed by
J. S. Furnivall on the basis of his research in Southeast Asia. It
has since been developed by M. G. Smith, P. van den Berghe,
and Leo Kuper, among others.[44] Furnivall describes the
characteristic features of plural society as (1) a society composed of disparate ethnic categories that live side-by-side,
because individuals of differeing ethnicity meet only in the
marketplace; (2) each ethnic category occupies a particular
place in the economic structure, with economic relations predominating over all other aspects of life, and (3) the component sections of the populations do not have a common "social will" or commonly agreed to set of values for checking
and guiding social action. The society is therefore held together only by external coercive power, usually, though not
necessarily, that of a foreign government.[45]

For Furnivall, pluralistic society derived from the disintegration of native cultures under the impact of capitalism,
which he saw as being virtually synonymous with colonialism. One permanent form of the disruption of native life was

42. For a good overview of the South African debate see Lawrence
Schlemmer, "Theories of the Plural Societies and Change in South Africa,"
Social Dynamics, 3, no. 1 (June 1977), 3–16.

43. John Rex, *Race Relations in Sociological Theory* (London: Weidenfeld &
Nicolson, 1970).

44. For the most authoritative but tedious statement see Leo Kuper and M.
G. Smith (eds.), *Pluralism in Africa* (Berkeley: University of California Press,
1971).

45. J. S. Furnivall, *Colonial Policy and Practice* (Cambridge: Cambridge University Press, 1948), pp. 199–204.

the substitution of the capitalist physical structure of existence—the introduction of the city as the center of productive life—for the system of villages serving largely self-sufficient agricultural communities. This strain toward centralization in colonialism is the basis of pluralism. Thus the critical feature of the plural society is the distinct pattern of economic behavior characteristic of colonialists and natives. While the initial application of the idea of the plural society was specifically in relation to colonial societies, it was gradually extended to give it applicability to all culturally heterogeneous societies. The latter view conceived of almost any cultural difference in social groups as a basis of pluralism.

M. G. Smith, one of the leading protagonists of the pluralist school points out that the plural society distinguishes itself by the specific arrangement of its cultural heterogeneity. All the cultural units, although autonomous, are bound together politically into a single polity. Such cultural diversity or pluralism is said to impose the structural necessity for domination by one of the cultural sections, usually a cultural minority. The integration of these various units is said to take place not on a voluntary basis but either by coercion or by force of economic circumstances. In the interests of the political unity of the whole, the former political institutions of the subordinate groups are inevitably repressed by the dominant minority. Given this situation, where there is hardly any value consensus, the social relations between groups deteriorate into an impersonal secondary type of contact. Coercion is inevitable according to the plural model.

Several of these theoretical assumptions are open to question: (1) It is doubtful whether cultural diversity or pluralism inevitably imposes the structural necessity for domination by a cultural minority. It could just as readily impose the necessity for equal representation of the various cultural sections. (2) The degree of autonomy of these cultural sections can be questioned, since they participate in common economic and political institutions and are subject to their dictates, particularly in industrialized, interdependent societies, such as

South Africa. Inclusion of blacks in the labor market with its own demands, makes the cultural autonomy of the preindustrial sector a waning phenomenon. However, there are also countertrends. As noted earlier, cultural differences are stressed by the ruling group precisely because members of the subject race have increasingly acquired the dominant culture and, based on these values, lay claim to its privileges. (3) Throughout the literature on pluralism, there is an underlying trend that "cultural diversity" is the main source of societal instability, that the colonial powers had served the purpose of holding together societies wrecked by very real cleavages, and that only an external power was capable of containing them. In this way, ethnic conflicts are hardly viewed as being related to questions of material equality, equal opportunities for all, justice, and discrimination. In short, the economic sector, the changing mode of production, is largely excluded from the analysis, or at best added as another variable and not as a constituent of ethnic cleavages. Cultural differences, and more especially the importance attached to such differences, are not conceived of as a rationalizing ideology for domination, but as constituting a force in their own right. The pluralist perspective tends to reify cultural differences as if they were immutable.

In this respect notions of pluralism serve the South African government well in the absence of a legitimating ideology of minority domination. Ideological insecurity is reflected in the frequent change of official labels for the subject population. What sounds like a surreal joke for those acquainted with the academic literature—the renaming of the "Department of Bantu Administration" (after "Native Affairs") into "Plural Relations"—indicates the perceived need for legitimation in line with acceptable outside norms. Moreover, "plural relations" conveniently redefines the new phase of interethnic collaboration between center and more autonomous periphery bureaucracies. The term obfuscates the very antipluralist policy of dismantling South Africa into more ethnically homogeneous independent units.

THE FOCUS ON CLASS FORMATION

Compared with the insistence on racism or cultural pluralism as the key to an understanding of the conflict, the emphasis on the beneficiaries of racial exploitation has superior explanatory value in understanding policy changes. Particularly in the revisions of several so-called "neo-Marxists" of differing outlooks, the focus on antagonistic capital interests in conjunction with state policies is far more pertinent than the hope for reconciliation and reasoning within a common humanity. It is fair to say that the earlier liberal optimism that industrialization will automatically be followed by democratization has been convincingly refuted in the last decade. Advanced capitalism and ascribed status allocation in a racial order are compatible, as South Africa demonstrates. Private capital may not reap the optimal profits under a system of restricted labor policies and substantial state interference, but it still yields sufficiently huge profit margins that would not have been possible in the first place without state suppression of effective bargaining and the low social costs of labor as a result of apartheid.

In this respect, many Marxist-inspired analyses, particularly of their favorite "ideal-type" subject, gold-mining, belabor the obvious. Where they fall short in most cases is in an adequate grasp of the psychological aspects of ethnicity versus class. Afrikaner nationalism, for example, served many purposes for its adherents. The variety of its meanings for those who embraced the ethnic outlook cannot be reduced to a rationale for economic exploitation. And yet the proponents of an exclusive class analysis view apartheid narrowly as a mere manipulative device for oppression and control of labor:

> From its inception it [apartheid] has operated simultaneously as an expression of the domination of capital in South Africa and as an expression concerned to reproduce [in changing forms] separate "racial" or "cultural" identities. Its real effects, as institutionalised through state policy are to perpetuate the oppression, uneven development, and

exploitation inherent in capitalist relationships; its ideological functions are to present those realities as forms of "racial" or "cultural" conflict, as "threats" to "group identities" which can be "solved" by varying modes of separation.[46]

Why should the independent role of beliefs not be granted, even in shaping an economic environment? Marxist interpretations of South Africa rarely go beyond the notion of base and superstructure. By mechanically relegating the realm of ideology to a mere reflection of underlying interests, Marxists usually ignore the subjective reality. A peculiar sterility, therefore, characterizes much of the recent leftist writing on South Africa. While their revelations of the structural forces in motion are indeed appealing, at the same time they are unsatisfactory in grasping the full picture of group behavior. Charles Lindblom recently felt the need to reject the popular misconception "that there exists some category of man's goals or aspirations that can be labelled economic." He reiterated that "people work, as well as buy and sell, in pursuit of goals as diverse as comfort, security, aesthetic pleasures, novelty, conformity, thrill, and diversion."[47] To dismiss such timely reminders as the false consciousness of bourgeois subjectivism may be as unnecessarily narrow as the usual neglect of insights from other scientific approaches. Official Marxism in Eastern Europe still excommunicates psychoanalysis from its tolerated methods. Similar dogmatism characterizes some of the radical South African studies although their authors are nonaffiliated academics.[48]

46. Martin Legassick and Duncan Innes, "Capital Restructuring and Apartheid: A Critique of Constructive Engagement," *African Affairs*, 76, no. 305 (October 1977), 464.

47. Charles Lindblom, *Politics and Markets* (New York: Basic Books, 1978), p. 9.

48. For example, in a special issue on South Africa of *The Journal of African Political Economy*, no. 7 (1977), in which a dozen Marxist-oriented authors collaborated, Afrikaner nationalism or ethnic belief systems in general were completely ignored. The reader who is interested in the finer semantics and historical details of the inner-Marxist debate may wish to consult various

47

In the orthodox version of the South African Communist Party (CPSA) the racism of white workers is blamed on temporarily successful manipulation or repressive state coercion that prevents free uncensored organization.[49] This bias of party Marxists, which "did not encourage theoretical debate" led a recent analyst to conclude: "Had the South African revolution produced its own Lenin he would undoubtedly have been drummed out of the CPSA."[50] What leading CP theoreticians such as Joe Slovo have written on South Africa remains so securely within the confines of doctrine, that they are safe from purges.[51]

An open Marxism on the other hand would not shy away from analyzing working class racism instead of redefining it as the "false consciousness" of a "labor aristocracy." The Cornwall miners did not become a "petty bourgeoisie" through their emigration to South Africa. They were still miners. The popular concept of "fraction" can also be applied to workers and need not be confined to capital interests. As Stanley Greenberg has argued, the trade union movement

---

articles in the British based *Journal of Southern African Studies, Economy and Society, New Left Review,* and, sometimes, *African Affairs.* The U.S. based *Journal of Southern African Affairs* on the other hand, espouses a less orthodox, more nationalistic, radical perspective. For a useful though not always accurate overview of the liberal-radical controversy see Harrison M. Wright, *The Burden of the Present* (Cape Town: David Philip, 1977). One founder of the "revisionist" South African historiography, F. A. Johnstone, has recently become very critical of Marxist political ideology (as opposed to methods), while other adherents of class analysis, such as Dan O'Meara in particular, have written some of the most insightful papers on early Afrikaner history. It is indicative though that almost all Marxist scholars concern themselves mainly with historical developments and hardly address themselves systematically to the contemporary scene.

49. H. J. Simons and R. J. Simons, *Class and Colour in South Africa—1850–1950* (Harmondsworth: Penguin, 1969).

50. R. W. Johnson, *How Long Will South Africa Survive?* (London: Macmillan, 1977), p. 25.

51. Joe Slovo, "South Africa—No Middle Road," in *Southern Africa: The New Politics of Revolution,* ed. Basil Davidson, Joe Slovo, Anthony Wilkinson (Harmondsworth: Penguin, 1976).

pursued different policies dependent on job security. The industrial unions favored strikes to limit black employment and prevent rival back unions from undercutting their privileges. For the artisan unions on the other hand, race was of lesser importance and they generally did not call for government interference on their behalf. More of such differentiation is the strength of an undogmatic focus on the political economy.

Many of the neo-Marxist studies note the extraordinary peaceful industrial relations between white unions and employers since the Rand Revolt of 1922 "on a scale unmatched in any advanced capitalist society."[52] This is explained by the obvious fact that the white workers receive "a proportion of the surplus generated by the forced labour economy." Nevertheless, such mere sharing in the benefits of exploitation by all major white sections would hardly have sufficed to suppress distributive conflicts between competing interests without the existence of a powerful ethnic ideology. Generally speaking, nationalisms do not only mobilize in-groups for the exclusion or conquest of outsiders, but above all impose discipline and pseudo-harmony on intragroup cleavages which in objective terms often exceed the in-group–out-group dichotomy. In the name of the higher spiritual goal and the psychological reward of belonging to the chosen in-group, sacrifices can be demanded, tensions pacified, and incompatibilities reconciled far beyond the dream of crosscutting interest group solidarity.

In the South African case, material rewards are at present only one part of the payoff that accounts for the maintenance of Afrikaner unity. Almost equally important would seem the cohesive power of a symbol system, rewards of esteem and status, the integrating role of ideology which is frequently underestimated, if not altogether rejected in economic analysis. Only a genuine synthesis of the interplay between

52. Martin Legassick, "Gold, Agriculture, and Secondary Industry in South Africa, 1885–1970: From Periphery to Sub-Metropole as a Forced Labour System," in *The Roots of Rural Poverty: Historical Background*, ed. Neil Parsons and Robin Palmer (London: Heinemann, 1977), p. 187.

ideology and economy, not the focus on either at the expense of the other, would seem to hold the key for deeper insights into the complex conflict.

In summary, Marxist analysis succeeds in penetrating beyond the symbolic structures with which groups interpret their changing reality. By not taking such ideological expressions as a given or "primordial" innate sentiment, the changing function of cultural identity can be discerned. The decoded symbols mostly reveal class interests hidden behind the proclaimed ethnic unity. Thus Marxist analysis can pinpoint the constituents of ethnic agitation. But this is where the usefulness of class analysis usually ends. What orthodox Marxism and most of its offspring fail to explain is why ethnic symbolism so easily succeeds in obscuring its beneficiaries. Class analysis remains mute or unconvincing on the crucial question as to why people everywhere are susceptible to the calls of agitators even though the mobilization goes against their real interests. To blame false consciousness begs the question.

THE COLONIAL ANALOGY

> *Bulala umulungu ("Kill the Whites")*—Popular slogan during Soweto upheaval 1976.

> *The interests of Southern Africa cannot be served by Russian, Cuban and American imperialist designs. . . . We must work at our own salvation. The problem is that the great powers will not leave us alone to do just that.*—Die Vaderland, March 16, 1977

In the colonial analogy, South Africa is considered the last outpost of an outdated system of alien rule. Its abolition is viewed as certain as the departure of the European powers from the rest of Africa during the process of decolonization since World War II. However, our argument doubts the applicability of this analogy in the case of South Africa, because of a different history of this society.

The early political independence of South Africa from colonial British rule—through the granting of self-government to the Cap Colony in 1853 and the establishment of a sovereign state in 1910—allowed the rise of a truly national bourgeoisie. Unlike other colonial societies, these national interests ensured the reinvestment of accumulated capital in the local economy instead of its being drained to the metropole. Because of their perceived permanent rather than temporary ties with the colonized land, the independent settlers developed early in infrastructure that became the basis of South Africa's industrialization. Abundant cheap labor, agricultural potential, and, above all, vast mineral resources (starting with the discovery of gold and diamonds) together with a pleasant climate and appealing landscape attracted further capital flows and a constant stream of skilled European immigrants. These factors combined later to create socioeconomic conditions different from the traditional colonization by a comprador class acting under the umbrella and in the interest of metropolitan capital. In this respect South Africa differs from all other British settler colonies, including Rhodesia, and particularly from Angola and Mozambique, as well as Algeria.

Above all, this rapid development of South Africa to an industrial empire took place in conjunction with an early anticolonial movement, that is, the bitter struggle between English capital and the indigenous farming group over state control. Only through state power could a weak and nascent Afrikanerdom hope to wrench a share from the giant foreign mining houses and move into other lucrative economic activities. Protectionist policies were a prerequisite for success in this endeavor.

Political power and substantial Afrikaner inroads into English monopoly capital, however, constituted only the outcome of a long process of ethnic activation. After the demoralizing defeat in the Boer War, a first phase of *cultural* "remoralization" centered around the suppressed Afrikaans language and heritage symbols. As will be shown in detail in subsequent chapters, *economic* mobilization ("buy Afrikaans") and the redirection of savings into exclusive Af-

51

rikaner institutions later in the 1930s facilitated primitive capital accumulation.

The success of the many campaigns by various Afrikaner organizations hinged on the psychological susceptibility for an ideal of collective sacrifice and solidarity, particularly among the growing dislocated and proletarianized Afrikaner work force in the cities. By their ideological inclusion into a larger ethnic unit, these poor whites were provided with much more tangible psychological rewards of belonging than a more abstract interclass and interrace solidarity could ever yield. This psychological security more than the material benefits attached to it, must be seen as the secret appeal of nationalisms everywhere. Even where material payoffs are missing, the rewards of belonging can substitute for the real advances for a long time. Therefore, the economic strides of an ethnically mobilized group can be considered more of a byproduct than as the main initial goal of this process, at least in the perception of the majority of group adherents.

Once cultural and economic mobilization was successfully achieved among Afrikaners a share in and later the takeover of exclusive central political power remained only a matter of time, given their numerical strength. The policies surrounding World War II split Afrikanerdom temporarily, but the forced isolation of South Africa from her European navel also helped to broaden the economic base of the emerging national bourgeoisie. With unchallenged political power at its disposal since 1948, Afrikanerdom could not only use the laws for further expansion but increasingly established itself as a parallel state-capitalism in addition to its takeover of the spreading public administration. Therefore, not only does South Africa politically constitute a sovereign state but also economically.[53] Her Afrikaner ruling tribe has, comparatively

53. It is indicative of the growing radicalization of African opinion that since about 1975 the legality and sovereignty of the South African state itself has been challenged. While the Lusaka Manifesto of 1969 carefully distinguished between the decolonization of Rhodesia and South West Africa on the one side and the elimination of racism in South Africa as a separate issue, a PAC manifesto now declares: "The certificate of respectability portrayed in

speaking, a lot more to lose than had any other European settler population in Africa, accentuated by the Afrikaner severance of ties with their European origin long ago. It is logical therefore to conclude that analogies with processes of decolonization elsewhere do not necessarily apply to South Africa.

A brief glance at the military situation can demonstrate this decisive difference and the fallacy of the domino theory, which views South Africa as the last colonial outpost that will inevitably fall after the surrounding white controlled enclaves have succumbed to African liberation. In all colonial wars of liberation in Africa (Algeria, Kenya, Mozambique, Angola) the local settlers could not sustain their rule without calling in the colonial army for help. The metropolitan forces were able to hold the indigenous insurgents off, but at a rising cost to the metropole.[54] This led to pressure on the settlers for a

the Lusaka manifesto that the racist regime of South Africa is an independent sovereign state is unjustified and unacceptable to the people of Azania." (Submission by Potlako K. Leballo to 1975 OAU Summit in Kampala, entitled "P.A.C. Case Against the Racist South Africa's Legal International Status of Independent Sovereign State.") It is unclear to what extent this document merely represents the view of its author or, as it claims, is shared by other African movements, particularly the ANC. The latter seems unlikely in light of the closer contacts that the ANC has with the signatories of the Lusaka Manifesto. The document, while arguing the continued colonial status of foreign Boer rule over African natives, is silent on the envisaged fate of the whites and does not even mention the other minorities. The submission concludes: "Our mandate and the views of our oppressed people are un-equivocal. Our struggle is for self-determination. To do so, we must over-throw the racist fascist colonialist regime of South Africa by force of arms. We reject outright any confusion or compromise with the enemy created by detente, dialogue or any contact. Our ultimate objective is for the seizure of political power, the recovery of our land and the means of production. For these reasons there can be no compromise whatsoever. We are fighting to the finish, even if it takes us over three hundred years–the struggle must con-tinue."

54. Contrary to frequent assertions, the Portuguese coup in April 1974 was not so much "stimulated by the increasing victories of the liberation movements in Mozambique and Angola" (Legassick, 1977, p. 196), but by the emergence of the European Common Market and the late entry of Britain, Portugal's most important trading partner. Vital membership of Portugal in

political handover of power, maintaining the traditional economic metropolitan relationships in a neocolonial guise. The local settlers, although furious about such a sellout, could not resist it because of their dependency on the metropolitan army. This classical constellation of decolonization does not prevail in South Africa. Even if there was a de Gaulle in sight in Washington, his control over Pretoria would be comparatively minimal, since the local ruling caste can, on the whole, take care of its military protection itself, short of a massive outside incursion backed by a major superpower.

In such a situation, African guerrillas "can no more defeat the South African army than El Fatah can beat the Israelis."[55] All the complex reasons for this assessment, which is shared by most knowledgeable observers, cannot be elaborated here. But one aspect of this power relationship, compared with the weakness of the colonial armies, is the relative absence of internal class cleavages in the citizen armies of both South Africa and Israel. They do not have a special Sandhurst-Oxbridge trained stratum of status-conscious professional officers imposed on the drafted ordinaries. Like senior appointments in the civil service, officers advance from the ranks, and the military bureaucracy is not as rigidly stratified and centralized in its command structure as was characteristic of the Portuguese army. With little graft in the relatively "classless" Afrikaner military establishment, comparisons

---

the promising trading block in which already 1.5 million Portuguese migrants (not to mention their dependents at home) made their living, became economically and politically incompatible with the commitment to a colonial empire in Africa. With the exception of Guinea-Bissau and Northern Mozambique, the war, though costly in terms of human lives in a small nation, had been going comparatively well for the colonial forces for the past two years before the Lisbon coup, with MPLA activity in Angola virtually at a standstill and the small-scale combat in southern Mozambique approaching more a stalemate than a defeat. It has been calculated by reliable observers that in Angola in fact more lives (approximately 70,000) have been lost through interfactional fighting after the Algarve announcement of political independence than in the thirteen years of guerrilla war before.

55. John de St. Jorre, *A House Divided: South Africa's Uncertain Future* (New York: Carnegie Endowment for International Peace, 1977), p. 131.

with the ill-motivated and corrupt colonial armies, fighting for a dubious cause in a foreign territory, frequently overlook the integration, high morale, and motivation of settler armies in South Africa and Israel alike. All these factors indicate the limitations of the colonial analogy.

Similar reservations have to be made against the conceptualization of white rule as domestic colonialism. First used by Karis, Carter, and Stultz in their analysis of Transkei,[56] the concept has since been applied to the U.S. ghetto,[57] Quebec, Northern Ireland, and even Stalinism.[58] In a particularly insightful analysis, Michael Hechter described the Celtic fringe in Britain as a question of internal colonialism. Hechter states the process in terms easily applicable to Afrikanerdom: "The superordinate group, now ensconced as the core, seeks to stabilize and monopolize its advantages through policies aiming at the institutionalization and perpetuation of the existing stratification system. Ultimately it seeks to regulate the allocation of social roles such that those roles commonly defined as having high status are reserved for its members."[59] However, while the internal colonialism analogy may fit many aspects of the dependency relationship, it deals only with two actors and ignores the crucial political role of the metropole in interfering with and mediating between the harsh domination of the settlers over the indigenous population in the process of decolonization. Furthermore, the logical conclusion from the

56. Gwendolen M. Carter, Thomas Karis, and Newell M. Stultz, *South Africa's Transkei: The Politics of Domestic Colonialism* (Evanston: Northwestern University Press, 1967). See also Harold Wolpe, "The Theory of Internal Colonialism: The South African Case," in *Beyond the Sociology of Development*, ed. Ivar Oxaal, Tony Barnett, and David Booth (London: Routledge, 1975), pp. 229–52.

57. Robert Blauner, *Racial Oppression in America* (New York: Harper & Row, 1972), chap. 3.

58. Alvin Gouldner, "Stalinism: A Study of Internal Colonialism," *Telos*, 34 (Winter 1977/78).

59. Michael Hechter, *Internal Colonialism. The Celtic Fringe in British National Development*, 1536–1966 (Berkeley: University of Colonial Press, 1975), p. 39. See also his "Group Formation and the Cultural Division of Labor," *American Journal of Sociology*, 84, no. 2 (1978), 293–318.

colonial analogy would be concomitant with political independence of the periphery from the center, the exact policy of Afrikanerdom!

Subimperialism has become another popular concept for the characterization of South Africa's regional role and international relationship. But at least implicit in the notion of subimperialism is the acknowledgment of South Africa's strength and endurance as the center of the periphery. It has long been pointed out that South Africa gradually assumes a similar function of economic dominance over a dependent hinterland as the United States has exercised for a long time vis-à-vis Latin America.[60] The deficiency of the subimperialism thesis lies in its assumption of a common imperialist interest, almost a conspiratorial design at the expense of the rest of the world. Samir Amin, for example, writes about Azania as "the heart of the citadel which comprises the *merging* of the interests of the Anglo-Boer settlers, of their State, and of American, British and European monopoly capital."[61] This perspective overlooks the serious rivalries between competing imperialist interests. Not only does it not come to grips with the continuing Afrikaner resentment of English influence inside South Africa, but also with the silent but no less bitter U.S.-French struggle over control in Africa or for that matter, established British interests and their challenge by German or Japanese competitors. Such rivalry has after all led different Western powers to back different local clients in regional wars (for example, in the Biafra secession) or caused alliances of other submetropoles with adversaries of their mentor (Israel and Kenya backing Ethiopia against Somalia for reasons of regional interests).

As the stronger, not the "weaker," partner in terms of local political control, South African state interests can dictate to a large extent the conditions for the operation of foreign capital.

60. Heribert Adam, *Modernizing Racial Domination: The Dynamics of South African Politics* (Berkeley: University of California Press, 1971).

61. Samir Amin, "The Future of South Africa," *Journal of Southern African Affairs*, 2, no. 3 (July 1977), 355. The literature on the theme of subimperialism is voluminous.

This alone causes frictions and contradictions between a local culture on the one side and managerial styles and policy preferences of the foreign partner on the other side, particularly when he is under public scrutiny for justification of differential practices. The split on the issue of black trade unions is a case in point, with the more farsighted foreign capital (see ECC code) favoring the expected stability through union discipline, while most local interests, fearing above all political repercussions of trade union organization, are strongly opposed.[62]

The different degrees to which foreign capital is willing to accommodate the peculiar demands of elite politics has also allowed the South African party to play various foreign competitors off against one another. In the past, the French were particularly apt in winning this game (see TV system) but have also lost out on other deals where the South Africans managed to find more willing German collaborators. In some cases, lucrative contracts with foreign private groups fell through for the paradoxical reason that the South African government wanted to teach the foreign government a lesson, softening it up for future deals by provoking internal pressure against "mixing business with politics." In the highly export-dependent European economies, even social democratic governments are usually more susceptible to employment/profit arguments of their home constituencies than the moral calls for boycott of distant dictators.

In short, these frictions have not caused divorces "within the family" and are unlikely to lead to any breakdowns despite the increasingly shrill rhetoric, but they do constitute

62. As a response to the accusation of discriminatory labor policies in 1977 it became fashionable for various organizations to devise codes of employment practices. However, they all amount to voluntary commitments by employers to improve working conditions. With the exception of the EEC code, they are particularly vague on African trade union recognition (i.e., the S.A. Urban Foundation Code) or did not mention this crucial issue at all—i.e., the initial U.S. "Sullivan" code—which, however, has been updated. The Urban Foundation Code, for example, allows wide interpretations, and the crucial issue of monitoring, let alone enforcing, the codes remain unresolved.

serious quarrels over styles and tactics of securing stability and predictability of investment risks.[63] It would, therefore, be more realistic to acknowledge that the assumed alliance with the outdated policies of the South African "partner" has also become a certain liability for the metropolitan side as well as a potential risk in light of the growing radicalization and (socialist) politicization of a restless labor force. No sinister imperialist ploy to collaborate in the oppression of black masses guides such decisions but reactions to promising opportunities in light of potential risks at home and abroad. By lumping together all Western states in an assumed alliance with the policies of the South African partner, the differential assessment of these liabilities by the metropolitan actors is neglected. Rather than the "merger" of outside "monopoly capital" with its South African partner, a growing cleavage can be expected, because the local section has not only most to lose but is also economically strong enough to resist the outside dictate for the time being.[64]

63. Rather than pull out, the approximately 1,000 foreign firms in South Africa have reacted to the perceived greater political risks by increasingly taking in local partners. This is seen as a less vulnerable position in a potentially deteriorating future when the South African partner can take over rather than finding an outside buyer in a less promising climate. It also avoids the expensive price of complete disinvestments, since there are restrictions on the legal capital transfer abroad. In addition, the local borrowing ability, which is based on the level of South African participation, is increased together with potential access to Afrikaans business and government orders in cases where the multinational is linked with Afrikaner capital.

64. This applies also to South Africa's greatest potential vulnerability, economic sanctions, and particularly a cutoff from vital oil supplies. There are several reasons why a declared oil boycott is unlikely to be enforced effectively and even in the improbable event of being imposed would hardly have the intended impact on the country's economy, let alone the intransigence of its politicians. (1) South Africa's energy needs rely only for one-quarter on oil. Unlimited coal reserves are available. (2) It is estimated that sufficient crude oil has been stored which presents a two-and-a-half years supply at 1977 consumption. (3) In case of sanctions this could be stretched until the second oil-from-coal plant at Louis Trichardt is in operation in 1981–82, which is planned to supply an equivalent of 28 percent of present domestic petrol demands, in addition to SASOL I with an output of 5 percent. (4) Finally, with oil having become a freely traded commodity on a competitive world

To sum up our argument: Geoffry Barraclough has recently called the United States–European–Japanese economic competition "the dominant factor in international politics."[65] From this perspective, metropolitan policy toward South Africa is very much shaped by the desire to outmaneuver imperial competitors for favorite access to the rich resources of Southern Africa. Similarly, Russian policy toward Angola, for example, has been motivated, far more than recognized, by the rivalry with China rather than by the East-West conflict. The unprecedented, intense involvement of five Western foreign ministers in the negotiations about a desert with hardly a million inhabitants (Namibia) reflects this interimperial competition for stakes in one of the few undemarcated rich regions. Multinationals, despite their global operations, still have a national base. Differential national recessions usually are first countered with renewed protectionism. Such constellations may well lead to a greater divergence of Western policy toward South Africa. The highly trade-dependent Western European economies, despite their social-democratic governments, can be expected to be more pragmatic in their dealings with white South Africa. The more autarkic North American policymakers, on the other hand, can afford a more principled moral stance, particularly in light of the racial issue in U.S. domestic politics. The United States, as the leading Western military power, is also facing the prospect of becoming involved militarily in case of a general escalation. This has

---

market, an embargo will almost be impossible to enforce against a ready fleet of sanction busters under many flags. International capital interests are so much intertwined with the South African economy—with the higher priced so-called spot market of oil readily supplying any demand—that oil sanctions are likely to be supported on paper only when substantial profits can be made. This calculation has not included the effects of an embargo on South Africa's client economies, including an independent Zimbabwe. The reluctance of the black states in South Africa's orbit to submit themselves as the first victims of an ineffectual boycott might well deter further its ultimate implementation. The main effect of a boycott lies in its psychological impact on the morale of white and black South Africans.

65. Geoffrey Barraclough, "Waiting for the New Order," *New York Review of Books*, October 26, 1978, p. 47.

caused ambivalence among some U.S. planners who previously regarded South Africa as *the* anti-Soviet ally in Africa.
Upon second thought it is now also argued that "the U.S.
needs to protect itself from a South African anti-communist
strategy which will pull the U.S. into a Southern African
conflict on the side of South Africa."[66]

In the final analysis, however, the economic interest in
political stability in Southern Africa is shared by all main
actors, particularly the front-line states. Their impoverish-
ment and locked-in dependency on outside links, including
"socialist" Angola and Mozambique, together with the basic
conservativism of the new African state bureaucracies, radical
rhetoric notwithstanding, restrain their willingness and
capacity to initiate or tolerate a real escalation with white
South Africa. Such a constellation lends itself to numerous
pragmatic ad hoc arrangements. Rather than comprehensive
final solutions, mutual blackmail and mutual considerations
of worse alternatives are likely to shape political responses
according to new challenges. Conventional notions of oppression versus liberation conceptualize undialectically a contest that is ongoing and whose outcome is never final.

66. William H. Lewis, "How a Defense Planner Looks at Africa," in *Africa: From Mystery to Maze*, ed. Helen Kitchen (Lexington, Mass.: D. C. Heath, 1976) as quoted by Barry M. Schutz, "Issues in U.S. Policy toward Africa," *Africa-Today*, 25, no. 3 (July–September 1978), p. 71.

3 Ethnic Mobilization and the Politics of Patronage Heribert Adam

It is one of the deep mysteries of Afrikaner Nationalist psychology that a Nationalist can observe the highest standards of behavior towards his own kind, but can observe an entirely different standard towards others, and more especially if they are not white.—Alan Paton

Of all the reviewed approaches in the literature on South Africa, the concept of ethnic mobilization would seem to be the key for an appropriate understanding of contemporary white South African politics. The notion may also be used to analyze processes of segmental exclusivism in general terms.

Ethnic mobilization delineates the process by which mere particularistic interests become a common cause. This cause then is embraced by most group members as their own entitlement against others. Adherents mobilize for sacrifice, group action, and the promise of a better future in the name of a common bond (language, religion, race, ancestry, sex). Multiple social attachments of individuals with members of excluded out-groups tend to become replaced with new intragroup relationships. Compared with the intergroup differences, intragroup conflicts are portrayed as minor. They merge into a common consciousness of a kind that subsumes formerly antagonistic interests in a new harmony. Class conflict, for example, is subjugated to the propagated need of group unity and, at the most, institutionalized within the in-group boundaries. Groups mobilized in this fashion represent powerful collective actors, as the history of nationalism has proved everywhere.

Ethnic mobilization of assumed homogeneous subgroups within a heterogeneous nation-state constitutes an equally promising device for a disadvantaged elite to redress elite grievances or defend an existing power position of exclusive patronage. Ethnic appeals to a common identity are particularly successful because they are based on a shared socialization experience, associated with early childhood comfort of security. The "emotional anchorage"[1] and symbolism of communal mobilization lend themselves far more easily to successful appeals of solidarity than calls for the unity of crosscutting class interests. This is subconsciously realized by union or even feminist organizers when they use familial notions of a *brother*hood of workers or *sister*hood of oppressed women.

Why interest groups can be cheated out of their collective advantages so easily by being manipulated with communal attachments represents one of the most crucial questions of political sociology. Perhaps, as Ernst Bloch suggested, the answer may lie in a utopian yearning that the ethnic mobilizers tap far more successfully than liberal universalists or orthodox Marxists. The symbols of communalism may fill a void in Enlightenment rationalism that the liberal and socialist dependence on reason overlooks. The waves of romanticism, mysticism, and nostalgia that periodically sweep the most enlightened societies reveal the thin layer of rationalism.

Popular support for racial exclusivism stands in the line of longings for harmonious and secure human relationships, particularly where the out-group represents no threat to the glorified in-group (anti-Semitism). In situations where the in-group directly benefits from the monopoly of resource control, on the other hand, racial mobilization is only irrational by utilizing invidious criteria with no meaningful distinctions in themselves. As organizing symbols for an exclusive "identity" in a particular context, racial notions may be as useful

1. E. K. Francis, *Interethnic Relations* (New York: Elsevier, 1976), p. 366.

and rational as any other aspect of primordialism.[2] In any case, a racial world view constitutes a reality of its own because individuals act according to their perception of reality no matter how fictitious their beliefs are. Once instilled through socialization into racist group conformity, racial beliefs are not easily discarded. Established cognition is largely immune against evidence to the contrary when it is reinforced by legitimate authority. For the racist individual such beliefs have their own logic and appear irrational only to the nonbeliever.

But what happens if the situational context of respective reference groups changes so that racial beliefs no longer serve the group interest but amount to an obstacle for new goals and strategies? The concept of ethnic mobilization suggests that because racial sentiments are not acquired biological predispositions of individuals and groups they can be readjusted and discarded according to changing circumstances. Much more than religious doctrine, which is perpetuated by scriptures and vested interests of its official interpreters in churches, ethnic and racial mobilization depends on its suitability and expediency in a specific sociopolitical environment in permanent flux. To consider racial perceptions as immutable qualities ignores their changing functions. Ethnic attachments persist, but only as long as they serve a purpose. Ethnic identities may lie dormant without being noticed. Whether and in which form they surface depend on the larger social context in which people find themselves. Above all it depends on whether there is a perceived need for ethnic identification and how mobilizers capitalize on these needs. Primordial ties generally act as shelter from an uncertain environment. The badges of cultural narcissism are donned as long as other identities and roles are denied. But as Daniel Bell aptly noticed: "The attachment to ethnicity may flush or

2. Rational is used here in the Weberian sense of achieving a given end with optimal means. Rationality in this formal sense does not imply any value judgement on the goals, it only describes the appropriateness of means to reach the end.

fade very quickly depending on political and economic circumstances."[3] For example, the initially unprejudiced but insecure immigrant to South Africa from Northern Europe changes quickly into an overconforming racist newcomer,[4] while the formerly stubbornly racist Afrikaner emigrant to Canada has little difficulty adjusting to a new liberal political culture. As tourists and even exiles outside South Africa, blacks frequently defend "their country" in a new-found identification, and "racist" South African whites in London often associate more easily with fellow black countrymen than with other Europeans. Such everyday life experiences only illustrate the floating nature of assumed identities according to context.

People's definitions of themselves and of others are shaped by the stage of the dominant political culture in which they act. The dominant definitions of the setting in turn derive from the complex process of interest perceptions by the more powerful groups. This has long been recognized in Marx's insight that the ruling values in any society tend to correspond with the norms of the ruling class. If past racism, therefore, no longer helps the dominant group survive why would a ruling group keep proclaiming its own death sentence? How South Africa will change from within, therefore, depends partly at present on how the leading opinion makers perceive the cost of racism or the advantages of abandoning past beliefs. How little or how much Afrikaner political culture is responding to its new challenges remains an empirical question, hardly answerable with notions of inflexible Calvinist character syndromes, references to primordial racial identities, or immutable "open" or "closed" cognitive structures. It is, therefore, more useful to ask how decisions are made and how interests are asserted than how rigid or dogmatic are individuals or groups.

The focus on ethnic mobilization must answer two seeming

3. Daniel Bell, "Ethnicity and Social Change" in *Ethnicity*, ed. Nathan Glazer and Daniel P. Moynihan, p. 171.

4. John Stone, *Colonist or Uitlander. A Study of the British Immigrant in South Africa* (London: Oxford University Press, 1973).

contradictions. (1) Do urbanization and secularization not diminish the significance of ethnic cohesion? (2) How can the focus on Afrikaner ethnicity be justified in light of the unquestionable fusion of Afrikaner and English-speaking whites into one beleaguered camp?

(1) It is a misconception to assume that urbanization, particularly in the first generation, will lead automatically to more liberal outlooks and an erosion of group cohesion. On the contrary, the insecurity in an unfamiliar environment may strengthen ethnic allegiance. All South African cities have typical Afrikaner suburbs with the familiar neighborhood of church and school. In many other parts of the world, sociologists belatedly notice the phenomenon of urban "ruralization" rather than the expected atomization of metropolitan neighborhoods.

(2) Despite the obvious tendencies toward elite fusion between the two white groups, the political culture of Afrikanerdom retains at present a considerable homogeneity in basic world views and social characteristics. Political behavior cannot be explored without taking full account of so startling a difference in most social indicators. Whether one takes different birthrates in both language groups, the degree of secularization and ethnocentrism, the economic status or educational standards, white cultural pluralism seems at least as important as the propagated black one. While more than 80 percent of both English and Afrikaners now live in urban areas, only one-third of the adult Afrikaners but two-thirds of the English grew up in the city.[5] The predominantly rural or small-town socialization of Afrikaners is reflected in the low 7.9 percentage of university graduates, compared with 11.8 percent in the English-speaking group. Twice as many Afrikaners as English concur with their respective religious denomination. Questions about bible reading and church attendance reveal even greater discrepancies: only 6 percent of

5. The figures and subsequent empirical data are derived from the "Freiburg Study." (Theodor Hanf et al., *Südafrika: Friedlicher Wandel?*, Munich: Kaiser 1978). The survey comprised a representative sample of 1,800 white voters and 205 interviews of members of the white elite.

Afrikaners admit that they never read the bible, three-quarters claim daily reading. If not piousness, such responses at the least indicate intact conformity. Among admired virtues, law, order, and traditionalism top the list among Afrikaners, while the English prefer liberal outlooks, such as tolerance and flexibility, among their favored politicians. In the representative sample of the Freiburg study, 43 percent of the Afrikaners, but only 11 percent of the English were members of a political party. Asked about the degree of identification with their respective group, only 15 percent of the Afrikaner, but half the English, deny such a bond.

Even Afrikaner political dissidents seldom denounce their cultural heritage. At the most, they call for a "relativisation of ethnicity," not its abolition.[6] The Stellenbosch philosopher Johannes Degenaar recommends: "A demystification of the concept of *volk* and the introduction of the more scientific concept of ethnicity which should be assessed realistically instead of either being ignored or deified, is necessary."[7] In the view of the ethnic establishment, too, political defiance does not relinquish eternal "blood ties." The dissidents are viewed as black sheep, unmercifully punished, but still part of the flock. Upon the death of Bram Fischer, the leader of the South African Communist Party, an Afrikaans paper mourned: "We who are of his blood but detest his politics cannot at his death escape the feeling of great compassion over a lost son who did not return."[8] The jailed poet Breyten Breytenbach, while serving a nine year sentence under the "Terrorism Act," is still awarded prizes by the Afrikaner literary establishment.[9]

Such intact group bondage at all levels makes for a unique political style. In terms of political parties, Hanf aptly characterizes the two political cultures as an almost one-party sys-

6. Johannes Degenaar, *Afrikaner Nationalism*, occasional paper no. 1 (Cape Town: Centre for Intergroup Studies, 1978), p. 39.

7. Ibid.

8. *Die Burger*, May 9, 1975.

9. For example, the 1978 Perskor prize of 2000 Rand handed over to Breytenbach's brother in the meantime.

tem versus the variety of English clubs. In the conservative British tradition the parties represent a loose alliance of notables to win an election; for Afrikanerdom the party is the emotional home of a mobilizing movement with mass membership. In the one case the funds for an election campaign come mainly from a few wealthy patrons, in the other instance, most supporters contribute time and money for *their* party. With such a cohesive constituency, leadership authoritarianism becomes superfluous. The recognized leaders can anticipate compliance because of common trust. The majority of National Party voters state explicitly that they would support the leadership in cases where they do not understand actions or even where they would disagree with decisions. Only 10 percent of Progressive Party voters express such readiness. Given the shared commonalities of a mobilized ethnicity, pride in advances of leaders of "our kind" satisfies identification needs.

The Freiburg study points out that the unity of members with widely conflicting views is ensured through two recognized postulates: (1) Instead of goals, only methods are open for questioning. Consensus about principles can always be assumed. Only the interpretation of doctrine is debatable. Legitimate intragroup dissent focuses on the best tactics to realize unquestioned goals. (2) The ethnic movement of Afrikanerdom insists on absolute loyalty to controversial decisions by the leadership. Once a dictum has been formally approved, criticism amounts to treason, because it would endanger unity.

Such a structure of political decision-making relegates national elections to periodic mobilizing rituals. Not even minor policy changes are determined by elections. Ethnic politics confines crucial decisions to trusted insiders. Since 1948 policy changes in white South Africa resulted from slow processes of Afrikaner in-group manipulation. Especially in the absence of a charismatic leader, such as Verwoerd had been, new policies emerged from the accumulating shifts within a small circle of opinion leaders. How they interpret the mood of their ethnic constituency matters more than how their loyal

followers demonstrate solidarity.[10] The ethnic leaders, therefore, possess substantial scope to initiate change. This lever-
age, however, is not recognized or conveniently denied by
apartheid critics as well as its leading proponents. Thus Colin
Legum writes: "Even if the prime minister and his cabinet
were to decide for hard-headed and practical reasons that a
radical readjustment of power were urgently necessary... ,
they would likely be blocked by their own parliamentary
caucus, which closely reflects the hard-line attitudes of the
Afrikaner electorate."[11] This assertion is empirically as incorrect as the excuses by ethnic leaders that they are restrained
by a prejudiced electorate. For South Africa, in particular, the
common experience that attitude changes follow policy directives applies, not vice versa. If the Freiburg study showed one
potentially significant result, it is that on several issues the
white—and even the Afrikaner—electorate, is ahead of the
leadership. Why then do ethnic leaders usually lag behind
their constituency?

Corporate groups select leaders differently from bureau-
cratically structured interest groups. Their leaders play different roles. Elite politics within Afrikanerdom as a corporate
group, with a mere democratic veneer of rank and file accountability, contrast with leadership opportunities and re-
sponsibilities in internal party democracies.

Among the many reasons for individual political stances at
the leadership level, opportunistic image-making in corporate groups represents an underestimated aspect. Jockeying

10. This makes the substantial literature on white voting behavior rather
irrelevant. What is highly predictable need not concern the attention of
sophisticated social scientists. But what is hidden behind the cloak of
rhetoric—why changing perceptions emerge and how they assert themselves—could be the revealing focus for exploring ethnic politics. In this
respect, the Freiburg study, too, describes perceptively, but gives little clues
as to *why* a polarization of opinion even in the inner Afrikaner leadership
circle (*binnekring*) took place. Opinion surveys, as useful as they may be, need
always to be backed up by structural analysis.

11. Colin Legum, "Looking to the Future" in *Southern African in Crisis*, ed.
Gwendolen M. Carter and Patrick O'Meara (Bloomington: Indiana University Press, 1977), p. 261.

for career advancement and vying for higher office by outmaneuvering potential rivals may frequently explain more specific actions than grand theories of class articulation. To be sure, such rivalry occurs within well-defined class and ethnic limits. However, how an ambitious politician articulates these interests, where he places himself in the spectrum from hawk to dove on which issue, which constituency he cultivates, and other idiosyncrasies of intraethnic interaction frequently determine short-term policy with far-reaching consequences. In corporate group politics, political actors are not merely mouthpieces of their constituency but once in power they also stamp courses with their peculiar brand of personality. While such considerations apply more or less to all societies with an open political system, there are crucial differences for a minority ethnic group in power.

Afrikaner leaders usually are chosen by acclamation, not by formalized competition within a democratic party bureaucracy as in Western states. The election of a prime minister is confined to a relatively small caucus. Split votes, as in the case of P. W. Botha, have been rare so far. A leader is chosen according to many criteria, but least in terms of his popularity among the electorate. He is also chosen for life or until he decides to resign. In interest groups, on the other hand. the figurehead (president, chancellor, prime minister) must lend himself to vote-catching in comparison with competing parties. Ethnic voting, especially in states where the ruling party is assured of victory at the polls, does not need outstanding campaigners, but credible representatives of dominant group sentiments. They rise in the party hierarchy because they have outmaneuvered ethnic rivals, not because they appeal to a nonexistent floating vote. They are delegates of consensual sentiments, not products of advertising campaigns. This informal selection procedure of ethnics compared with the different qualities of leaders of heterogeneous interest groups, called parties, gives the ethnic political actor more scope but also constrains him at the same time. He can rely with greater assurance on the unquestioned trust of his people, who view him as one of their own, regardless of his specific action. The loyalty of the clan, tied together by an overriding communal attachment, encompasses relatively blind approval of the legitimate group leadership. The ethnic leader is not primarily judged according to the goods he can deliver, as in an interest group, but more according to how well he represents psychological group values, particularly the promise of security. The authority of such a father figure to command obedience remains unquestioned. There are no polls in South Africa with which cabinet ministers need to test their popularity, as in Western democracies. At the same time, *broedertwis*, the rivalry of brothers, can be vicious. Seldom carried out in the open, the upstarts have a permanent duty to prove their trustworthiness. If rumors of betrayal spread, careers end. Bold steps can be deadly. Broederbond membership operates on the blackball system, which ensures conformity. Such intraethnic structural constraints, more than intellectual rigidity, explain why the National Party leadership is so hypnotized by its rightwing challenge, while it ignores its far stronger liberal opposition.

The constant official reiteration that nothing has changed, that traditional policy is upheld, is a prerequisite for the gradual abdication of sacred principle in ethnic politics. Each Afrikaner politician has to operate under an impeccable ideological camouflage in line with approved tradition that does not lay him open to charges of deviance by his rivals.

The adoption of rhetorical facades for domestic use contrasts with the comparative openness with which leading Afrikaners discuss alternatives with a foreign visitor who is not apt to exploit the frankness locally. It is not enough to explain such schizophrenia as a calculated device to dupe the foreigner with a veneer of pragmatism. If impressionistic evidence is at all a reliable guide, the two political "identities," so to speak, are held simultaneously. The impression of double-talk with which most foreign observers are struck derives from the corporate constraints of ethnic politics not necessarily from the contradictory views of its actors. Therefore, ideological utterances are notoriously unreliable evidence for actual political behavior, unless interpreted in the context of ethnic politics.[12] More and more the speeches have become cynical cloaks under whose protective communal umbrella personal rivalries are fought, with the contenders merely manipulating rank and file allegiance. Many surveys have in fact proved that the Afrikaner electorate would go a long way with radical policy changes. Afrikaner political actors have not thrown their authority behind more pragmatic approaches because of the restraining system of ethnic politics. Pressure groups outside the communal framework cannot form constituencies on which a more courageous leader could rely. He is, therefore, vulnerable to rival contenders for office if he tries to move outside accepted principle. Ethnic politics, as embodied in Afrikanerdom, rewards the conformist at the expense of the prophet, and the rewards are substantial for those who stay within the safe limits of approved norms.

While individual corruption is infrequent, group patronage substitutes for it.[13] In the perceptions of ethnics in power, procedures and bureaucratic regulations lose their universal applicability. Policy is made for the consolidation of the group as the highest priority to which other considerations must be bent and accommodated. The law itself represents a mere means to the end of enhancing ethnic patronage. The law has lost is inviolability and can be broken with impunity if it comes into conflict with legitimate group interests. In the

12. The ideological camouflage under which Afrikaner politicians operate resembles the perfected Nazi practice of giving atrocities euphemistic labels. And yet there is the crucial difference that most Nazi leaders believed in their racial supremacy for its own sake while Afrikaners use racial policies primarily to entrench their weak in-group in anticipation of a powerful challenge. The Nazi anti-Semitism vested on an irrational premise of a Jewish threat which was elevated to a convenient scapegoat for maintaining cohesion. The Afrikaner "racism" is based on the rational fear of losing out and, one would expect, is open to compromise.

13. For a fine general conceptual analysis of ethnic patronage see Robert Jackson, *Plural Societies and New States*, Research Series no. 30 (Berkeley: Institute of International Studies, 1977).

"fight for survival no rules apply," declared Mulder when his Information Department was criticized for illegal actions.[14] The dismissal of the main actors in the scandal resulted more from their alleged personal or moral corruption, not unequivocally from their illegal defense of group interests. Legalism still applies to individual behavior but is easily suspended if group/state interests are at stake. Such ad hoc actions, however, cannot be openly admitted, since it would alienate those excluded from the ethnic benefits. However, when challenged from within, a twinkle in the eye refers to the common spoils.[15]

In the ideology of the ethnic mobilizers the *volk* as a whole, not individuals or sections within it, are supposed to benefit from unity. Historically, Afrikaner workers were brought into the fold and wooed away from socialist flirtations by the expectation that no individual group member would capitalize on ethnic solidarity. Mobilization in this spirit of *Volksgemeinschaft*, which is supposed to transcend class strife, demanded strict behavioral codes for group representatives. Ostentatious display of wealth, the conspicuous consumption of English class society with private schools, and elaborate status symbols were considered alien and divisive to a people on the move. Simplicity, modesty, and honesty ranked high among the desired virtues of those entrusted with political power. This very trust in the leaders resulted from their image as ordinary, down-to-earth *volk* members, rather than distant figures on a remote throne. Unlike Nazi leaders and other despots who were hiding their private vices behind a public mask of infallibility and inaccessibility, Afrikaner leaders were supposed to share their frailties in the communal tradition of equals. Poor golfing or hearty drinking

14. *South African Comment and Opinion*, May 12, 1978.

15. In this vein a cabinet minister answered his critic (on the trivial issue of illegal drilling operation in the Kruger Park) publicly in Parliament: "Say we have broken the law. Say we have infringed the law. Haven't we done it for the benefit of an undertaking like ISCOR? All right, say we have given wrong answers: is it still necessary to kick up this tremendous rumpus?" (*Star Weekly*, March 17, 1978).

of public figures merely proved that they remained "one of us." Hitler, for example, never even allowed himself to smoke in public. In this vein, the trusted code of honor that traditionally governed the relationship among rank and file settlers extended to the Afrikaner leaders. They were not exempt, but rather more closely subjected to a strict ethnic legalism which applied to everyone regardless of rank and status in the group. Without such codes of conduct the momentum of mobilization could not have been maintained and cleavages would have widened at an early stage. In light of the overall weak Afrikaner power base, legalism also provided much needed legitimacy vis-à-vis the other ethnics, particularly the English.

However, the intrawhite legalism had long been abandoned in white-black relations and where the treatment of more radical activists, regardless of color, was concerned. Beginning with the cynical abolition of the limited black franchise in the Cape, Afrikaner nationalism sacrificed the last vestiges of a universal rule of law in the 1960s when the African Nationalist resistance had been legally suppressed. In public pronouncement, the security of the (Afrikaner) state was declared of a higher priority than the rule of law.

In the 1970s several powerholders (Mulder, van den Bergh, Rhoodie) assumed that the legalism could also be abolished with regard to the English opposition by secretly funding an English newspaper (*The Citizen*). Moreover, and most significantly, for the first time the large-scale use of state-patronage for personal enrichment was revealed.

In this respect, the so-called Information affair constitutes a test case for the continued strength or weakness of traditional ethnic mobilization in light of increasing ethnic secularization. The controversy deserves detailed treatment as a case study that illuminates issues which may split or erode the ethnic movement.

It is indicative that both sides in the quarrel accepted the myth of the "classless" heritage as the norm for proper conduct. Ethnic authenticity was claimed by those for whom no rules apply in the struggle for group survival as well as by

73

rivals who stressed intragroup legitimacy in pursuing their own empires. For the sake of clarity, the two Nationalist camps may be roughly distinguished by the relative labels "political compromisers" or "modernizers" versus "Apartheid hardliners" or "traditionalists." The irony of the affair lies in the fact that the conservative "hardliners" became associated with graft and corruption while the more progressive "compromisers" or "modernizers" could fall back on ethnic traditions of legalism to outmaneuver their rivals. The whispered knowledge of violations of the traditional codes of moral conduct was left to simmer for several years. The personal enrichment from state funds by cronies, the flouting of budgetary rules and administrative neglect, but, worst of all, rumored licentiousness of public figures could then be played up like a well-staged drama in the contest for Vorster's successor. Along another historical cleavage, the numerically dominant Transvaal regional nationalism lost out against its Cape counterpart, because its leading contender, Mulder, became tainted with dishonesty and impurity. A symbol of the true faith and impeccability, Treurnicht, was elected by the Transvaal caucus in revenge for its earlier defeat.

What structural conditions and interests does such infighting reflect? At the ideological level, which arguments are used by the contending factions to gain legitimacy? What is the likely outcome of the discord in the ruling oligarchy?

The illegal use of state funds for party political purposes undermined the desired all-white unity. The new-found trust of Anglo-whites in nonpartisan Afrikaner administration was at stake.[16] Therefore, it was possible to let heads roll in the name of incorruptible procedures: "A purge of elements . . . who have imperilled our precious national unity has become imperative."[17]

16. A later survey by *Rapport* indicated that English-speaking support for the National Party dropped from 31.6 percent to 19.3 percent as a result of the scandal. As expected, the great majority of Afrikaner Nationalists replied that they had not lost confidence in the government. (Quoted in *Star Weekly*, December 23, 1978).

17. *Beeld*, November 1, 1978. In their own interests Afrikaner papers led the patriotic moral posturing. There is concern about their all-decisive circu-

In the name of eradicating, "the spiritual rot"[18] of competitors, the new leadership could defeat its opponents and yet retain legitimacy. The personalized drama played in the foreground of course shed only dim light on the real issues occurring backstage: these are, how far and how fast the government (1) adjusts to the rising cost of traditional apartheid, (2) engineers a more liberal control of black labor against the objections of white unions, (3) politically accommodates representative urban Africans in addition to Coloureds and Indians, and (4) seeks international support in return for internal ideological compromise. In the code words of the domestic debate this is presented as how far economic problems can be reconciled with political ideology and how much principles should be adapted to reality.

As will be shown in greater detail later (chapter 8) these issues are intertwined with vested organizational interests. After the entrenchment of Afrikaner power, bureaucratic empires have grown which increasingly have come into conflict with each other. For example, with the ill-fated "outward policy" under Vorster and the subsequent internationalization of the Southern African conflict, Pretoria vastly expanded its bureaucracy of intelligence personnel under a newly created Bureau of State Security (BOSS), renamed Department of National Security (DONS), after the retirement of its first head, Hendrik van den Bergh. Extended propaganda efforts of the Information Department provided employment for more than five hundred people by 1978. Suave technocrats and cosmopolitan operators with a playboy image, such as Eschel Rhoodie, were appointed as managers from outside the civil service, against the opposition of the influential Civil

---

lation figures. A government-subsidized daily, regardless of its Nationalist bent (*The Citizen*), undercuts the sacrosanct market-mechanism as an unfair competitor. Although in English and initially aimed at the most vociferous government critic (*The Rand Daily Mail*), there was suddenly no longer any guarantee that secret government funds would in future not also undermine the fledgling press critics on the Afrikaner side.

18. *Beeld*, November 27, 1978. Other concepts used in accusations included "moral nihilism" and "law of the jungle." See letter by Professor F. J. J. van Rensburg to *Die Burger*, November 7, 1978.

Service Commission. The patronage of the minister, Mulder, meant a break with the traditional seniority principle.[19] Other conflicts originated from the new style of influence peddling. The Foreign Affairs Department favored *winning* support abroad according to established methods, the new advertisers believed in *buying* the unobtainable ware at any price. South African diplomats in Washington for example, trained in the propriety of the trade, were frequently surprised—and embarrassed—about the activities of aggressive lobbyists from well-connected U.S. law and public relations firms, directly hired by the parallel bureaucracy at home. International propaganda activities, such as large-scale schemes to entice visitors, were carried out by front organizations, such as the disbanded Foreign Affairs Association.[20] The deception was considered necessary because of the pariah status of official South Africa. Without the neutral image, fewer foreigners would dare to touch the outcast.

Since much of the slick propaganda and intelligence activity was carried out in secret, the normal control mechanisms did not apply to the great discretionary powers of the unorthodox operators. At the end they were accountable only to themselves.

However, such a system of individual integrity has long

19. It is ironic that Rhoodie was appointed in the place of the incumbent Barrie, who later became auditor-general and wrote the first report about the irregularities of the Information Department. It is said that many tipoffs to newspapers came from wives of civil servants, phoning from call-boxes.

20. The revelations about state-funding of front organizations brought other bodies concerned with foreign affairs under renewed suspicion, particularly the Pretoria based Africa Institute and the Institute of International Affairs, affiliated with Witwatersrand University. The university's director, John Barratt, stated that the Institute is "poor but pure." The question of funding seems irrelevant however, since all academic institutions in South Africa are paid for out of the public purse. What would matter is the independence of the academic researcher from the government as sponsor in terms of accountability, censorship, and open publications. In this respect, South African non-Nationalist academics have a rather impressive record while many committed Nationalist academics unconditionally support the government anyway, which makes specially government designed social science research almost superfluous.

become undermined by the spoils of power and affluence. The concomitant ethnic secularization in parts of the *volk* are no longer guarantees that traditional trust can ensure reliability. The entrusted upholders of security easily become a corrupt source of insecurity. Unreliable values of past communal mobilization conflict with the organizing principles of rational, modern bureaucracy and accountability. Ambivalent selection criteria of honesty are reasserted nevertheless, indicating a continued belief in the strength of mobilized ethnicity. The Erasmus Commission of Enquiry even subjugates the merit principle to a vaguely defined loyalty test:

> In order to ensure security, such administration must be entrusted to honourable people, tried and tested, and whose integrity has withstood the tests of time and rectitude. Appointments on the consideration of friendship or political expediency, and even insight and intelligence, but without regard to the honesty of the person concerned, may not take place.[21]

The former head of BOSS, H. van den Bergh, exposed by the commission as arrogant and power-hungry, clearly was such a "tried and tested" individual. Nonetheless, the honesty test in the name of communal integrity allows the rival empires within Afrikanerdom to define for themselves who is trustworthy according to specific sectional interests and conflicts about appropriate strategies of group survival.

The conflicting notions about the most expedient tactics to counter rising costs no longer represent mere ideological differences about the purity of the faith, such as the Hertzog split in the late 1960s. Advocacy of different strategies now cuts across the vested interest of the security apparatus. While the Security Police tends to favor the traditional methods of repression, the upper ranks of the military seem to be more aware of the nonmilitary aspects of counter-insurgency. This results partly from the more sophisticated

21. Quoted in *South African Digest*, December 8, 1978, p. 3.

professional training of the higher military brass, in which university graduates predominate. They know, for example, the lessons of Vietnam and anticolonial struggles. Far fewer graduates are to be found in the Security Police, which draws its recruits from the ordinary ranks of comparatively unsophisticated policemen. Their obsession with conspiracies and agitators, conflicts with the more political and international considerations of the military. In the latter's view, Soweto, the Biko death, and the bannings of October 19 reflect police bunglings which directly led to the arms embargo. The internationalization of the Southern African conflict since 1974 together with the rise of the former Defence Minister to the premiership in 1978 meant an increase in the influence of the military in South African political decision-making and a comparative decline in the independent power of the police establishment.

Are these cleavages likely to lead to further splits or new alliances within the threatened camp? The "disturbing indications of confusion and disunity," which Afrikaans papers diagnosed "as a result of the information drama," nevertheless have not caused organizational splits.[22] As the South Africa correspondent of *The Economist* probably correctly observed: "Anywhere else this would cause a political party to break apart, but the pressures on the Afrikaner Nationalists to remain united are enormous."[23] The increasing divergence of interests and attitudes within Afrikanerdom is reconciled in a different way. For the time being, the cleavage is institutionalized within the Nationalist Party without organizationally splitting the ethnic movement. Such an internal division with a front of unity still guarantees more rewards for both "modernizing compromizers" and "hardline traditionalists" than an open split.

The traditionalists could not hope to retain or share political power in the case of a breakaway. None of the other white factions could coalesce with them. Barring a rapid deterioria-

22. *Die Vaderland,* November 8, 1978.
23. "Transvaaler's Revenge," *The Economist,* December 2, 1978, p. 66.

tion of the white security situation, the constituency of the hardliners would be confined mainly to white unions and sections of the apartheid bureaucracy. For the more pragmatic Afrikaner compromisers, a coalition with the English opposition parties seems at present neither necessary nor expedient.[24] As long as past mobilization guarantees the discipline behind the legitimate party leadership, the ethnics within the fold can be more easily manipulated than ethnic outsiders. Besides, in a coalition with the heterogeneous English parties, the present incumbents would have to share power on a far broader basis than in an uneasy truce with intraethnic opponents. This is not to say that with rising costs a broader white alliance of national unity—perhaps even including a small black middle class in an "internal settlement"—should be ruled out as a possibility. However, at present, expectations of new party coalitions underestimate the advantages of continued Afrikaner organizational unity for all factions as well as the psychological obstacles to any Afrikaner breakaway.

Mobilization of the disadvantaged instilled in its members a particular approach to power. They view political and economic power as the essential prerequisites for group existence. Afrikaners are taught that their ability to realize themselves depends on group membership and that the survival of the group depends on its acquisition and maintenance of control. This contrasts with the liberal approach to authority. The supreme doctrine in the liberal perspective maintains that government infringement on individual liberties must be minimal. The protection from unwarranted state interference is considered crucial. In the view of mobilized ethnics, on the other hand, the very capture and expansion of state power guarantees individual fulfillment through group affiliation. State and society appear as identical. The crucial separation of the two spheres in the post-Enlightenment era of bourgeois development does not exist for mobilized ethnics in power.

Different relationships to power between those who pos-

24. The leader of the opposition, Colin Eglin, added to the defeat of his own wishful thinking by publicly prophesizing such a likelihood.

sess it by virtue of acquired "right" (the wealthy English in South Africa) and those who aspire to power or need to consolidate their newly gained achievement against group challengers (Afrikaners) are reflected in different political socialization. Suspicious vigilance is stressed in the one tradition, obedience to group authority in the other. Even Afrikaner political dissidents do not escape this experience. They seldom engage in the moral gestures of protest that characterize English liberals but view power more cynically as the manipulation of group sentiments. The liberal dissenters, by contrast, place trust in reasoning and individual virtues of a common humankind rather than opportunistic motives of group affiliation. Donald Woods, for example, in all sincerity, indicts apartheid with the statement that South Africa's "problems" are not unique. A multiracial society, he says, handled with good will and honesty, is not a problem.[25] The experience of ethnic mobilization allows the victors, with equal sincerity, to view such appeals to good will as naive calls for surrender.

A world view that employs collective filters such as "identity maintenance" only registers that the very group existence is based on exclusion. It continues at the expense of those who do not belong. The ethnics in power can therefore perceive their challengers only in terms of their own experience of successful mobilization. If there is one theme with which many Afrikaner politicians and academics are obsessed, it is the insistence that their adversaries would certainly behave in identical ways as they themselves did in achieving and consolidating power. The reiteration in Afrikaner speeches to foreigners, that "we know the Africans," reflects the projection of their own group socialization into the threatening out-group.

Such projection of Afrikaner mobilizing experience is not adequately described as "fear of revenge," which would imply punishment for past actions. The certainty of losing out

25. Donald Woods, "The Indictment" *New York Review of Books*, May 4, 1978, p. 25.

in a collective competition comes closer to explaining the refusal to accede to any formula of majority rule or one man one vote. As a South African ambassador explained privately: "We are prepared to divide power but not to share it."

This policy of excluding ethnic outsiders from meaningful participation in decisions about the distribution of the national cake perpetuates unequal racial opportunities and the racial attribution of differential life-chances. However, such exclusion is hardly explained by the traditional notion of racism, in the sense of considering racial outsiders as biologically inferior or unworthy of membership in the privileged group. On the contrary, it is because of the perceived superiority of the adversaries in terms of numbers and competitive advantage that the ethnic minority in power excludes the competitors from a fair share. How little racism depends on the characteristics of the discriminated but on their structural relationship to the superordinate group has perhaps never been better highlighted than by the statement of former Australian premier Alfred Deakin about the Japanese: "I quite agree . . . that the Japanese are the most dangerous because they most nearly approach us, and would, therefore, be our most formidable competitors. It is not the bad qualities, but the good qualities of these alien races that make them dangerous to us."[26]

Can mobilized ethnicity be successfully institutionalized in the interest of a ruling minority? An outright negative answer would seem premature. Much would depend on the options available, on who actually benefits from such an arrangement, compared with alternatives. If we see South Africa as consisting of competing groups, suppressed or mobilized on an ethnic basis for access to political and economic power, we can then explore the crucial questions, namely, which policy the power-holding group will adopt when it is sufficiently threatened. Can the ethnics demobilize in the sense of redefi-

26. Robert A. Huttenback, *Racism and Empire: White Settlers and Coloured Immigrants in the British Self-Governing Colonies 1830—1910* (Ithaca and London: Cornell University Press, 1976), pp. 283–284.

ning group boundaries? Can the symbols and the emotional apparatus of past mobilization give way to hitherto inconceivable paradigms? Which rival interpretations of identity are advocated by whom and in whose interest? A detailed historical analysis of different Afrikaner self-concepts should shed light on the chances of ethnic demobilization.

4   The Growth of Afrikaner Identity
Hermann Giliomee

Like the trim outline of Table Mountain seen from afar, Afrikaner identity appears to be a well-defined feature of the South African political landscape. Yet a look at history shows that this identity was much more blurred than this appearance suggests; indeed its boundaries were often adjusted in order to fit historical circumstances and social contexts. Even now, Afrikaner identity may be going through a decisive phase of redefinition and change.

It is not predictable how a group of people existing within a common cultural and kinship network will formulate its political identity and goals.[1] Ethnic groups require leaders who inspire them to think and act collectively in politics. Such leaders in turn depend on favorable social conditions in which men could be persuaded to shelve their individual and class differences for the sake of group mobilization. Ethnic identification occurs most strongly where a collection of individuals come to consider themselves communally deprived and believe that mobilization as a group would improve their position or where persons seek to protect the privileges they share with others against those who do not have them or whom they are exploiting collectively. The Afrikaners have

1. My theoretical understanding of group identification has been influenced most by Herbert Blumer, "Race Prejudice as a Sense of Group Position" in *Race Relations: Problems and Theory*, ed. J. Musuoka and P. Valien (Chapel Hill: University of North Carolina Press, 1964); Heribert Adam, *Modernizing Racial Domination* (Berkeley: University of California Press, 1971); and Nathan Glazer and Daniel P. Moynihan, *Ethnicity: Theory and Experience* (Cambridge, Mass.: Harvard University Press, 1976).

known all these: the gradual awakening of ethnic consciousness, the leaders who fostered or fragmented it, the bitterness of being a despised minority, and, at present, the challenges to the privileges they enjoy as the dominant group in a deeply divided society.

The main contention of this chapter is that South Africa's institutionalized racism (the policies that distribute power, wealth, and privileges unequally on a racial basis) can best be understood as the product of the Afrikaners' conception of their distinct place in the social structure. They have come to regard "group-belongingness," group mobilization, and the defense of the group position as positive responses that occur universally. Discrimination and prejudice are seldom justified as ends in themselves but as the inevitable consequence of the maintenance of ethnic rights and interests. In such a context discrimination and prejudice often rest more on the construction of group rights than on fear or scorn of an out-group.

This analysis attempts to outline the development of the Afrikaners' conception of themselves, with emphasis on the political self-conception. For this reason, considerable weight has been attached to the pronouncements of political leaders who sought to stimulate group concepts and articulate the group's characteristics, rights, and ideals. It is a survey of how Afrikaner identity has been shaped by both these conscious self-definitions and the social matrix of South Africa.

SETTLEMENT, SLAVERY,
AND THE FRONTIER, 1652–1899

The Europeans who immigrated to the Cape during the seventeenth and eighteenth centuries derived from several countries. They came primarily from the Lowlands where national boundaries were less clearly defined than elsewhere. Nonetheless these settlers shared certain characteristics. Although French and especially German were widely spoken at the early stages of settlement, Dutch was the common language. The settlers had the Christian faith in common and, while they belonged to different denominations, they were all

84

Protestants. Lastly, they were all white, as distinct from the brown Khoisan hunters and herders, whom they encountered in the vicinity of the Cape, and the black and brown slaves, whom they imported from Africa and the East.

During the first two centuries of settlement, the colonists' sense of their identity was shaped by their European heritage (culture, ideas about race, and such) and material forces (economic conditions and demographic ratios) that reinforced each other. Generally speaking, Europeans were cultural chauvinists who looked down upon the "heathen," "primitive," or "barbarous" indigenous people of the colonies in which they settled.[2] While this was true of European colonizers everywhere, there were also differences among them. Some scholars have concluded that seventeenth-century Dutch and English colonists were more "racist" than their Spanish and Portuguese counterparts since they came from countries already advanced on the road of capitalism and democracy. Here society was not regarded as a complex feudal hierarchy of social ranks but mainly of two classes: the respectable burghers and the despicable poor. In their colonies they more readily divided society into rigid racial categories. There is also some evidence that the somatic norm (aesthetic response to different physical types) of the Dutch and the English—the "whitest" of Western Europeans— differed from the darker Iberians. Dutch and English colonizers tended to exclude persons of mixed ancestry from their ranks whom Iberians accepted.[3]

It is a debatable point whether there existed at the seventeenth-century Cape a consciousness of race in the modern sense of the word. All that one can say is that the Euro-

2. For the case of British colonizers see Winthrop D. Jordan, *White over Black: American Attitudes Toward the Negro, 1550–1812* (Chapel Hill: University of North Carolina Press, 1968).

3. This paragraph and the next couple of pages draw heavily on Hermann Giliomee and Richard Elphick, "The Structure of European Domination at the Cape, 1652–1820," in *The Shaping of South African Society 1652–1820*, ed. Richard Elphick and Hermann Giliomee (London: Longman, 1978), chap. 10. Full references are in the chapter cited above, consequently none is given here.

peans (used here and subsequently coterminously with whites) were aware of their color and of the way color and culture generally corresponded with each other. But even so, a consciousness of race does not ensure that it would remain an important part of a group's identity. Racial consciousness needs the proper social conditions to stay alive and become rooted. If, for instance, the majority of white men at the Cape for demographic reasons had been forced to marry blacks, the settlers' consciousness of race would have been eroded. At the Cape this racial identity was not only retained but reinforced by the colonial context.

First it was fostered by the administrative structure of the Cape Colony. The Dutch East India Company distinguished consistently among four legal categories: (1) Company servants, (2) freemen (also called free burghers), (3) slaves, and (4) "aliens" (the Khoikhoi and Bushmen). The Company did not consider "whites" or even "Europeans" as a distinct official category of people. Indeed, manumitted slaves, the so-called free blacks, were legally the equal of any white belonging to the category of either Company servant or freeman. There is no evidence of discrimination against free blacks in the seventeenth and early eighteenth centuries. However, in an important sense the Company's policies did strengthen racial consciousness. The Company recruited almost exclusively whites as servants and as immigrants. From the outset the officials and the community of free burghers created in 1657 to farm the land given out by the Company were, with few exceptions, white.

In the course of the eighteenth century the white Company servants and free burghers drew nearer to each other. From their ranks came the politically dominant class in society. Although some top Company officials considered themselves superior, they needed the burghers as much as the burghers needed them. Outside Cape Town, the only centers of authority were the *drostdys* (magistracies) of Stellenbosch (established 1679), Swellendam (1746), and Graaff-Reinet (1786). Assisted by only four or five policemen, the *landdrosts* (sheriffs) were forced to rely on burgher officers called fieldcornets to enforce the laws and to mediate in disputes between the colonists and their slaves or indigenous laborers. The Company was also dependent on the produce of the free burghers who supplied Cape Town and the passing ships with wine, bread, and meat. To facilitate production the Company accorded the burghers special privileges: only they could hold land under the landholding system of the colony or exercise burgher rights such as practicing a "burgher craft or occupation" (in practice this meant farming) or holding office (heemraad, fieldcornet, and so forth).

The burghers put a wider interpretation on these rights. They assumed that they were entitled to special protection by the government and to a special legal status above that of slaves and Khoikhoi. Although the Company would never specifically state that the burghers had a superior legal status, in reality it upheld a social hierarchy with officials and burghers at the top and Khoikhoi and slaves at the bottom. Thus the group that later became known as the Afrikaners increasingly considered political privilege as a crucial element of its position in society. And because very few black free burghers emerged, this came to be perceived as white privilege.

The nature of the Cape economy was even more important than the administrative structure in shaping the social order. The primitive Cape economy lacked an export staple that could compete overseas. There was hardly any local industry. In its own interests, the Company in the seventeenth and eighteenth centuries thwarted the emergence of local industry. Consequently there were few occupational opportunities for colonists. In Cape Town they could become clerks in the Company service, keep boardinghouses, and engage in trade. Beyond Cape Town, farming was virtually the only occupational opportunity. From 1700 overproduction of wheat and wine and the lack of careers stimulated cattle farming beyond the arable lands of the southwestern Cape. It was mainly the surplus white population—the young, the poor, and the landless—who participated in the rapid expansion of *trekboer* pastoralists.[4] In the south they reached the Little

4. This is a controversial issue but see the conclusion of Leonard Guelke on the topic in *The Shaping of South African Society*, chapter 2.

Karoo in the 1730s and then expanded toward the Fish River. In the north they penetrated the Oliphants River Valley (1720s), Roggeveld (1740s), Nieuwveld (1760s), and reached the Camdebo (Graaff-Reinet) areas of Bruintjeshoogte and Zuurveld by the 1770s, roughly at the same time as the southern stream.

Whites dominated the economic life of the Cape. While not all the whites were rich, virtually all the rich were white. With the exception of some free black slaveowners, the slaves were all held by Company servants and white free burghers. In Cape Town, whites were the main traders and providers of services. Outside the capital they were the agents of expansion and held almost all the land given out under the colony's landholding system. The expanding frontier bred the expectation that every son would one day have his own farm.[5] No white working class developed: a white who did not hold land farmed as a member of an extended family or as *bywooner* (tenant farmer). Manual work in the service of someone else was considered as unfit for a freeman. In the southwestern Cape, slaves provided manual and skilled labor; in the interior Khoikhoi and, later, Bantu-speaking Africans served as farm laborers. Since land was freely available during much of the eighteenth and nineteenth centuries, the pattern of a slender superstructure of white landholders controlling brown and black labor was extended over a vast area. No economically successful non-European group—for instance, the free blacks in Cape Town or the Bastaards on the frontier—emerged to break down the order of whites predominating over browns and blacks. Their numbers remained small for both material reasons (the simple nature of the economy, which provided few intermediate jobs) and cultural reasons (for example, the failure of the church to promote manumission).[6]

The sex ratio of the white population at the Cape was as

5. P. J. van der Merwe, *Die Trekboer in die Geskiedenis van die Kaapkolonie* (Cape Town: Nasionale Pers, 1938), p. 185.

6. This argument is put forward in detail in Giliomee and Elphick "Structure of European Domination at the Cape."

important as the administrative and economic contexts in shaping the social structure of Cape society. By 1770 the sexual ratio of the white population had declined from 170 to 144 males for every 100 females. These ratios allowed most white men except the poorest to find white wives.[7] Although it was fairly common for poor whites to cohabit with nonwhites, a rather small minority of Cape marriages was mixed.[8] As a rule their offspring fell into the nonwhite group. Although some fair-skinned nonwhites succeeded in "passing" for white, this did not occur on a significant scale.

Culturally, whites considered themselves to have a special claim to the Christian religion and literacy—two of the main attributes of what they regarded as civilization. The few clergymen—by 1790 there were still less than ten—concentrated their activities on the officials and burghers. Baptism and elementary literacy remained extremely important as cultural symbols through which group membership was expressed. In sum, members of the white group enjoyed more status than others. People who were rich and white had the most status; those who were nonwhite and poor had the least. Political and economic dominance, cultural and racial exclusivism, and social status all contributed to the racial order of society, which after a period of flux in the seventeenth century, became stabilized in the course of the eighteenth century.

In this period, too, the group that later became known as the Afrikaners increasingly conceived of themselves in egalitarian terms. The interplay of weak government control and the continuing availability of land produced a socially mobile white group who accepted their fundamental equality as Europeans. W. S. van Ryneveld, who rose to the position of president of the Court of Justice, said early in the nineteenth century: "Among the true inhabitants of this colony there is no real distinction of ranks among the white

7. Robert Ross, "The White Population of South Africa in the Eighteenth Century," *Population Studies*, 29, no. 2 (1975), 217–30.

8. F. C. de Bruyn "Die Samestelling van die Afrikaner," *Tydskrif vir Geesteswetenskappe*, 16 (1976) and personal communication.

population."[9] The traveler George Thompson observed in the 1820s that there was little or no gradation among the white population. "Every man is a burgher by rank and a farmer by occupation."[10] This egalitarianism was of special significance for the social order: Europeans who saw other Europeans as their equals were inclined to see non-Europeans as their inferiors.

In a sense the social order of the colony was also a class order in which the rich and powerful were white and the poorest and most helpless (slaves and Khoikhoi) black or brown. But this class order broke down in the middle. While a considerable number of poor were white and some freemen were nonwhite, they did not form a coherent class. The poor whites tended to identify strongly with the richer strata and insisted on the protection, respect, and rights due to burghers. In general, they received this acceptance and protection from both the government and the rich colonists. The government issued a proclamation that no slave might jostle a European even if he was of the meanest rank. The colonists readily accepted poor whites but not blacks or even Bastaards as *bywooners*. For this reason it makes more sense to analyze the Cape social order in racial rather than in class terms.

But while there was a racial order, it would be simplistic to regard this society as a racist one. Cape society in the eighteenth century was more complex and influenced by some other considerations as well. First, relations were to a large extent determined by the status differences between masters and slaves. Second, the prerogatives and privileges of the white elite were only gradually converted into the "racial" rights of the entire group. Third, though color marked social status, it was possible for individual members of the subordinate racial group to acquire some social status—free blacks, for instance, by marrying whites. At the same time discrimination and prejudice against blacks was not aimed at

9. W. S. van Ryneveld "Schets van den Staat der Kolonie in 1805," *Het Nederduitsch Zuid-Afrikaansch Tydschrift*, 8 (1831), 124.

10. George Thompson, *Travels and Adventures in Southern Africa* (London: H. Colburn, 1827), vol. 2, p. 275.

TABLE 1   Population at the Cape, 1670–1820

Year	European Free Burghers	Free Blacks	Burgher's Slaves	Khoikhoi and Bastaards
1670	125	13	52	*
1711	1,693	63	1,771	*
1750	4,511	349	5,327	*
1798	c. 20,350	c. 1,400	25,754	14,447
1820	42,975	1,932	31,779	26,975

*Not enumerated until 1798.

Source: Hermann Giliomee and Richard Elphick, "The Structure of European Domination at the Cape, 1652–1820," in The Shaping of South African Society 1652–1820, eds., Richard Elphick and Hermann Giliomee (London: Longman, 1979), Chap. 10.

individuals simply because they belonged to a certain racial group but occurred because these blacks rebelled when their racial and social positions were too rigidly linked. It was in such a context that we find the first recorded statement expressing racial animosity at the Cape. Made in 1706 by some wealthy farmers who dreaded the rise of a rebellious class of poor freemen of mixed racial origin, it denounced the "Kaffirs, Mulattoes, Mesticos, Casticos, and all that black brood living among us, who have been bred from marriages and other forms of mingling with European and African Christians [colonists born in Europe and at the Cape]. To our amazement they have so grown in power, numbers and arrogance, and have been allowed to handle arms and participate with Christians in . . . military exercise, that they now tell us that they could and would trample on us. . . . For there is no trusting the blood of Ham, especially as the black people are constantly being favoured and pushed forward."[11]

The European migrant stock farmers, who faced various Bantu-speaking African chiefdoms in the late eighteenth and

11. Cited in Giliomee and Elphick "Structure of European Domination."

entire nineteenth century, carried with them to the frontier a well-developed sense of group position.[12] It is sometimes claimed that their Calvinist faith determined their relationships with the indigenous peoples and lay at the root of their "racism." The argument is that they saw themselves as a community of the elect with a God-given mission to establish their control over the land and the natives, who were viewed as heathens damned to servitude.[13] This is to mistake rationalization for motivation. Calvinism as a force shaping Afrikaner identity is more important for what it did not accomplish than for what it did achieve. Unlike Catholicism in Latin America, it did not emerge as a countervailing force against the rise of a racially exclusive society. This was not because of any fundamental dogma but because of its lack of a centralized organization (like the Catholic Church) and resources. For the rest, the history of European colonization shows that it does not matter materially whether colonizers are Calvinists or Catholics. What is crucial is whether they enjoy enough power to acquire the land, cattle, and labor of indigenous peoples.

The frontier in South Africa was in fact the scene of less prejudice than the established parts of the settlement.[14] In what can be called the *open frontier*, which lacked authority over all inhabitants in the frontier zone, there was a measure of political and social fluidity. Colonists without the means to use coercion effectively had to attract indigenous labor. The people in their service could more properly be called clients. Frontier colonists were also sometimes forced to shed their prejudices in order to establish military or sexual alliances across racial lines. There was an uncertainty of status: whites were not all masters; nonwhites were not all servants. This

12. This is further developed in Hermann Giliomee "The Cape Eastern Frontier 1770–1812," *The Shaping of South African Society*, chap. 7.

13. For a recent statement see Ruan Maude "The Myth of White Meliorism in South Africa," in *South Africa: Economic Growth and Political Change*, ed. Adrian Leftwich (London: Allison and Busby, 1974).

14. I discuss the frontier theory in South African historiography in "The Development of a Racial Order," manuscript, 1978.

produced the paradox of, on the one hand, a greater degree of cross-racial cooperation, especially in the military field, and on the other hand, violence as different groups attempted to find a footing on which they could base their relationship. On the *closed frontier*, in contrast, where whites had succeeded in establishing undisputed control, a different set of relationships and a much more caste-like social structure prevailed. As indigenous laborers lost the ability to resist or escape, the master-client relationship changed into labor-oppression, serfdom, and, in extreme cases, slavery. It was only after the frontier had closed that nonwhites were consistently seen as black and racially inferior.[15]

In the records there is no evidence of widespread racist thinking in the first half of the eighteenth century. After c.1770, when it did start to appear, it occurred most often as a reaction to challenges to the social order whether it be on the frontier or the settled parts. There were two periods in which the colonists experienced an acute sense of insecurity and "racial disorder." The first crisis, between 1780 and 1810, sprang from a shortage of land after the frontier had begun to close. This was aggravated by the insistence of the government and the missionaries that the Khoikhoi should receive equal protection from the courts. In the Western and Eastern Cape there were signs that some Khoikhoi and slaves were no longer prepared to accept European hegemony. At the root of the colonists' expressions of hostility was the concept that they occupied a special place in society.

First, there was a sense of superiority: the other group was deemed inferior. When Governor Janssens visited the East-

15. The relationship between Bastaards and whites on a frontier that had closed was described by an official as follows: "the one is proud and assuming because white; the other abject and diffident because coloured and curly haired; the one is permitted by the Government the independent possession of land which to labour to his heart's content; the other knows of no such privilege beyond the possession of it on common with others upon mere suffering of the Government, and has all the feelings of an outcast.... The feelings of subjection... has so wholly pervaded their habits of thought that they had become deplorably servile." GH 28/71, Moffat-Rawson, March 12, 1856, enclosure to no. 82.

ern Frontier in 1803 he remarked of the whites living there: "they call themselves people and Christians, and the Kaffirs and Hottentots heathens, and on the strength of this they consider themselves entitled to anything."[16] There was also a secular rationalization of white superiority. In the Western Cape, Sir Robert Wilson remarked on the colonists' notion that nature had drawn a fixed line between white and black and had destined the blacks to be subservient for all time.[17]

Second, there was the view that the "inferior" social groups are intrinsically different and alien. Landdrost Alberti of Uitenhage complained in 1803 that it was impossible to persuade the colonists that the Khoikhoi were equally entitled to the protection of the law since the colonists held the view that heathens were not truly human although they could not be classified with animals either.[18]

Third, there was the concept of a prior claim to certain privileges and benefits. On the Eastern Frontier literacy and the Christian faith were considered the cherished privileges of the white group. When the missionaries Read and Van der Kemp started to work among the Khoikhoi in the vicinity of Graaff-Reinet in 1801, strong dissatisfaction arose among the frontier farmers. In his notes on a rebellion that broke out in June 1801, Van der Kemp mentions that the rebels were aggrieved among other reasons because "the Hottentots and Caffres... were instructed by us in reading, writing, and religion, and thereby put upon an equal footing with the Christians."[19]

The second crisis in social relationships occurred between

16. *Belangryke Historische Documenten over Zuid-Afrika*, vol. 3, ed. G. M. Theal (London: Clowes, 1911) pp. 217–22.

17. Cited by Michael Streak, *The Afrikaner as Viewed by the English* (Cape Town: Struik, 1974), p. 20.

18. J. S. Marais, *Maynier and the First Boer Republic* (Cape Town: Maskew Miller, 1944), p. 73.

19. *Transactions of the Missionary Society*, vol. 1, pp. 481–82. At the base of the opposition to literacy there may also have been the fear that this could endanger the pass system. For a fuller discussion of the crisis of the period 1780 to 1810 see Giliomee and Elphick "The Structure of European Domination."

1828 and 1838 when threats to the colonists' group position and security played an important part in precipitating the Great Trek. Ordinance number 50 (1828) and the emancipation of the slaves (1833) abolished the legal lines of distinction between Khoikhoi, slaves, and whites. Although in practice the class order did not change, the rise of a new legal dispensation was traumatic. *Gelykstelling* (equalization), as the colonists called it, seemed to lead inevitably to *gelykheid* (equality) and the disintegration of the social order. Coupled with this was the breakdown in security. Bands of Khoikhoi and Xhosa wandered through the eastern districts and occasionally pilfered cattle. Not only was the social order endangered; law and order, as the colonists perceived it, was breaking down. Writing on the causes of the Great Trek, C. Buchner, a frontier field cornet; Karel Trichardt, a Voortrekker leader; and Anna Steenkamp, niece of another leader, all touched on these themes. Buchner declared: "The unbridled conduct of the blacks here goes against the grain of the Afrikaners and this alone, and nothing else, is the motive for the removal."[20] Karel Trichardt stated: "The main objection to the new dispensation was the equalisation of coloured people with the Whites."[21] To Anna Steenkamp, the Great Trek had been caused not so much by the emancipation of the slaves as by "their equalisation with the Christians, in conflict with the laws of God and the natural divisions of descent and faith, so that it became unbearable for any decent Christian to submit to such a burden; we therefore preferred to move in order to be able the better to uphold our faith and the Gospel in an unadulterated form."[22]

In the Free State and Transvaal Voortrekker settlements their concept of themselves as a group separate from and superior to the nonwhites was incorporated in legislation. In the daily struggle for survival in the midst of an overwhelm-

20. Cited by C. F. J. Muller, *Die Oorsprong van die Groot Trek* (Cape Town: Tafelberg, 1974), p. 208.
21. Gustav S. Preller, *Voortrekkermense* (Cape Town: Nasionale Pers, 1920), p. 4.
22. Ibid., pp. 30–31.

ing majority of people who were different in color and culture some colonists developed the notion that they were a chosen people. They tended to apply the precepts of the Old Testament to themselves: Like the people of Israel, they were the chosen ones who had been forbidden to mingle with the heathen Canaanites (or the race of Ham). Some considered it their vocation to civilize and Christianize the blacks.[23] Among the average burghers, however, this found little response; their sense of superiority and of mastery carried much more weight. They were unwilling to promote education among the subordinates because this would cause the blacks to consider themselves as their equals. For the same reason they were opposed to missionary work among blacks.[24]

THE RISE OF A NATIONAL CONSCIOUSNESS
IN THE EIGHTEENTH AND NINETEENTH CENTURIES

The notion of the Dutch- and later Afrikaans-speaking colonists that they formed a distinct group was not shaped purely through interaction with blacks. Equally important was the gradual psychological disengagement from Europe. In the course of the eighteenth and nineteenth centuries they came to see themselves as an indigenous ethnic group with a distinctive national character and culture. In the 1770s a traveler observed: "The first Europeans in the Colony, which comprised various nationalities, have in the course of time intermingled to such an extent that they have become indistinguishable from each other. Even most of those who were born in Europe . . . have so to speak exchanged their national character for the character of this country."[25] Isolation, ad-

23. F. A. van Jaarsveld, *Lewende Verlede* (Johannesburg: Afrikanaase Pers, 1961), pp. 228–58.

24. H. J. van Aswegen, "Die Verhouding tussen Blank en Nie-Blank in die Orange-Vrystaat," Ph.D. dissertation, University of the Orange Free State, 1968, two volumes.

25. J. S. Stavorinus, *Reize van Zeeland over de Kaap de Goede Hoope* (Leyden: Houkoop, 1798), p. 309.

ministrative neglect, and an economic policy designed exclusively in the Company's interests fostered individualism and a sense of independence.

At the same time identification with the Netherlands as a fatherland weakened or disappeared. In contrast to the high officials, the ordinary burgher began to turn his back on Europe as the eighteenth century wore on. This is clearly evident in the struggle of the Cape Patriots who aimed to improve the political and economic position of the burghers. In the Burgher Petition of 1779 "fatherland" still referred to the Netherlands; by 1785, when it became clear that few of their demands would be granted, this term denoted the Cape Colony.[26] Thrown back on their own resources, the colonists forgot about Europe and came to realize that they were of Africa—their only true home. On the eastern frontier, Marthinus Prinsloo and some other colonists referred to themselves just before the turn of the century as "true natives of our true fatherland."[27]

The process of becoming indigenous or Africanized found expression in the term "Afrikaners," by which the colonists came to refer to themselves. The first evidence of its use to describe a white occurs in a document of 1707. It records that Hendrik Bibault, a young white man born at the Cape, protested when the landdrost of Stellenbosch attempted to flog him as punishment for rowdy behavior in public. From his words, "I am an Afrikaner, even if the landdrost flogged me to death ... I will not be silent."[28] It is not clear whether he merely wanted to indicate that he was a native of Africa (in contrast to natives of Europe), or whether he wished to convey the concept of an Afrikaner as a person holding certain rights and a status which the landdrost ought not to ignore. From the last quarter of the eighteenth century onward the

26. Coenraad Beyers, *Die Kaapse Patriotte* (Pretoria: Van Schaik, 1967), pp. 194–96.

27. Hermann Giliomee, *Die Kaap tydens die Eerste Britse Bewind* (Cape Town: Hollandsch Afrikaansche Uitgevers Maatschappy, 1975), p. 28.

28. J. L. M. Franken "Hendrik Bibault of Die Opkoms van'n Volk," *Die Huisgenoot*, September 21, 1928.

term "Afrikaner" for the colonists became firmly established. Discussing the Cape colonist, the traveler De Jong remarked in the 1790s: "He is proud of the name 'Africaan'; Citizen of the Cape he deems a title of honour."[29] Some contemporary observers, such as De Jong, applied the term to the white inhabitants of the colony but others used it to encompass blacks as well. Even Cape-born slaves were sometimes called Afrikaner slaves.[30]

At the time of the British conquest of the Cape (1795 and, after the Batavian interlude, again in 1806) many prerequisites for the awakening of a national consciousness were present: a distinctive spoken language, a single religious faith, a common historical heritage, and the consciousness of belonging to a separate ethnic group with a special status in a slaveholding society. On the other hand, there were few educational and church facilities where a national consciousness could be propagated; there were almost no intellectual leaders and no press to stimulate awareness. One could hardly say a national consciousness had emerged by 1806 though there was, perhaps, a sense of common heritage and destiny.

In the course of time the new rulers attempted to recast political and social institutions in a British mold. During the first half of the nineteenth century English became the language of the public service and judiciary. Afrikaners on government bodies such as the *Hof van Landdrost en Heemraden* and the *Raad der Gemeente* were replaced by predominantly English-speaking magistrates and town trustees. In Cape Town and environment the Afrikaners came under strong pressure to abandon language and customs for English cultural and social values. As a result some prominent Afrikaans families became fully anglicized or semi-anglicized, the so-called Anglo-Afrikaners.

In contrast other leading Afrikaners, resentful of the fact

29. Cornelius de Jong, *Reizen naar de Kaap de Goede Hoop . . .* , 1791–1797 (Haarlem: Bohm, 1802), p. 134.

30. Giliomee, *Die Kaap*, pp. 28–29; *De Zuid-Afrikaan*, October 29, 1834, D. J. Kotzé, *Positewe Nasionalisme* (Cape Town: Tafelberg, 1968).

that they were treated by the British as "minors," "wastrels" and "mentally deficient,"[31] continued to stress their own "nationality"—or to use a modern term—their ethnicity. In 1835 Adv. Denyssen declared that it was of the utmost importance that Afrikaners should retain their "nationality." Although they no longer lived in a Dutch colony they had by no means become a new people with different minds or feelings: "Even if man so wishes, he cannot so lightly forget the past, nor shake off the mores of his ancestors."[32] In the same year the Dutch newspaper *De Zuid-Afrikaan* wrote: "It is an error we have frequently opposed, to suppose that as British subjects we are compelled to adopt a British nationality. A colonist of Dutch descent cannot become an Englishman, nor should he strive to be a Hollander."[33]

The "nationality" of the colonists in the Cape comprised firstly a cultural element. Dutch (or Afrikaans) remained the home language of probably the majority of Afrikaners. Although English had become the language of public life by 1870, the Afrikaners insisted that Dutch remain the language of the Dutch Reformed Church, by far the most important social institution in the Cape Colony. Language and religion were seen as vital elements of ethnic identity.[34] A second component was a sense of belonging to a superior social class, elevated above the blacks whose ancestors had been slaves. When *De Zuid-Afrikaan* in 1857 analyzed the reasons for the declining standards of the government schools, it cited as the first cause that "there was no distinction between social classes in government schools, as is proper in any well-ordered society, and which, for local reasons, becomes even more marked in colonies." The paper objected to the practice of teaching

31. J. C. Visagie, "Willem Frederik Hertzog, 1792–1847," M.A. dissertation, University of South Africa, 1971, p. 125.

32. D. Denyssen "Voorlezing," *Het Nederduitsch Zuid-Afrikansch Tydschrift*, 12 (1835), 29–48.

33. Cited by J. du P. Scholtz, *Die Afrikaner en sy Taal, 1806–1875* (Cape Town: Nasou, 1964), p. 83.

34. Scholtz, *Afrikaner en sy Taal*, pp. 112–30, 156–62.

"along with the children of white farmers, the children of servants who had been their slaves only shortly before."[35]

As in the settled parts of the colony, a national consciousness only gradually matured on the frontier. The Great Trek (1834–54) was not the result of a national consciousness among the Afrikaners.[36] A leader such as Andries Pretorius did have a sense of belonging to a "freeborn people" which had the right to cast off British rule.[37] But the Voortrekkers did not emigrate as a nation. They considered themselves, as Hendrik Potgieter put it, as "free citizens who could go where they chose without prejudice to anyone."[38] Initially they referred to themselves mainly as "emigrants," sometimes more closely defined as "Dutch-Afrikaans Emigrants."[39] In contrast to the Voortrekkers, the *trekboeren*, who were part of a separate expansion process, saw themselves primarily as loyal British subjects and repeatedly requested that they be recognized as such by the colonial government.

Whereas slavery and settlement stimulated a racial consciousness, the Afrikaners' clash with British imperialism brought the concept of a distinct white political entity to the fore. The annexation of Basutoland (1868), the diamond fields (1871), and the Transvaal (1877) shocked Afrikaners throughout South Africa into the awareness that they were a spiritual entity—people sharing the same interests, language, faith, and destiny.[40] However, while a national consciousness had now definitely emerged, the Afrikaners were still far from united and there were important differences of views as to who was an Afrikaner. In the political context of the Cape Colony with a parliament elected on a color-blind basis, this

35. Cited by Scholtz, *Afrikaner en sy Taal*, p. 106.

36. For a discussion of this issue see Muller, *Die Oorsprong van die Groot Trek*, pp. 208–22.

37. M. C. E. van Schoor "Die Nasionale en Politieke Bewuswording van die Afrikaner in Migrasie en sy Ontluiking in Transgarieb tot 1854," *Archives Year Book for South African History*, 2, (1963), 49.

38. Ibid.

39. van Jaarsveld, *Lewende Verlede*, pp. 173–200.

40. F. A. van Jaarsveld, *Die Ontwaking van die Afrikaanse Nasionale Bewussyn, 1868–1881* (Johannesburg: Voortrekkerpers, 1957).

became a matter of vital concern. For the Afrikaner Bond, founded in 1880 and soon becoming the first major Afrikaner political party, a crucial issue was whether it would mobilize the Afrikaners exclusively or whether it would attempt to attract votes from across the lines of color and culture. Since membership of the Bond was restricted to Afrikaners, the definition of Afrikanerdom reflected various political strategies. For S. J. du Toit the concept "Afrikaner" had an exclusive connotation: It denoted someone of Dutch or Huguenot descent who spoke neither English nor Dutch but Afrikaans, which was now also emerging as a written language. On this foundation Du Toit built a structure of exclusivity: The Afrikaner had to follow his own political course, preserving his distinct culture.[41] Du Toit distinguished among three kinds of Afrikaners: those with English hearts, those with Dutch hearts, and those with Afrikaans hearts, the only true Afrikaners. Someone who was not opposed to the British annexation of the Transvaal was not an Afrikaner; those who sympathized with the Transvaal had "true Afrikaner hearts." "True Afrikaners" were those who were not ashamed of being known as such, who sympathized with the Afrikaans cause, and who stood for their people and their fatherland.[42]

In contrast, Hofmeyr's definition of the concept "Afrikaner" was inclusive. He rejected Du Toit's language qualification and claimed for the Afrikaner also the cultural heritage of the English section of society. An Afrikaner could be either English- or Dutch-speaking. Politically he defined an Afrikaner as "anyone who, having settled in this country, wishes to remain here to help to promote our common interests and to live with the inhabitants as members of one family."[43] The constitution of the Afrikaner Bond, adopted in

41. W. K. Hancock, *Smuts: The Sanguine Years* (Cambridge: Cambridge University Press, 1962), pp. 24–25; T. R. H. Davenport, *The Afrikaner Bond* (Cape Town: Oxford, 1966), pp. 51–53, 327.

42. van Jaarsveld, *Ontwaking*.

43. J. H. Hofmeyr, *Het Leven van Jan Hendrik Hofmeyr (Onze Jan)* (Cape Town: Van de Sandt de Villiers, 1913), p. 574.

1883, provided that: "The Bond knows no nationality what-soever, except that of the Afrikaners, and considers as belonging to it anyone, no matter of what descent, who seeks the welfare of South Africa."[44] On this basis Hofmeyr constructed a policy of cooperation between Dutch and English "Afrikaners." Where did the blacks fit in? Here Hofmeyr was ambivalent. He firmly supported the color-blind franchise, but he made it clear to a deputation from the Cape Coloured community, who were predominantly Afrikaans-speaking, that they could not be treated as social equals of whites. He also discouraged them from becoming members of the Afrikaner Bond.[45]

In the Transvaal, too, there were different views as to whom political rights should be granted and how the term "Afrikaner" should be defined. Stressing the independence of Transvaal and isolation from the Cape Colony, Paul Kruger argued that the Afrikanerdom in Transvaal consisted only of the "old people of the country." They were also God's People: He had led them from the colony as His chosen people and had given them liberty; they had been tried and tempered but were also blessed if they were faithful to Him. To make the Republic grow "on the roots of our national history" only Afrikaners and Dutch immigrants should be allowed to assimilate with "God's people." The others should be regarded as "strangers" and foreigners.[46] But who was an Afrikaner? For Kruger it was obviously any white who spoke Afrikaans or Dutch. This was too wide a definition for Schalk Burger, chairman of the Volksraad, who declared that the word "Afrikaner" had to be interpreted as meaning "Transvaler": even an immigrant from the Cape Colony or the Free State was a stranger.[47] On the other hand General Piet

44. Hofmeyr, *Leven*, p. 712.

45. Hofmeyr, *Leven*, pp. 341–42; Davenport, *Afrikaner Bond*. pp. 276–80.

46. J. Albert Coetzee, *Politieke Groeperinge in die Wording van die Afrikaner-nasie* (Johannesburg: Voortrekkerpers, 1941), pp. 247–56.

47. C. T. Gordon, *The Growth of the Boer Opposition to Kruger, 1890–1895* (Cape Town: Oxford. 1970). p. 10.

Joubert, advocating the political unification of all Afrikaners in South Africa, considered foreigners as potential Afrikaners, including English-speaking "Afrikaners."

During the late nineteenth century the Afrikaners of the Cape Colony advocated the integration of the Afrikaners and the English on the basis of a broad national unity. The Jameson Raid, however, altered this perception. They now desired the mobilization of all the Afrikaners across South Africa on an ethnic basis.[48] The term "Afrikaner" was given an exclusive connotation as a result of growing anti-British and anti-imperialistic sentiments. To Paul Kruger, "God's People" were persecuted by the "Beast" (the English), who had done them injustices and had deprived them of their rights, their language, and their liberty.[49] The anti-imperialist tract *Een Eeuw van Onrecht* (A Century of Wrong) stated that the "solid white aristocracy," into which the Afrikaner people had developed, had been wounded by the British government. The Afrikaner would, however, persist in his struggle for liberty, and in the end, "Africa for the Afrikaner" would triumph from the Zambezi to Simon's Bay.[50]

Afrikaner nationalism was greatly strengthened by the Anglo-Boer War and by the struggle to preserve the Afrikaans culture and identity in the face of Milner's aggressive policy of Anglicization. Though some feared that the Afrikaners were doomed to extinction others expressed the belief that out of the ashes of defeat a new people would rise. President Steyn, who was the most respected Afrikaner leader in the decade before Union, propagated the view that the "Boerevolk" of the two old Republics had to die in order that a larger Afrikaner nation might be born in a new South Africa.[51]

48. J. C. Smuts, *'n Eeu van Onreg* (Cape Town: Nasionale Pers, 1899 and 1939), p. 28.

49. van Jaarsveld, *Lewende Verlede*, pp. 201–07.

50. Smuts, *Eeu van Onreg*, pp. 1–3, 57.

51. J. J. Oberholster and M. C. E. van Schoor, *President Steyn aan die Woord* (Bloemfontein: Sacum, 1953), pp. 15–16, 135–47. For an analysis of the fas-

AFRIKANER IDENTITY
IN THE TWENTIETH CENTURY

Different contexts shaped Afrikaner identity during the first half of the twentieth century. First there was the new political framework of the Union of South Africa, a member of the British Empire. The force of rapid industrialization left a deep imprint on Afrikaners who increasingly were being drawn or pushed to the cities. At the beginning of the century only 10 percent of the Afrikaners lived in cities and villages; in 1911 this figure had risen to 29 percent; in 1926 to 41 percent; and in 1960 to 75 percent.[52] The new industrial context called for new strategies: some Afrikaners abandoned their ethnic identity, others chose to underemphasize it, while still others decided that the assertion of Afrikaner identity would be the most advantageous course.

The Union of South Africa was a compromise between the determination of English-speaking whites to maintain the "British connection" (the link with the Empire) and the deep desire of the vanquished republican Afrikaners for independence. The South African Party, which held power from 1910 to 1924, and the United Party, which ruled from 1934 to 1948, were imbued with this spirit of compromise. Although the background, interests, and outlook of their members were highly diverse, these parties tried to integrate the white population into a nation consisting of the two white language groups. They were prepared to deemphasize distinctions between these groups and strove toward greater homogeneity and mutual understanding. Their leaders, Generals Botha and Smuts, saw Afrikaners and English-speaking whites as

---

cinating discussion of the Afrikaner military leaders on whether the Afrikaners should fight the Anglo-Boer war "to the last drop" or bow to superior force, see André du Toit, "Confrontation, Accommodation and the Future of Afrikanerdom," *Outlook* (October 1977), pp. 147–52, 160.

52. F. A. van Jaarsveld, *Stedelike Geskiedenis as Navorsingsveld vir die Suid-Afrikaanse Historikus* (Johannesburg: Randse Afrikaanse Universiteit, 1973), p. 16.

flowing together in "one stream." Botha wished to "create from all present elements a nationality; whoever had chosen South Africa as a home should regard themselves as children of one family and be known as South Africans."[53] For some "Sap-Afrikaners," as they were called, the new political order meant only accepting the British monarch as sovereign, for others it even meant the abandonment of parochial sentiments and loyalties in favor of membership in a magnificent worldwide civilization. Thus a Dr. Niemeyer proclaimed at the time of Union: "We are all Britishers alike now. We have all accepted the British, and the majority of us... wish to form one nation with you, to the glory of the British Empire."[54]

A growing group of nationalists led by General Hertzog and Dr. Malan rejected these strategies. Unlike the participants in the rebellion of 1914, Hertzog recognized the legitimacy of the new South African state. However, he insisted that it should develop a separate and independent political identity within the British Empire. And within the South African polity the Afrikaners should retain their unique "nationality." In stressing separateness, Hertzog staked a historical claim: He described the Afrikaners as pioneers of the "South African civilisation." Because this group had played such a special role he was not prepared to have it assimilated, along with new arrivals and with those who had a double identity through their ties with England.[55] A minister of the Dutch Reformed Church, Malan was inclined to appeal to metaphysical notions. He viewed the continued existence of the Afrikaners as a separate entity, as part of a divine dispensation. In 1915 he stated: "Ask the nation to lose itself in

53. C. P. Mulder and W. A. Cruywagen, *Die Eerste Skof van die Nasionale Party in Transvaal, 1914–1964* (Johannesburg: Voortrekkerpers, 1964), p. 13; Hancock. *Smuts*, p. 361.

54. Sheila Patterson, *The Last Trek: A Study of the Boer People and the Afrikaner Nation* (London: Routledge and Kegan Paul, 1957), p. 97.

55. C. M. van den Heever, *Generaal J. B. M. Hertzog* (Johannesburg: A. P. B., 1943), pp. 301–11.

some other existing or as yet non-existent nation, and it will answer: by God's honour, never."[56] He argued that the Afrikaner had a full right to cling to his nationality as something upheld by God through the years. National unity dared not be emphasized at the expense of a duality of the white population.[57]

Hertzog and Malan proposed that the streams of English and Afrikaner nationality should flow apart until the Afrikaner stream developed to the level of the English. There was also a white and black stream. Hertzog saw the differences in terms of civilization: The whites were the bearers of civilization; the blacks stood only on the first rungs of the "civilized ladder." It was the duty of the white to protect "civilization" through the so-called civilized labor policies, while at the same time helping the "natives" to make the "transition between semi-barbarism and that of civilization."[58] Hertzog regarded the Cape Coloureds as already part of the white nation, politically and economically, although not socially.[59]

Hertzog and Malan from an early stage employed language as a mobilizing tool. In 1908 Malan stated: "Raise the Afrikaans language to a written language, let it become the vehicle for our culture, our history, our national ideals, and you will also raise the people who speak it. . . . The Afrikaans Language Movement is nothing less than an awakening of our nation to self-awareness and to the vocation of adopting a more worthy position in world civilisation."[60] After the founding of the National Party in 1914 the Botha government

56. *Glo in u Volk: Dr. D. F. Malan as Redenaar, 1908–1954*, ed. S. W. Pienaar (Cape Town: Tafelberg, 1964), p. 16.

57. A. H. Marais, "Die Politieke Uitwerking van die Verhouding van die Afrikaanssprekende tot die Engelssprekende, 1910–1915, Ph.D. dissertation, University of the Orange Free State, 1972, p. 588.

58. *Gedenkboek Generaal J. B. M. Hertzog*, ed. P. J. Nienaber (Johannesburg: A.P.B., 1965), pp. 233–42.

59. C. M. Tatz, *Shadow and Substance in South Africa: A Study in Land and Franchise Policies Affecting Africans, 1910–1960* (Pietermaritzburg: University of Natal Press, 1962), p. 46.

60. Pienaar, *Glo in u Volk*, p. 175.

came under frequent attack for having failed, for the sake of conciliation with the English, to press for equality of rights for Afrikaans. Through Botha's onestream policy, it was alleged, the tender plant of Afrikaans culture would be swamped by the all-powerful English world culture. Only by keeping the cultural lives of the Afrikaners and English in two separate streams would Afrikaner nationality be maintained and developed.

The Nationalists also appealed to the psychological needs that ethnic identification met. For many Afrikaners there could be no question of conciliation with the English while the memories of conquest in war and concentration camps were still fresh in their minds. For Afrikaner Nationalists the alienation, anxiety, and insecurity of the new order could only be reduced within the womb of ethnic collectivity. Only by stressing their ethnic identity could the humiliation of defeat and the cultural chauvinism of the English be overcome.

Ethnic identification, then, sought to attain political and cultural goals and meet diverse psychological needs. It was more than a struggle for material rewards, but the outcome of the Afrikaners' struggle in the economic field would be decisive in determining whether they would see themselves primarily as an ethnic group or as a class. In the twentieth century, Afrikaners who had been forced to migrate to the cities often entered the job market on the lowest rungs, hardly any higher than the equally unskilled black labor force and far beneath the skilled English worker. Viewed from a Nationalist perspective, the dominant feature of the South African economy was the vast gap between Afrikaner and English wealth (the ratio of the per capita incomes of the Afrikaner and English is estimated to have been as high as 100:300 in 1910).[61] But from a class perspective the obvious characteristic was the cleavage between the capitalists and workers in a system that exploited the largely unskilled and proletarianized Afrikaner and black labor.

For various reasons the Afrikaner workers ultimately as-

61. Personal communication, J. L. Sadie.

sumed an ethnic rather than a class identity. The racial values formed in the eighteenth and nineteenth centuries militated against a class coalition across racial lines. However, more important than abstract racism was the existence of a split labor market in which whites, who were expected to maintain a distinctive standard of living, had to compete with blacks who did not have to meet such expectations. Afrikaners objected to competition with blacks not so much because they were black but because they were offering their labor at a cheaper rate than whites could socially afford. For instance, in the cities blacks were prepared to do unskilled manual labor for two shillings a day during the period 1900 to 1940; competing white workers were unwilling to accept a daily wage of less than three shillings and six pence, or sometimes five shillings.[62] When blacks in the 1930s and 1940s entered the semi-skilled ranks in industry at rates lower than that established for white workers, the same objections against cheap labor were raised. In denying that this amounted to racial discrimination, Malan argued that "the white is really discriminated against in the labour market when he comes into competition with the non-white. The white man, because he is white, is expected—whatever his chances in the labour market—to maintain a white standard of living . . . you can understand that in the circumstances the competition for the white man is killing."[63]

The political order formed another obstacle to a class identity. In 1910 every white male was given a vote. Most Afrikaner workers looked to political action to promote their material interests. They did not identify from the outset with the Nationalist movement and its attempt to establish separate Christian-National trade unions. Many joined the English-speaking white workers in the trade union movement and the Labour Party. However, they gradually lost their tenuous identification with the white working-class movement as they came to regard the Labour Party as an ally

62. J. Lever, "White Strategies in a Divided Society: The Development of South African Labour Policy," unpublished paper, p. 3.

63. House of Assembly debates, 1939, col. 5524.

of British imperialism and the trade union movement as being led by foreigners who in some cases concluded agreements with management against the workers' interests.[64]

In 1937 out of 118 trade union organizations about 100 had non-Afrikaner secretaries although the majority of members were Afrikaners. These trade union leaders fatally underrated the force of ethnic sentiments. One of the few who did realize this was E. B. Sachs, a well-known English trade union leader who was most successful in fostering a class consciousness among Afrikaner workers that transcended racial cleavages. He stated: "The workers' organisations looked upon the Afrikaner people with an air of disdain.... The Labour Movement... failed almost entirely to try to appreciate fully the development, tradition, sentiments and aspirations of the masses of Afrikaners ... as a people which suffered cultural, economic and political oppression. People of a ruling race, including even class conscious workers, usually fail to understand the feelings of a conquered nation, of an oppressed people."[65]

In the 1930s the Afrikaner's quest for identity entered a new stage when the United Party was established, fusing Hertzog's National Party with the pro-Empire South African party of Jan Smuts. Equally significant was the vast influx of Afrikaners in the 1920s and 1930s into industry in semi-skilled operative positions (see chapter 6). For the followers of Malan's "purified" National Party, fusion constituted a material threat. They anticipated that big capital, especially mining capital, would become predominant in the United Party. This would split the whites into a capitalist and working class and would enable the capitalists to replace un- or semi-skilled Afrikaner workers by cheaper black labor. Moreover, South Africa's almost neocolonial economic dependence on the British Empire would increase and would make a mockery of formal political independence. The attack on the joint

64. Dan O'Meara, "Analysing Afrikaner Nationalism: The 'Christian-National' Assault on White Trade Unionism in South Africa, 1934–1948," *African Affairs*, 77, no. 306 (January 1978), 45–72.

65. *Forward*, July 15, 1938.

enemies of imperialism and capitalism was led by a group of men usually labeled in a class analysis as "petty bourgeois": Afrikaans lawyers, teachers, professors, and lower-level civil servants whose career opportunities were limited by the increasing influence of the English language and imperialist values under United Party rule. Especially in the Transvaal this group was politically isolated because farming capital in the north supported the capitalist United Party. This left the white workers as the only potential political ally. For the petty bourgeoisie, fusion posed the threat of the Afrikaner workers becoming denationalized in the process of mobilizing themselves on a class base. Should this happen, there was no hope of an Afrikaner party winning power and using the state to promote the interests of the Afrikaners at large and those of the petty bourgeoisie in particular.[66]

An orthodox class analysis, however, does not provide an adequate answer to the question of why the "purified" version of Afrikaner nationalism became a driving force in such a comparatively short time. As important as material interests were cultural and psychosocial fears and needs to which a strategy of ethnic mobilization could address itself. Fusion presupposed competition on an equal footing of the young and fragile Afrikaans culture with the rich British world culture. The purified Nationalists claimed that this would end in the Afrikaans culture being swamped. Fusion also embodied reconciliation with English-speaking South Africa. The Nationalists argued that this was a chimera before the Afrikaners had asserted themselves economically and culturally against the richer and more worldly wise section of the white population. Lastly, fusion represented the strengthening of the political ties with Britain and an entrenchment of the duality of national and imperial symbols. For the Nationalists

66. This paragraph and the preceding one are based on two excellent studies by O'Meara, "Analysing Afrikaner Nationalism," and "The Afrikaner Broederbond 1927–1948: Class vanguard of Afrikaner Nationalism," *Journal of Southern African Studies*, 3, no. 2 (1977), 156–86. It will be seen that my analysis differs from O'Meara in that I attach separate weight to the factors of ethnicity and class.

these imperial symbols did not evoke a sense of pride in membership in the British Empire but reminded them on the contrary that their nation had not yet taken its place in the row of independent nations of the world.

To understand these Afrikaner goals and sentiments, they should be viewed within the context of the deep psychosocial fears and resentments that many Afrikaners experienced in the 1930s and 1940s. The dislocation of rapid urbanization at a comparatively late stage instilled in them a deep sense of insecurity. In a society in which urban and capitalist values predominated, the Afrikaners not only were from a rural origin and the poorest white group but also were perceived as culturally backward and lacking in sophistication. It was middle-class Afrikaners, particularly educators and clergy, who were most attracted to a strategy of ethnic mobilization to overcome the deep feelings of insecurity and social inferiority that plagued Afrikaners. It was they who disseminated the ethnic gospel that self-realization and human worth could only come through group identification and assertion. It was because the 1930s was such a traumatic period for these Afrikaners that they would be so attracted to the radical "solution" of apartheid.

Both Hertzog and Malan tried to mobilize the electorate by exploiting the concept of Afrikanerdom and both defined it in ways that suited their political strategies. Hertzog, in attempting to build a cross-ethnic middle-class base wished to make the term an inclusive political concept. He proclaimed the rise of a "new Afrikanerdom" consisting of Afrikaans and English-speaking whites—"equal Afrikaners"[67]—who subscribed to the principles of South Africa First, and of full equality between the two white groups. In contrast, Malan's political strategy was to unify politically the Afrikaners who constituted more than 50 percent of the electorate. For the Cape Nationalists, who dominated the party, an Afrikaner

67. For an analysis of statements such as these see D. J. Kriek, Generaal J. B. M. Hertzog se Opvattings oor die Afrikaans-en Engelssprekendes na Uniewording," Ph.D. dissertation, University of Pretoria, 1971.

was someone whose home language was Afrikaans. Religion and political views were not qualifying factors.[68]

Malan's Purified National Party hoped to mobilize the Afrikaners by staking group claims based on the notion that Afrikaners occupied a special place in the South African society. Politically it rejected the compromise of Fusion and called for republican independence. It argued that until a republic had been established justice would not have been done to the Afrikaners. National unity was only possible if the English-speaking section became part of the new South African nation of whom the indigenous Afrikaner people was the core. In the economic field the Afrikaners were urged to unite as an interest group to close the gap between Afrikaner and English wealth and to protect the poor white from competition with blacks, which could lead to the disintegration of the white race and "semi-barbarism." Culturally, the party demanded a two-stream approach entailing mother-tongue education and separate educational, student, cultural, and religious societies in order to restore the Afrikaners' self-confidence and liberate them from their sense of inferiority.[69]

The most significant achievement of the National Party in the 1930s was to rally most of the intellectual elite of the Afrikaners behind its cause. These men were "cultural enterpreneurs"[70] who made extensive use of the Afrikaner Broederbond to ideologize Afrikaner identity and history. This northern-controlled secret organization with extensive influence in Afrikaner educational institutions believed that only by imbuing the Afrikaners with the sense that they were members of an exclusive *volk* could they be mobilized to pursue the National Party goals aimed at safeguarding the future of Afrikanerdom. The Broederbond spread the doctrine of Christian-Nationalism, which held that nations were prod-

---

68. Phil Weber, *Republiek en Nasionale Eenheid*, Hertzog Memorial Lecture, University of Stellenbosch, 1973.

69. See Malan's series of articles entitled "Op die Wagtoring," published in *Die Burger*, particularly the articles published on December 16 and 23, 1933.

70. The term is used by Crawford Young, *The Politics of Cultural Pluralism* (Madison: University of Wisconsin Press, 1976), p. 45.

ucts of a Divine Will, each with a diversity of allotted tasks and distinguished from each other by their separate culture. From this followed that certain political, cultural, and spiritual values were a prerequisite for membership in the Afrikaner ethnic group. These were predominantly bourgeois values with little appeal for workers. Concerned with winning their support, Broederbond thinkers such as Nico Diederichs and Piet Meyer defined the *volk* almost in preindustrial terms: The Afrikaners were an organic unity in which workers and capitalists had an assigned place and function with corresponding rights and duties. To these thinkers true Afrikaners would never exploit a fellow Afrikaner but would protect and support him.[71]

The cultural entrepreneurs also ideologized Afrikaner history. A recent study by Dunbar Moodie points out how central events in the Afrikaners' history such as Blood River, the Wars of Independence, and the concentration camps were woven together in a "sacred history" in which God had repeatedly revealed Himself to the Afrikaners as a chosen people. Moodie argues that the sacred history constituted a civil religion and that after the emotion-charged commemoration of the Great Trek in 1938 the ordinary Afrikaner had made the main themes of the civil religion part of his own emotional identity. Indeed by 1938 "most Afrikaners believed that they belonged to an elect People."[72]

Moodie's work is the most sophisticated on Afrikaner ideology yet, but it is difficult to imagine the majority of Afrikaners at this stage conceiving of themselves as an elect people with a sacred history. Cultural entrepreneurs may spice their speeches with such notions but for an audience it was enough to be told that they were a separate people with particular interests that could best be promoted through mobilization. By 1938 the feeling of belonging to a distinct political entity had grown considerably but it only made a major breakthrough after 1939 when a rival political identity

---

71. O'Meara, "Analysing Afrikaner Nationalism."
72. T. Dunbar Moodie, *The Rise of Afrikanerdom* (Berkeley: University of California Press, 1975).

was crippled. This was Hertzog's concept of an Afrikaans- and English-speaking *volk* united in a new Afrikanerdom which was shattered in 1939 when the Smuts faction of the United Party took South Africa into World War II on the side of Britain. It rekindled all the old anti-British and antiim- perialist sentiments and was ultimately decisive in persuad- ing the majority of the Afrikaners to go it alone politically.[73] Afrikaners now more readily accepted civil religion as part of their identity, but even leaders did not subscribe as faithfully to its tenets as historians imagine. Malan, leader and prophet of the Purified Nationalists, remarked by 1946 that the Af- rikaners did not, as outsiders alleged, consider themselves as a uniquely chosen people.

> The truth is that the Afrikaner... generally speaking re- tained his sense of religion. As a natural consequence his nationhood is rooted in religious grounds: in his personal fate, as in that of his people, he sees the hand of God.... But that he claims this as his exclusive right and thus raises his people above others as God's special favourite is a false and slanderous allegation.[74]

In 1948 the Afrikaners won exclusive political power. In the standard literature the common assumption is that they could only do so by exploiting the Afrikaners' racist sentiments. From this perspective the election of 1948 was clinched by the ideology of apartheid. There are serious problems with this interpretation. In the political campaign preceding this elec- tion, Nationalists often suggested that racial policies should not be allowed to become a political issue between the two parties. Some argued that the only hope South Africa had of solving its racial problem lay in taking the issue out of politi- cal contention.[75] The electoral victory was in fact ensured by a

73. See the argument of Newell M. Stultz, *The Nationalists in Opposition, 1934–1948* (Cape Town: Human and Rousseau, 1974).

74. See his unpublished manuscript "Op die Wagtoring," c.1946, D. F. Malan collection, Carnegie Library, University of Stellenbosch.

75. Stultz, *The Nationalists in Opposition*, pp. 136–43.

decisive measure of Afrikaner unity. The appeal of the apartheid platform to classes such as the workers and the farmers was no doubt an important factor in attracting support for the National Party, but equally important were the party's demands for South African national independence, its promotion of Afrikaner business interests, and its championing of the Afrikaans culture. Or to put it differently, apart from "putting the Kaffer in his place," 1948 also meant to the Afrikaners—particularly the professionals, educators and civil servants—"getting *our* country back" or "feeling at home once again in *our* country."

With single-minded vigor the National Party set out after its victory to entrench its political control. In its endeavor to make the country safe for Afrikanerdom it set up a bulwark of restrictive racial legislation. However, no laws could ultimately prevent the growing dependence on a voteless labor force and the consequences flowing from that. This realization only gradually penetrated. Twenty years after the electoral victory an Afrikaans paper editorialized: "Every white person will have to be made to recognise that there is a race problem in South Africa. How this knowledge can be brought to the whites is a problem nobody has as yet solved."[76]

POWER, UNITY,
AND IDENTITY, 1948—78

After 1948 Afrikaner political power and ethnic unity gradually reinforced and consolidated each other.[77] It has often been assumed that the cohesiveness of the National Party should be ascribed to a rigid adherence to the ideology

76. *Die Transvaler* cited by William R. Frye, *In Whitest Africa* (Englewood Cliffs, N.J.: Prentice-Hall, 1968), p. 104.

77. F. van Zyl Slabbert "Afrikaner Nationalism, White Politics, and Political Change in South Africa," in *Change in Contemporary South Africa*, ed. Leonard Thompson and Jeffrey Butler (Berkeley: University of California Press, 1975), pp. 3–19. This short piece is the best analysis of the sociology of Afrikaner nationalism.

of apartheid. However, central to the party's concerns was not so much the apartheid ideology but the need to maintain Afrikaner unity as a prerequisite for the promotion of Afrikaner interests. If there was any dominant ideology it was one that stressed the values of *volkseenheid* (folk unity), which transcended class or regional (the North-South antagonism) differences, and *volksverbondenheid*, the notion that the realization of the full human potential comes not from individual self-assertion but through identification with and service of the *volk* (people).[78] The indispensable support English-speaking whites provided in maintaining the racial order worked against advocating Afrikaner hegemony too openly. But the same purpose was served by espousing Afrikaner unity. The policy of apartheid should be seen as an instrument that structures the South African polity in such a way that it fosters and conceals Afrikaner hegemony.[79] However, it is unity that is of decisive importance rather than the official policy that is not considered untouchable.

To ensure that a sense of ethnic identity remains the major determinant of political behavior in a changing world, the values of the group and its attitudes toward other groups are constantly redefined. Such redefinitions draw on new insights into the causes of past conflicts and future challenges to the Afrikaner power structure. In the thirty years that the Afrikaners have held exclusive power their ethnic identifications have remained constant. Nonetheless in different times different aspects of their identity were stressed. During the period 1948–59 the central theme in the Afrikaners' self-concept was the paradox of an insecure white people in need of legislation to ensure its survival. Their thinking was racist

78. For a further analysis see A. James Gregor, *Contemporary Racial Ideologies* (New York, 1968), pp. 221–76. Gregor gives a succinct account, based on primary sources, of the ideology of apartheid. My analysis differs from his in that I do not consider separate development as the dominant ideology.

79. André du Toit "Ideological Change, Afrikaner Nationalism and Pragmatic Racial Domination in South Africa," in *Change in Contemporary South Africa*, p. 37.

to the extent that miscegenation was considered an evil that would lead to the degeneration of their race. Absent, however, was the belief that the superior will naturally prevail over the inferior. The Afrikaner politicians of 1948–58 were a rising middle class who feared their English and black adversaries as much as they distrusted their own lower class to maintain separateness and purity of race. They had to be educated in a proper sense of color to maintain proper behavior; and they had to be instructed along the paths of apartheid to ensure that the white man would remain master. To allow social intercourse would be to allow familiarity to breed, blurring the sense of color distinctions. Legal lines had to be drawn in order to establish white as well as black in their "proper" place in society.

In the legislation two considerations were inextricably linked: without a privileged position the Afrikaners could not survive as a separate people; without safeguarding the racial separateness of the people a privileged position could not be maintained. The words of J. G. Strijdom illustrate this connection: "If the European [white] loses his color sense, he cannot remain a white man.... On the basis of unity you cannot retain your sense of color if there is no *apartheid* in the everyday social life, in the political sphere or whatever sphere it may be, and if there is no residential separation... South Africa can only remain a white country if we continue to see that the Europeans remain the dominant nation; and we can only remain the dominant nation if we have the power to govern the country and if the Europeans, by means of their efforts, remain the dominant section."[80]

The outcome of these views was the Mixed Marriages Act (1949) and Immorality Act (1950), which prohibit sexual intercourse across racial lines; the Population Registration Act (1950), which compels every citizen to have an identity certificate showing his "race"; and the Reservation of Separate Amenities Act (1953), which segregates post offices, stations, trains, park benches, hospitals, beaches, and swimming

80. Tatz, *Shadow and Substance*, p. 133.

pools. The Group Areas Act provided for separate residential areas for lower class Afrikaners unable to "buy their apartheid." Political power was safeguarded by removing the Coloureds from the existing voting rolls, thus forestalling a Coloured-English coalition, which in theory was strong enough to end Afrikaner rule.

Verwoerd's term as prime minister (1958–66) saw a shift in attitudes. With the color lines firmly drawn, the Afrikaners, who had gained full political independence with the establishment of the Republic (1961), now emphasized their separate nationhood rather than their separateness as a race. In line with the universal rejection of racism, government spokesmen did not view blacks as innately inferior. Rather than different races they were considered different nations even if they did not agree with the official definition of their identity. Like the Afrikaners, they simply had to accept the values of ethnic identity and ethnic identification in evolving toward a separate nationhood. The unspoken assumption was, however, that their historical and cultural heritage made them unprepared to exercise political power too soon. Because of these differences, contact between the various peoples had to be restricted to the minimum since it would deter the nonwhite peoples from evolving along their own lines. Bedazzled by Verwoerd, many Afrikaner intellectuals for a decade believed with some fervor that apartheid was the restructuring of South Africa according to a vision of justice, all with a view to lasting peace, progress, and prosperity. For this brief period there was indeed a sense of purpose, dedication, and destiny.[81]

Under Vorster there has been a further shift. Having made great material progress, the Afrikaners of the 1970s increasingly see themselves as a politically based class with vested interests. There was little to fear of the deracializing and denationalizing influences that haunted them in the 1950s. Their ethnicity was now expressed in identification with the South

81. W. A. de Klerk, *The Puritans in Africa* (Harmondsworth: Penguin, 1975).

African state and the symbols of the state which had become fully Afrikanerized.[82] At the same time they no longer believed the rhetoric of the 1960s that apartheid will bring about the social harmony of "separate freedoms." It has become much clearer that apartheid maintains white power, wealth, and privileges—usually subsumed under the code words "white identity." Economic discrimination is no longer justified in ideological terms but in terms of the "economic" or "political realities" that do not allow the gap between black and white wealth to be narrowed more rapidly. Racist rhetoric is seldom heard in the public life, nor is the unspoken assumption of Verwoerd that the historical differences of blacks will impede their progress. Instead Vorster has emphasized that differences do not constitute inferiority. He frequently states that "the policy of separate development was conceived not because we considered ourselves better than others . . . we created the policy of separate development because we maintained that we were different from others and valued that difference, and we are not prepared to sacrifice that difference."[83]

No longer is there a biological justification of white domination; instead history is called in to legitimize group claims. Whereas during the first half of the century whites argued that in view of their superior civilization they had the right to rule over all of South Africa, Vorster claimed that whites have the *historical* right to maintain their sovereignty in "white" South Africa: "We have our land and we alone will

82. Stanley J. Morse, J. W. Mann, and Elizabeth Nel, "National Identity in a 'Multi-National' State: A Comparison of Afrikaners and English-Speaking South Africans," *Canadian Review of Studies in Nationalism,* 2, no. 2 (1977), 225–46.

83. Hermann Giliomee, "The Development of the Afrikaner's Self-Concept," in *Looking at the Afrikaner Today,* ed. H. W. van der Merwe (Cape Town: Tafelberg, 1975), p. 27. The Minister of Justice, Mr. Kruger, told Chief Gatsha Buthelezi recently: "I accept you as my brother. I accept the black man of Africa as my black brother. . . . But he's a different nation and this is the whole point and that nobody can go against history. . . ." *The Star,* December 3, 1977.

have the say over that land. We have our Parliament and in that Parliament we and we alone will be represented."[84]

Afrikaner Nationalists can now criticize the apartheid policy in a forthright way without being considered disloyal as long as the criticism is considered to serve the purpose of internal peace and prosperity. A leading editor could write with reference to the failures of apartheid: "Human plans are not sacrosanct. If they do not work they must be changed and refurbished. To elevate them to the status of untouchable truths and eternally valid slogans, might be politically expedient in the short run but would be nationally harmful and disastrous in the long run."[85] Gerrit Viljoen, head of the Afrikaner Broederbond, stated: "Apartheid is not an ideology nor a dogma. It is a method, a road along which we are moving and is subject to fundamental reassessment."[86]

Despite the waning belief in separate development as a "solution," the distinct historical heritage of the Afrikaner still exercises a powerful influence. This heritage manifests itself in various values and myths born in the successful strategy of mobilizing themselves as a people against British imperialism. Except for the gross inequities in the allocation of funds, Afrikaners generally do not consider it an injustice that browns and blacks are compelled to attend their own schools and live in their own group areas. They tend to project on them their own history of resistance to elitist and denationalizing strategies, and of fulfillment by encapsulating themselves in their own schools and residential areas.

However, within the ranks of all those who consider themselves Afrikaners, cleavages are widening. Although more than 80 percent still support the National Party, they have different perceptions as to how the survival crisis of the Afrikaners should be met, what aspects of Afrikaner identity should be stressed, and how this identity should be preserved. In political terms there can be said to be three dif-

84. Ibid., p. 28.

85. *Die Burger*, September 25, 1972.

86. John de St. Jorre, *A House Divided* (New York: Carnegie Endowment, 1977), p. 13.

ferent ways in which Afrikaners identify with the group. First, there are those who see the Afrikaners as an exclusive *volk*, a creation of God sharing a definite genetic character, a distinct cultural heritage, and common conservative values, people who support the National Party as protector of these values. Even Afrikaans-speaking whites who do not share these values or who oppose the party are excluded. The historian Gert Scholtz has expressed this attitude as follows: "a nation is a spiritual entity. If you don't subscribe to its principles, you belong to another group."[87] Since the 1930s leading members of the National Party and Broederbond have strongly propagated this identity, which restricts membership of the *volk* in terms of certain exclusive political and spiritual values.[88] It is still being disseminated in some schools and universities and by organizations such as SABRA, FAK, and the Rapportryers. However, such exclusivity belongs more properly to a minority that still is in the process of mobilizing the group. Today aspects of it have become an embarrassment. Metaphysical notions of *volksiel* (soul of the people) and the Afrikaner's vocation in South Africa are beginning to disappear. The identification with the Afrikaners' history—a central element of this exclusive identity—is on the decline. One indication is the steady decrease, since the advent of the Republic, in the number of Standard 10 pupils who study history at school. A recent study analyzing this gave as one of the main reasons "the modern precedence accorded to material values and specialization trends for the occupational order." It led "the majority of young people to display a primary interest in the so-called 'bread and butter' subjects."[89] "Bread and butter" concerns

87. Cited in Jim Hoagland, *South Africa: Civilizations in Conflict* (London: George Allen and Unwin, 1972), p. 42.

88. For a perceptive discussion of Afrikaner education with special reference to the doctrine of Christian-Nationalism which underpins this exclusive identity, see John David Shingler, "Education and Political Order in South Africa, 1902–1961," Ph.D. dissertation, Yale University, 1973.

89. C. R. Liebenberg, *The Teaching of History at South African Secondary Schools* (Pretoria: Human Sciences Research Council, 1972), pp. 23–24.

aside, it has become clear to the Afrikaner rank and file that their interests and privileges no longer safely rest on exclusive Afrikaner power serving an exclusivist Afrikanerdom. The future will almost certainly see a further broadening of the group-concept.

A second pattern of identification is that of the political leadership, who sees the Afrikaner as the core of the *white* South African nation embracing all whites and sharing the same privileges. It differs substantially from the vision of Hertzog in the 1930s of coequal Afrikaners and English components forming the "Afrikaner nation." Though it is seldom articulated, the underlying assumption presently is that the interests and values of the Afrikaners are supreme. While such a group base is in some respects a more viable one than the first, it still is a racially exclusive one. Indeed, by excluding the Afrikaans-speaking Coloureds—sometimes referred to as "brown Afrikaners" by Afrikaans writers—but including the English, this concept defines the values of Afrikanerdom even more explicitly in racial terms. Connie Mulder, former leader of the National Party in the Transvaal, has articulated this as follows: "We do not only want to survive in South Africa. We want to survive as a white *volk* and retain our identity. We will keep all measures to maintain this because we want to survive as a white *volk* and not as a coloured *volk*" [*kleurvolk*].[90]

"Afrikaner identity" in this and the previous instance refers to much more than the Afrikaans language and culture. It is, in fact, a political code word that relates to the status which accompanies political domination and to the range of ethnic interests, privileges, and spoils, of which crucial ones, such as career chances in the civil service and public corporations (see chapter 6), depend on political control and the policy of separate development, which ensures Afrikaner hegemony. Here two of the most basic misconceptions about the identity and ideology of the Afrikaners can be noted. The first is the advice given to the Afrikaners by outsiders that they should

90. *Die Burger*, September 13; 1978.

learn to maintain their identity without laws and that they could do so in an open society without costs to the group. The second is that apartheid is not just a policy but an ideology fervently believed in by the Afrikaners" and so inflexibly adhered to that it "has led to a totalitarian exercise of power."[91] One look at the Afrikaners' structural position in the South African society shows that the existing laws and regulations are indeed protecting an identity such as the one covered by the code word discussed above. And an investigation of the Afrikaners' political system would show that a rational calculation of ethnic interests rather than ideological zealotry underpins the exercise of power by Afrikaner nationalists. (See chapter 8)

Third, there are also those Afrikaners, particularly among the business elite, professionals, academics, and writers, who identify with the group not because it is the politically dominant group or because it serves their own interests. They do, however, feel attached to the Afrikaans culture and involved with the Afrikaner people in the struggle to introduce a greater measure of freedom and social justice in the South African political system. To them, Afrikaans as language would best be promoted by the vigor of its literature while the interests of the Afrikaner middle-class would best be served by de-ethnicizing the South African political, economic, and social system. Thus they are not nationalists in the sense that they feel that the ethnic group should invariably receive their highest love and loyalty or be their main source of identification. Much rather would they see their Afrikanerhood as one of several loyalties and identifications. Anton Rupert, the Afrikaner business leader, has expressed this in the following terms: "I am a man with a Christian conscience, child of Christian civilization. I am Afrikaner-born. I am a South African. I belong to the Western world. I am a world citizen."[92] In political terms these Afrikaners see the Afrikaner *volk* as an

91. Derek Heater, *Contemporary Political Ideas* (London: Longman, 1974), p. 74.

92. Anton Rupert, *Progress through Partnership* (Cape Town: Nasionale Boekhandel, 1967), p. 12.

interest group (with claims to protection of its language rights, sharing political power and enjoying, on the principle of merit, the prosperity of the country) within an expanding South African nation encompassing also black and brown people. In such a society, class interests would increase and ethnicity would decrease as a primary category of politics. As a result Afrikaners would increasingly experience a "blurred two-ness,"[93] conceiving themselves as both Afrikaners and South Africans. Being Afrikaners—or to use a less loaded concept: being Afrikaans—they would take pride in their cultural heritage; being South Africans they would share with others the sense of belonging to a new political "peoplehood" based on middle-class values and interests.

At the moment supported by only a small majority, such an identification may gain wider support in the politics of survival. Recently some politicians and editors have argued that the present crisis could best be met by alliances across ethnic lines. Thus an ex-editor of *Die Burger* remarked that the greatest need of the Afrikaners "now seems to be to define the common aims of all peoples sharing their land with them. The most obvious of these must surely be the defense of a common civilization."[94] And *Die Vaderland* stated that the new constitution confronts the Afrikaners with the decision of "whether it will continue to exclude, on grounds of colour, people who fully accept its language, culture and traditions."[95] But working against the growth of such an inclusive concept is the racialized political structure of South Africa.

A rough gauge of the relative strengths of these identifications and the values that they represent are the findings of recently conducted opinion surveys. How exclusive are the Afrikaners politically? In the early 1960s Verwoerd declared that only whites constitute the South African nation. In a sample of Afrikaners interviewed in 1972 some 45 percent of

93. Harold R. Isaacs, *Idols of the Tribe* (New York: Harper, 1975), pp. 194–95.

94. Piet Cillié, "The Case for Africa's White Tribe," *Saturday Evening Post*, May 1977.

95. *Die Vaderland*, March 15, 1978.

Afrikaners indicated that they would call an Afrikaans-speaking Coloured an Afrikaner. When the survey was repeated in 1977 this figure had risen to 52 percent.[96] Another survey undertaken in 1975 showed that 47 percent of a sample of Afrikaners thought that Coloureds should be allowed to represent Coloureds in Parliament.[97] How strong is the traditional concept of the white man as being entitled to a privileged position in the job market? According to a study of Market and Opinion Surveys only 32 percent of Afrikaners in 1974 agreed with the statement that nonwhites should be trained for the same jobs as whites in industry and receive the same pay. In October 1976 some 42 percent of Afrikaners agreed to the abolition of Job Reservation, and in October 1977, 62 percent found acceptable the admission of nonwhites to the same jobs as whites and 62 percent accepted the principle of equal salaries for whites and nonwhites.[98]

These attitudes may simply indicate a greater measure of sophistication among Afrikaners who wish to broaden the political and economic bases on which their power rests without, however, widening ethnic boundaries. According to the Freiburg survey the opposition to social integration remains strong with only between a fifth and a third of the Afrikaners interviewed in 1977 favoring admission of blacks in the same churches, to all cinemas, to certain white schools, and to white recreation areas.[99] But also here there is a trend toward greater openness. In a South African survey the Afrikaner support for the abolition of the Immorality and the Mixed Marriages Act has grown from roughly 12 percent in 1974 to just over 20 percent in 1977.[100] The Afrikaners, to be

96. Lawrence Schlemmer, "Change in South Africa: Processes, Opportunities and Constraints." Paper delivered in April 1978 to be published in *Optima.*

97. *The Star,* May 2, 1975, quoting Market Research Africa.

98. Schlemmer, "Change in South Africa."

99. Theodor Hanf, Heribert Weiland, and Gerda Vierdag, *Südafrika: Friedlicher Wandel?* (Munich: Kaiser, 1978), chapter 7.

100. Schlemmer, "Change in South Africa." In the social field two trends can be discerned that suggest a greater degree of openness than the above figures indicate. First, the resistance seems to be against "forced" integration

sure, are still determined to retain their politically dominant position in society. In the sample of the Freiburg survey some 90 percent of Afrikaners rejected the notion of a federal state in which power is shared and no group dominates.[101] Why this fear of black majority rule? In a survey conducted in 1977 the question posed to another sample of Afrikaners was what would be the most likely outcome if blacks were to govern South Africa. The two propositions winning most support were: (1) the order and security of our society would be threatened (80 percent), and (2) the jobs and work security of whites would be threatened (37 percent). Only 14 percent indicated that they most feared that the language and culture of the Afrikaners would be threatened.[102]

Taken together these findings suggest a distinct but not yet decisive shift away from an identity that rests on exclusivity and privilege toward an orientation in which culture, merit, and free association are preferred to race as the basic ordering principle of society. At the same time, however, identity for the large majority of Afrikaners means more than cultural affiliation or their immediate material interests. It rests on the notion that their ethnic group has a claim to a distinct place in the country that they regard as their own. To "maintain their identity"—the present shibbolith of white South African politics—means for the majority of Afrikaners to retain political control over "their" affairs and through that their present

---

not voluntary integration. In a Market and Opinion Survey of 1975, only 6 percent of Afrikaners were in favor of all hotels in white areas being opened to nonwhites. However, 51 percent were in favor of the proposition that the license holder of a hotel should have the liberty to choose whether he would like to open the hotel to all population groups. Second, Afrikaner attitudes change as the policies change. Whereas only 4 percent of Afrikaners in 1970 were in favor of competition between whites and blacks in all kinds of sport, 50 percent agreed with mixed sports at club level in 1976 after the government had introduced the new sports policy. In 1977, 61 percent found blacks and whites together in sports teams acceptable.

101. Hanf, Weiland, and Vierdag, *Südafrika: Friedlicher Wandel?*, chapter 7.
102. Schlemmer, "Change in South Africa."

class position.[103] However, it is exactly these claims that are challenged by both the black opposition within and the world outside. As a result the Afrikaners are at the moment engaged in the painful process of redefining the inner, non-negotiable core of their identity as they prepare to meet these challenges.

103. For recent critical analyses of the phenomena and rhetoric of Afrikaner Nationalism see René de Villiers, "Afrikaner Nationalism," in *Oxford History of South Africa,* ed. Monica Wilson and Leonard Thompson (Oxford: Clarendon, 1971), pp. 365–424; Johannes Degenaar, *Afrikaner Nationalism* (Cape Town: Center for Intergroup Studies, University of Cape Town, 1978); and André du Toit, "Black and White Identities and the Prospects for Peaceful Accommodation in a Changing Society," paper presented to the "Road Ahead Conference," Grahamstown, July 1978.

5 Survival Politics: In Search of a New Ideology Heribert Adam

Once a revolution has taken place, the major problem for any chiliastic regime is how to maintain enthusiasm. Revolutionary regimes must therefore try to sustain the zeal by maintaining an atmosphere of war, by mobilizing emotions against an outside or internal enemy, or by some kind of "revitalized faith."—Daniel Bell[1]

In his thorough sociological study of Afrikaner ideology, Dunbar Moodie has shown that the civil theology most adequate to the exigencies of the 1930s was an interpretation "which was tight enough to unite Afrikaners and yet loose enough to allow considerable difference of opinion on practical matters."[2] While the same functional needs for a proper ideology remain for the 1970s and 1980s, "civil theology" can no longer fulfill this task. This is mainly due to increased secularization and value changes in an urbanized life, which have diluted traditional culture with the corruptive spoils of affluence. Moodie appropriately concludes that the exigencies of Afrikaner power have changed the debate from one between rival social metaphysical interpretations of Christian Nationalism (Kuyperianism, neo-Fichteanism, Volkskerk) to that of "the very continuance of ideology itself."[3] Such considered findings are confirmed by similar observations of

1. Daniel Bell, "The Return of the Sacred?" *British Journal of Sociology*, 18, no. 4 (December 1977), 419–49.
2. T. Dunbar Moodie, *The Rise of Afrikanerdom: Power, Apartheid, and the Afrikaner Civil Religion* (Berkeley: University of California Press, 1975), p. 104.
3. Ibid., p. 288.

"outsiders" who returned after a lengthy exile. In the assessment of Ezekiel Mphahlele: "Until a decade ago one would have categorically said that the Boer masses all sincerely and passionately shared the thoughts and feelings of the elite who talked kultuur, mother tongue, religion and so on. Today I would not be so sure. Because of the white alliance and the filtering of other noises from the Western world outside, it may only be the Boer intellectual elite who refuse to stop at political and economic victories and keep the ancient fires alive."[4] However, such impressionistic evidence is not confirmed by systematic attitude surveys. And yet both observations are not necessarily contradictory, as a closer analysis of the ongoing redefinition of ethnic zeal will show.

On the one hand, there is considerable evidence of a dwindling interest in traditional Afrikaner mobilization. The quaint rituals and emotional speeches on memorial days only demonstrate that the spirit of the Voortrekkers is as dead as the two monuments in which the past advancements are now enshrined. Symposia are still held on "The Afrikaner in the City," but this time with the aim of marketing culture in the packages of PR campaigns: "Culture in an attractive wrapping that is suited to the character and way of life of the modern Afrikaner ought—even in the year 1978 and subsequently—to find a ready market."[5]

On the other hand, such trends do not indicate the irrelevance of ethnicity. All empirical evidence confirms a highly cohesive ethnic outlook.[6] The apparent contradiction reflects the continual redefinitions of the ethnic content. A ruling ethnic minority has to constantly compromise its principles in order to cope with a stronger reality. Doubts among the *volk* arise because the cultural tenets are interlocked with political strategies.

4. Ezekiel Mphahlele, "South Africa: Two Communities and the Struggle for a Birthright," *Journal of African Studies*, 4, no. 1 (Spring 1977), 21–50.

5. *Beeld*, March 1, 1978.

6. See particularly the Freiburg study. In this most systematic and thorough survey, ethnic factors accounted for surprisingly high correlations on almost every attitude questioned.

If the latter have to be jettisoned in favor of more expedient policies, uncritical dedication to the entire ethnic world view could become affected. It is the failure of apartheid as the promised political solution that gives rise to some doubts about the future course of ethnic politics. Two comments, typical of many that recurred in private conversations, may suffice to illustrate the perplexed longing for a new faith in an ideological vacuum:

> It is in times like these that a nation needs a vision, such as the one we had when we seized upon the idea of separate freedoms. Then, too, we were aware of the dark times that lay ahead, but somewhere in the tunnel we saw a glimmer of light and we made our way in that direction. Now we find ourselves once more in such a tunnel.[7]

Voices from the English-speaking white sector express an equally ambivalent conjuration for ideological guidance, as if such legitimacy could be invented with goodwill overnight:

> White South Africans, more than most, need a race policy they can believe in. An ideology they can clutch at and lean on as the going gets tough. Apartheid was such a concept and it has served the Afrikaner well for nearly three decades. Now confidence in it is ebbing, not least among Afrikaners themselves. It would be an act of supreme statesmanship for Mr. Vorster now to seek a new faith, a new principle, a new dispensation that can carry the Republic forward for the next three decades. And this time to seek it with the help of the Brown and Black men with whom, willy nilly, we have to share this troubled land—in prosperity and peace or in poverty and bloodshed.[8]

An ethnic oligarchy searching for legitimacy is constrained by various circumstances in its attempt for ideological re-

7. *Rapport,* January 2, 1977.
8. *Financial Mail,* April 15, 1976, p. 210.

mobilization. Ideology for what? With Afrikaner political power vis-à-vis the English consolidated, the new task has become that of soliciting the active collaboration of the English section in the maintenance of Afrikaner dominance vis-à-vis the blacks. Civil theology, therefore, let alone the exclusivist symbols of the past Afrikaner mobilization, could not provide the ideological paradigm for a common white cooperative effort. On the contrary, emphasis on Afrikaner exclusivism and reminders of the past intrawhite struggles served only to antagonize the newly wooed ally. But neither could the cherished folk traditions be abandoned in the name of all-white unity. Not only had they acquired a life of their own as sacred parts of a glorified history, but to jettison Afrikaner exclusivism would have invited splits among the Nationalists with much more widespread appeal of accusations of betrayal and capitulation than the Herstigtes could muster. In addition, while courting the English vote, the Nationalists had no intention of sharing political power with their former adversary. Even if they all joined the ruling party, decisive policy was to be made for and within exclusive Afrikaner circles. The Broederbond has yet to admit a single non-Afrikaner convert. At most, the National party thus far is prepared increasingly to involve trustworthy non-Afrikaners in the administration of the state to placate English support. The alleged expertise and the image of English patriots, who had ingratiated themselves, proved useful in selective cabinet positions (Finance, Tourism, Indian Affairs) where a more cosmopolitan background could harness goodwill. The inclusion of some token English converts in the ruling machinery also provided public rewards for veteran supporters, inviting more of the same from ambitious upstarts, without relinquishing any Afrikaner control or redefinition of priorities. After all, Afrikaner capital is still locked in a more silent competition with its imperial rival despite increasing mergers and joint ventures. Advances of Afrikaner economic power through the public corporations (parastatals) and by way of redirecting national income into sectional support, still left the private English capital in a dominant, though reduced, position. But despite this ongoing conflict, Afrikaner power needed now more than ever before, the support of all whites. The new need derived from the exigencies of a war economy. With the direct exposure of South Africa to hostile military forces, after the collapse of the Portuguese colonial empire, a new constellation had developed that required unity of all white sections as a minimal prerequisite for effective countermobilization. With a drafted army of civilians, for example, resentment of the government as sectional, even by a small part of the population, could have severe effects on the morale and efficiency of the military. Not having a fifth column within its ranks, has always been the strength of a settler regime.

This need for collaborative unity needed a new motivating ideology in the 1970s. It had to embrace the sacred Afrikaner symbols without alienating those excluded. It had to disguise the furtherance of Afrikaner power while at the same time mobilizing for sacrifice by all whites. The new rationale had to allow for the accommodation of all sectional interests, while simultaneously obscuring the underlying antagonisms. Hence, differential sacrifice and rewards among the white community could result in potential disintegration. This danger had to be overcome by an explanation sufficiently powerful to disregard self-interest or at least tolerate imposed restrictions.

At the same time the new ideology could not afford to be completely out of tune with the international context, despite the pariah role of South Africa. Her continuing dependence on Western support and inclusion in the global network of Western interests demanded a rationale for white hegemony that (1) does not differ at home and abroad and (2) is "marketable" internationally, that is, that it solicits a minimum of basic understanding and sympathy among "reasonable" people who at least would not be embarrassed to support a justifiable cause, regardless of its implementation locally.

How could a cause that optimally fulfills all the functions of external consistency with internal, nonsectional mobilization be defined? It would appear obvious that neither theological motivations of Afrikaner Calvinism ("civilizing mission of a chosen people") nor an overtly racist rationale ("keeping standards against primitive natives") could provide this motivating legitimacy. For a while, a blind anticommunism was emphasized as a common bond of all those supporting the status quo. But since it lumped together the most impeccable foes of communism, from high clergy to liberal capitalists, it could appeal only to the most unenlightened. Neither was such a stance consistent with an international scene in which the Cold War had given way to detente and collaboration between the superpowers in stabilizing regional conflicts. If nothing else, the Carter administration has at least shocked Pretoria into the realization that even some conservative Americans considered their bandied brand of anticommunism as a liability and prescription for further radicalization of previously pro-Western black sentiment.

To conceive of an ideology as being consciously invented by a braintrust or some other deliberate conspiracy would be misleading. A legitimating rationale gradually emerges through constant repetition and refinement by opinionmakers. A new formula "catches on" while older interpretations fade out because it reflects better the changing needs of its adherents.

Since neither ethnic chauvinism, cultural purity, nor anticommunism continued to provide the needed rationale, a formula has emerged in response to the new exigencies that appears to fulfill all the divergent functions discussed so far. This formula is the *idea of survival.*

The ideology of survival implies an unquestioned threat. An enemy exists by definition, regardless of the specifics that are under attack. Who has time to bicker about policy changes when a gun is pointed at you? Survival means countering a challenge to life itself, the safety of sleeping securely at night. With such appeals to universal protection needs, the leadership can advertise controversial constitutional proposals. As Vorster presents them in a full page advertisement of the National Party: They "are more important than the advent of the Republic because it concerns your future. It will determine how long you will survive in this country; how long you will be safe in this fatherland."[9]

Survival is thereby defined in biological terms; the survival of privileges need not be raised. Survival as well as identity represent respectable code words, vague enough to allow the leadership to manipulate their specific meaning. Yet they signal sufficient emotional appeal to rally the faithful behind those who promise relief from insecurity. For political leaders the secret of successful mobilization with survival politics lies in creating anxieties in the first place and then offering the way out for the frightened. The world as a jungle of black and white, Marxist aggressors at the throat of industrious farmers, effectively obfuscates an unjust reality for the Afrikaners themselves as well as an ambivalent outside world.

Survival politics allows the leadership to determine internal changes without laying itself open to charges of betrayal of doctrine: "If there are practices and matters that would lead to our destruction rather than assure our survival, we must look at them with meticulous honesty."[10] The same message by editor Dirk Richard asserts succinctly: "Survival must be subject to adaptation."[11] Survival is sufficiently serious to permit officeholders to manipulate domestic priorities on the basis of alleged superior information. It has become their prerogative to define "essential interests" in cases of ambiguities:

> It is not always easy to determine precisely what is of importance for survival. That is where it is necessary to conduct the debate more openly and more searchingly. I personally believe that there are numerous matters which could be changed without affecting our survival, indeed, which must be changed if we are to survive.[12]

On the other hand, if the debate gets out of hand, the threatening enemy can be redefined to restore unity: "For the

9. *Weekend Argus*, November 5, 1977.
10. Pik Botha, *Rapport*, editorial, January 1, 1978.
11. Dirk Richard, *Die Vaderland*, August 22, 1977.
12. Pik Botha, ibid.

total onslaught on South Africa has now also become an onslaught from within. It has already succeeded in sowing the seeds of disunity."[13] Therefore, rallying behind the party leadership against the agitators, whoever they are, has become the duty of all true patriots, because: "The National Party is the guarantor of white survival in a turbulent subcontinent and the opposition and other enemies will exploit every little crack."[14]

The chief of South Africa's military General M. Malan now mobilizes the public for "total war." He refers repeatedly to the "problem of reconciling democratic principles with total strategy" and concludes: "I must emphasise that the overriding consideration is survival. Survival concerns every citizen in South Africa directly and personally."[15] Survival needs caused a unique imposition of citizenship on unwilling whites while at the same time willing blacks are deprived of their South African birthright. Mobilization for "total war" could no longer afford the exemption of a large section of immigrants who refrained from acquiring South African citizenship. A new law specified that aliens under 25 years old with a permanent residential permit will automatically acquire South African citizenship after two years. Hence, they become eligible for military service. Those who refuse will forfeit their residential rights. The new regulation was passed despite its likely effect on an already dwindling immigration figure in order to separate "the sheep from the goats"[16] and eliminate the military disadvantage of South African born youth.

Will the same survival needs also apply to new political dispensations across the color line? While the army increasingly enrolls blacks in its ranks, sometimes against the opposition of rural commandos, the political deracialization still remains the center of the dispute within Afrikanerdom. It is on this issue that the advocates of the new ideology clash

13. *Die Vaderland*, November 8, 1978.
14. *Beeld*, November 22, 1978.
15. General M. Malan, *Sunday Times*, March 13, 1977.
16. *Rapport*, February 26, 1978.

with the proponents of traditional policy in the name of survival. The politics of survival is invoked in determining "whether white and black can work out a new deal for our co-existence in peace and friendship."[17] "Joint survival" calls for an alliance of white and "moderate blacks" against "militant, radical Marxists." Strengthening the legitimacy of non-Marxist black nationalists becomes for the first time an urgent necessity: "On the part of the whites generally and of the Government in particular action must be taken in such a way that the moderates among the black leaders (i.e. Buthelezi) must have their hands strengthened among their own people. That would be the best strategy against the extremists."[18] Co-optation strategies, however, also include a hitherto sacrosanct redefinition of group boundaries, "the question of whether Afrikanerdom will be prepared to open its ranks to people of other colours."[19]

But survival pleas also signal weakness. The defensive stance implicit in the notion affects morale. It must therefore be offset by a climate of hopefulness and optimism about the future. The more pragmatic ideologues clearly sense this need. Connie Mulder is reported as saying that he was tired of predictions that death lay around the corner, and he rejected the creation of a psychosis of panic among the people. "From to-day there can be only one slogan: 'It can be done.'"[20] What can be done is left to individual interpretation though not to individual action. Such mobilizing cries recognize and reflect a threatened in-group morale. Leaders of all beleaguered states in recent history painted a picture of imminent victory in the realization of approaching doom. A common slogan of revolutionary movements after shattering setbacks also is: "The struggle continues! Victory is certain!" In order to combat such crisis of morale, it does not suffice to assail defeatism. Every sophisticated army commander

17. *Beeld*, March 28, 1978.
18. *Die Vaderland*, March 14, 1978.
19. Ibid., March 15, 1978.
20. C. Mulder as quoted in *The Star Weekly*, April 8, 1978, p. 7.

knows that the more defecting soldiers are court-martialed, the more the purpose of the punishment is undermined.

A much more promising propaganda device attaches the symbolism of morbidity to the enemy, who is portrayed as "on the way out." The "vigorous" in-group is only threatened by a "spent force." In the case of South Africa Mulder says, she must do all in her power to prevent herself from becoming "one of the last victims of a *dying* liberalism of the Western world."[21] The former emotional secession from the British empire has now turned into gratifying defiance of the world:

> "World opinion is no longer the yardstick," declares the semi-official South African Broadcasting Corporation, "if the election demonstrated anything, it is the determination of the nation to act in the best interests of South Africa— whatever the effect on world opinion. If by so doing world hostility is intensified, so be it. For too long the attempt to satisfy world opinion has limited our freedom of action.[22]

However, the posturing against foreign interference in South Africa in reality barely hides the need for more Western involvement in the survival of white South Africa. It is because of the new Western ambiguity toward a discredited ally that isolationism and defiance are glorified as state dogma, when white South Africa in fact becomes daily more dependent on allied outside support.

In a drifting ship many want to save their skin first, regardless of customary morality. Yet changing the course does not guarantee hope in the eyes of those responsible for the wreck. Irreversible outside hostility is falsely asserted in order to rally the doubtful behind the official defiance. "We have no hope of satisfying the world by concessions on correction," declares the chairman of the Broederbond.[23] The sole alterna-

21. Ibid.
22. *Current Affairs*, December 2, 1977.
23. Gerrit Viljoen, *The Star Weekly*, May 20, 1978.

tive is posed as capitulation or Afrikaner self-determination. However, as already pointed out, the sacrifices of self-reliance can hardly instill enthusiasm or even confidence in the certain success of survival ideology.

Survival is inextricably bound to its opposite: disaster. Whatever the individual may conceive of as disaster, the mere thought of such an event will initiate frequent protective behavior: money abroad, career planning for a potential emigration, or cautious investment decisions in immovable goods. It is this erosion of confidence that has afflicted white South Africa since the Soweto unrest of 1976. No statistics reveal the massive contravention of ever tighter currency regulations or the increasing number of South Africans who explore alternatives abroad without formally declaring their intentions to the authorities. The rapidly increasing emigration represents only the top of an iceberg of self-doubt.[24] Therefore, survival ideology also undermines its very objective of defiant mobilization. It starts a process of attrition in the minds of the more intelligent sectors of the populace.

A static "siege-culture" always embodies its dynamic opposite: the avoidance of surrender through new initiatives. This will spiral when the prospects of more civil unrest and escalation of dissent have mandated the use of scarce resources to deal with the upheavals to such a degree that a sense of despair will become more widespread. A system in such a "legitimation crisis"[25] and under the pressure of scarce

24. Surveys reveal that the majority of English-speaking white graduates contemplate career prospects abroad. This prompted some university officials to issue a letter to all newly admitted students that the institution is training professionals for service in South Africa. There is of course no way to stop this costly ongoing exodus short of cutting all ties with the outside world through a Berlin wall. However, the loss of white South Africa does not always mean the gain others had hoped for. Declaring that "significant numbers" of South African Jews had emigrated recently, Johannesburg Rabbi Norman Bernhard assailed local Jews who identify themselves with Zionism and then go on aliyah to the United States, Britain, Canada, and Australia. (*Jerusalem Post*, International Edition, April 12, 1977, p. 3.)

25. On this concept see the "landmark in critical social analysis": Jürgen Habermas, *Legitimation Crisis* (Boston: Beacon Press, 1975), from which many

material resources survives only by permanently incorporating elements of the rejected system in order to ease the strain. Domination under threat can perpetuate itself and extend its options by itself insisting on social change. To control inevitable change rather than to resist it seems therefore to have become the latent thrust of Nationalist policy.

However, this endeavor needs the isolation from outside interference in order to retain sole control. Given the dependency on outside allies and their interest in "meddling" in South African affairs, a suitable defensive weapon lies in discrediting the moral right of interference. Such posture points, above all, to the double standards of the accuser. This portrays the defendant in the role of an unjustified victim. The historical crimes of fellow settlers lend themselves to beg absolution from the contemporary sins:

> South Africa is the victim of an historical guilt-feeling in the West. South Africans were the only white people to establish themselves outside Europe who continued to flourish without killing off all the indigenous people or reducing them to a minority in their own country. This happened with the Indians in North America, the Eskimos in Canada, Lapplanders in Sweden, Aborigines and Maoris in Australia and New Zealand and the Aztecs and Incas in South America. It is now the descendants of these murderers of peoples who criticise the Afrikaner today, citing high morality and Christianity.[26]

The propaganda goes to any length to prove the double standards without noticing the absurdity of the accusations. A good example is the frequent equation of European terrorist fringe groups with broad-based liberation movements against racial hegemony that have been bestowed with international legitimacy.

---

of my own theoretical constructs and ideas are derived, though, I hope, in a more readable form.

26. Gerrit Viljoen, *The Star Weekly*, May 20, 1978, p. 9.

Why do Mr. Vance and Dr. Owen not insist that West Germany should negotiate at higher level with the Baader-Meinhof gang? And why does Dr. Owen not negotiate with the Irish Republican Army.[27]

Thereby Afrikanerdom traps itself in its own propaganda. A hostile outside world is obscured by a verbiage that no longer distinguishes between friend and foe. In the tradition of the U.S. lunatic fringe groups, labels are bandied about that make even the founder of the Trilateral Commission look suspicious:

To say outright that Professor Brzezinski is a Marxist is perhaps too drastic, but the degree of tolerance he displays towards Marxism is surprising for a man who should be strongly committed to the Western ideology.[28]

Similar examples of bizarre portrayals of a threatening reality could fill a long list. They are supposed to reinforce the theme of self-reliance and uncompromising vigilance. Since nobody else can be trusted, the unity of the *volk* remains the only guarantee for survival. But the effort still lacks a mobilizing goal. It is only wedded to the defense of the *status quo*. At the same time, the mobilizing manipulation allows for flexibility and abrupt changes, if the need arises.

Survival ideology also lends itself to international marketing without being inconsistent with the mobilizing practice at home. To struggle for survival fits an appealing underdog role for eliciting sympathy abroad. To an American television audience, the South African spokesman pleads: "Please understand the dilemma of the people who, irrespective of the colour of their skins, only want to survive.[29] One is hard

27. *Die Vaderland*, April 17, 1978.
28. *Current Affairs*, October 14, 1977.
29. *South African Digest*, February 24, 1978. Former banker Jan Marais states: "We need a saleable survival package." *Financial Mail*, September 1978, p. 1066.

pressed to imagine any other statement that would reveal a deeper crisis of legitimacy for an ethnic oligarchy.

The absence of successful ideology beyond mere survival crucially weakens the white cause. Novelist Dan Jacobson has observed "that a minority in such a situation is worth backing only when it expresses or embodies moral and political principles which other states feel they cannot, for their own sake, allow to go under."[30] The widespread public support for Israel, regardless of her intransigence, flows from such sources. Israel solicits empathy because she stands for the minority right to live after experiencing the most systematic genocide in history. Israel succeeded in keeping this memory of the holocaust alive at home and abroad.[31] Israel can offer the Western world the continuous exorcism from fascism. By not succumbing to the lure of Arab money and tolerating her defeat, the Western countries reassert the heroic principles of the allied war, apart from pursuing their own interests in the region.

With the visit of Vorster to Israel in 1976, Afrikaner opinion-leaders tried to mount this bandwagon of world sympathy for the underdog, some anti-Semitic sentiments in part of the *volk* notwithstanding. However, despite the obvious analogies of the two threatened pariahs among numerically superior adversaries, Afrikanerdom lacks the moral principles worth defending. The unquestioned right of survival is seen by the Western world as insufficient for backing a racial minority. Only survival under nonracial sociopolitical conditions can be expected to solicit more sympathy for Afrikaners. Unlike Israel, which symbolizes idealism, white South Africa embodies the worst kind of materialism. And as

30. Dan Jacobson, "Among the South Africans," *Commentary* 65, no. 3 (March 1978), 32–48.

31. When the U.N. passed its Zionism-racism equation, Israel found herself threatened with a similar ideolgical reversal. Her hysterical reaction to the resolution must be understood in this context. For complex reasons, Israel and her powerful lobby abroad quickly managed to overcome this attack on the very rationale for her existence.

much as the so-called Christian world engages in similar immoral profiteering, as useful a moral cause comes to symbolically reiterate a lost principle. For historical reasons, Israel lends itself to such secularized repentance. But the anti-Semitism and holocaust do not compare with the barbarism of the Boer War, especially since the losers had soon turned the table. Unlike Israel, therefore, South Africa represents in the public image the worst kind of immorality after colonialism and the fascist holocaust: racism. Instead of defending such a minority, its political downfall is called for by all principled persons.

In about 1975—when Pik Botha made his famous speech at the United Nations that South Africa would henceforth start abolishing racial discrimination—the Afrikaner leadership seem to have realized what their public relations experts had advised long ago. Visible signs of racism had become untenable. They gradually turned out as not only embarrassing for forging neocolonial relationships with black Africa, but they also were perceived as an insult to the dignity of all black people everywhere. Moreover, putative racism proved not only a diplomatic liability but a mortal danger to the domestic stability in light of the war mobilization. It was in this climate that the Afrikaner elite, ahead of English-dominated regions, slowly began the excruciating process of dismantling social apartheid in some public facilities and in sport. What appeared to Afrikanerdom as a giant step forward in regaining Western acceptability merely meant symbolic redecoration of a facade to politicized blacks at home and informed observers abroad. No redistribution of white power and wealth was contemplated.

And yet an attrition of an entrenched outlook and life-style had been started. Once in motion it is more difficult to stop at will when it encounters more fundamental obstacles of white privilege. Such attempts will likely cause greater contradictions. The inner logic of this process challenges previously insurmountable barriers, not the least by politicizing through frustrated expectations. Thus the existing disposition of power becomes inherently unstable. Soweto represented one manifestation of this new constellation in which Afrikaner power has been put on the defensive ideologically, although de facto it could restore its supremacy without difficulties. Never before however, was the resentment of the racial order so deep and so widespread internally and considered untenable among South Africa's Western allies. The Afrikaner hope that the Bantustan scheme would find recognition has fallen by the wayside. Worse still, the blueprints of decolonization, which Afrikaners unilaterally imposed from above, are increasingly doubted among the ruling group itself as a practical solution to the demands of urban Africans. The search for a successful legitimizing ideology and a vision for the future appears further than ever away from fruition.

In summary, survival lacks the vision of a resurrectional, national ideal, which fascist ideology could exploit. Nor does survival comprise a restorative ideal. Mere survival as a mobilizing concept represents the barest common denominator of a threatened oligarchy, which is bound together by little more than privilege maintenance. Will such an outlook suffice to bear the rising costs of racial polarization? In the long view, can a drafted army be motivated to risk lives in a civil war of resistance against obvious injustice? Despite the pervasive indoctrination with powerful images of peace-loving defenders against bloodthirsty terrorists, there are limits to the manipulation of the white electorate itself. Unless substantial racial reforms parallel the mobilization for a war economy, the difficulties with the morale of the heterogeneous ruling group in the absence of a truly unifying ideology could prove costlier than the abandoning of racialism. Therefore, the hypothesis may be ventured that the pace and scope of racial reforms increase with racial polarization and rising costs of traditional apartheid.

Rather than encapsulating themsevles in a beleaguered fortress, the Afrikaner elite is searching clumsily for possible breakthroughs in any direction. Which one the Nationalists will finally choose under sufficient pressure only depends on the quarrels about viable strategies among themselves, but hardly on an inflexible Calvinist character guided by a divine

143

mission. It depends above all on interests, affected differentially by the rising costs of racial polarization. How these interests can assert themselves within the decision-making process, how successfully they can manipulate their cause, in short, how much power the advocates of one strategy can muster against their opponents, will decide policy. Within the corporate politics of Afrikanerdom, such interests are articulated by powerful political entrepreneurs. These several dozen figures in the center of opinion-making as politicians, journalists, academics, but above all, senior civil servants in the higher echelons of the administrative and economic state bureaucracy bring into the decision-making their own ethnic socialization and individual outlooks. To reduce such idiosyncratic divergence about strategies solely to different material class interests may satisfy a dogmatic mind but hardly explains an open-ended reality, where policy outcomes frequently indeed hinge on personality characteristics.

Barrington Moore has stressed intrabureaucratic competition in the context of East European political systems in terms easily applicable to the corporate politics of Afrikanerdom:

> The policy that is presented to the public as the outcome of rational discussion is actually very much the product of the system of rivalries, hostilities and shifting clique relationships among these figures at the apex of the system and their institutional supporters lower down in the bureaucratic hierarchies.[32]

Many conventional studies on the foreign or domestic policy of Western states overlook that such alleged cohesive designs hardly exist except in the neat order of the researcher. No longer does a coherent ideological blueprint effectively guide or determine South African policy. It is this constellation that makes exact forecasts on the basis of rhetorical pronouncements or professed survival ideologies largely a game of crystal-gazing.

32. Barrington Moore, *Injustice. The Social Bases of Obedience and Revolt*, (White Plains, N.Y.: M. E. Sharpe, 1978), p. 504.

6 The Afrikaner Economic Advance
Hermann Giliomee

This chapter describes the economic advance of the Afrikaners during the twentieth century, focusing on the crucial interrelationship between ethnic mobilization and political power in this advance. By 1974 the Afrikaners had risen from a poor, underdeveloped population group to a prosperous bourgeoisie.[1] The new relationship between Afrikaner and English capital as well as the emerging class cleavages within Afrikanerdom are analyzed in chapter 7.

THE AFRIKANERS'
ECONOMIC POSITION, 1910–24

The white Afrikaans-speaking population group entered the Union of South Africa in 1910 with its economic position far from secure. The discovery of diamonds and especially gold in the nineteenth century were transforming a largely subsistence rural economy into an industrial economy firmly tied to British imperial interests. By 1910, foreign capital completely

1. I am indebted to J. L. Sadie of the University of Stellenbosch for permission to consult his unpublished study "The Afrikaner in the South African Economy," manuscript, dated January 15, 1966, prepared for the Canadian Royal Commission on Bilingualism and Biculturalism. The best published overview of the Afrikaners' economic advance is by David Welsh, "The Political Economy of Afrikaner Nationalism," in *South Africa: Economic Growth and Political Change,* ed. Adrian Leftwich (London: Allison and Busby, 1974), pp. 249–85. See also S. Pauw, *Die Beroepsarbeid van die Afrikaner in die Stad* (Stellenbosch: Reddingsdaadbond, 1946); E. P. du Plessis, *'n Volk staan op* (Cape Town: Human and Rousseau, 1964), and S. van Wyk, *Die Afrikaner in die Beroepslewe in die Stad* (Pretoria: Academica, 1968).

dominated the mining industry. Industry and commerce in the cities and even shops in rural areas were almost exclusively in the hands of non-Afrikaners. Skilled occupations in the northern provinces were filled by English-speakers organized in English-led trade unions, while the artisan guilds of Cape Town were the preserve of the Coloured and the English. The English also dominated the public sector. By 1912 some 85 percent of the civil servants were English-speaking. Even in the Afrikaans rural areas, English civil servants and teachers were prominent. In view of their economic position there was the expectation among many English-speakers that their capitalist and cultural values would continue to transform the South African political life.

In contrast, the Afrikaners as individuals experienced critical times. As the frontier closed toward the end of the nineteenth century the rural poor, particularly the small subsistence farmers, were pushed off the land. The rinderpest epidemics of the 1890s and the ravages of the Anglo-Boer War accelerated the flow of poor Afrikaners to the cities. In general, they were so destitute and lacking in industrial or vocational skills that little, apart from their sense of being white men, distinguished them from the Africans in the cities. As De Kiewiet wrote: "At the base of white society had gathered, like a sediment, a race of men so abject in their poverty, so wanting in resourcefulness, that they stood dangerously close to the natives themselves."[2] But as a farming group the Afrikaners also had strengths. Four-fifths of the farm land was in the hands of Afrikaners, of whom some had accumulated considerable capital. By 1910, commercial farming was benefiting from the expansion of the internal market through the development of the mining industry and from the growing export market for commodities such as wool. Together with mining interests, agricultural capital predominated in the South African Party that ruled South Africa after the establishment of Union in 1910.

Less afflicted by the political and economic upheavals the

2. C. W. de Kiewiet, *A History of South Africa: Social and Economic* (Oxford: Oxford University Press, 1957), pp. 181–82.

Afrikaners in the North had suffered since the 1890s, the Afrikaners in the South tended to support the ethnic movement led by Hertzog, who broke with the South African Party in 1914. It was also in the South that the first enterprises in the so-called first Afrikaner economic renaissance were launched from 1915 to 1918. After the rebellion of 1914, the *Helpmekaar* (Mutual Aid) organization was founded to pay the fines of the leaders. When the fund attracted 190,000 pounds within two months, the idea arose to use it to establish Afrikaans enterprises that would provide Afrikaners with employment and a training in business skills. The leading role was played by some professional men in the Western Cape who enjoyed the financial support of a few wealthy farmers in the region.[3] Between 1915 and 1918 they founded, in the face of strong opposition and even boycotts by some English firms, a publishing house, Nasionale Pers, which printed the first nationalist newspaper, *Die Burger*, and the insurance companies Santam and Sanlam.

In the same period the cooperative movement in agriculture was launched. The most important of these cooperatives was the K.W.V. (Koöperatiewe Wijnbouwers Vereeniging). A burial society, Avbob (Afrikaanse Begrafnis Onderneming Beperk), was formed and, like Sanlam and Samtam, started to attract the savings of Afrikaners. Some of these enterprises openly appealed to Afrikaner sentiment and solidarity. Sanlam's chairman, describing the firm as a "genuine Afrikaner people's institution," asked Afrikaners who wished their people to become economically self-reliant to support these firms. Some time later the Afrikaner Teacher's Association recommended Sanlam's policies to their members. As San-

3. A study is needed of the wealthy Cape farmers and professional men who played such a crucial part in the Afrikaner movement of the early twentieth century. Apart from analyzing their material interests and ideological commitments, it should also investigate the psychological makeup of men politically rather more mature and self-confident than the northern Afrikaners. They were from a region that had been colonized for more than a century by the British. It is often men who have moved furthest along the road of colonization (anglicization in this case) who turn away and then present the first serious challenge to the integrationist assumptions of the colonizers. See Albert Memmi, *The Colonizer and Colonized* (New York: Orion Press, 1965).

lam grew to become a giant corporation it instilled in Afrikaners a sense of self-confidence: It proved that they could run a successful business.[4]

A more important group asset than these fledgling enterprises or even agricultural wealth, was the political power of Afrikaners. In 1911 the Afrikaners over twenty-one represented just over 50 percent of the total white adult population. They were a force every politician had to consider. They could make claims on the state to be provided with education and job opportunities which the Coloureds, not to speak of Africans with their limited franchise, could not do. But this did not mean that the Afrikaners' concerns were always those of the state. The strength and weakness of Afrikaner political power manifested itself most clearly within the context of the state's relationship with the gold-mining industry. This industry directly employed 23,600 whites in 1910.[5] As the most important single source of government revenue, it helped to finance the employment of thousands more. Via its backward linkage effect, it provided jobs in the railways and service industries. The government was obliged to provide conditions in which the mining industry could operate profitably. However, any impression that it had sold out to big business would alienate large sections of the electorate. What made its dilemma more acute was that the mining industry wished to cut costs by decreasing its dependence on the white labor force it considered as overpaid, while the white miners militantly defended their position.[6]

In 1922 the gold miners struck in protest against the management's attempt to reduce the mines' dependence on "overpaid" white labor. Afrikaners, according to a commission report, constituted the largest part of the strikers.[7] The

4. Welsh, "Political Economy," pp. 253–54.

5. Francis Wilson, *Labour in the South African Gold Mines* (Cambridge: Cambridge University Press, 1972), p. 157.

6. For a class analysis of this struggle see F. A. Johnstone, *Class, Race and Gold* (London: Routledge and Kegan Paul, 1976).

7. Union of South Africa, *Report of the Martial Law Inquiry Judicial Commission* (Pretoria, 1922), pp. 16–17.

government intervened against the white workers because it could not afford to lose the income from the mines or the foreign investment they attracted. Contrary to the standard historical interpretation, the Afrikaner-dominated Pact government, consisting of a coalition of Nationalists and Labour which came to power in 1924, did not herald a victory for the workers over the mining industry. The white workers did not receive a raise in wages, which would have had a ripple effect in the economy. Average wage rates actually remained well below the average that had prevailed before the 1922 strike. The total number of whites employed in the mines remained throughout this period below the numbers employed in the years immediately following World War I, while the ratio of whites to blacks employed in the mines averaged 1:9.3 in the late 1920s, compared to 1:8.3 in 1921.[8] However, the mining interests also had to pay a price. During subsequent decades the gold mining industry against its will had to subsidize to a large extent the civilized labor policies, state aid to farmers, and the program to diversify the economy by promoting local manufacture and industry.[9] The cornerstone of this program was the state-owned Iron and Steel Corporation (ISCOR) established in 1928 against the strong opposition of mining capital. With laissez-faire notions on the decline, the Afrikaners increasingly began to look to the state as an instrument to promote the wealth of their group.

FROM PACT GOVERNMENT
TO NATIONAL PARTY RULE, 1924–48

The Pact government was eager to promote white employment and wages but not at the cost of capitalist growth. Despite the fact that the white workers were well represented in

8. Robert Davies, David Kaplan, Mike Morris, and Dan O'Meara, "Class Struggle and the Periodisation of the State in South Africa," *Review of African Political Economy* no. 7 (September–December 1976), p. 10.

9. Davies et al., "Class Struggle," p. 10.

the government, wages of the white labor force in the private sector did not increase. This was not only true of the mining industry but also of manufacturing. White wage rates in this industry, which had been reduced after the 1922 strike, did not return to their pre-1922 levels under the Pact government.[10] While not prepared to interfere with wage levels, Hertzog's National Party was not insensitive to the large numbers of poor and unemployed Afrikaners.

Capitalist development and rural poverty led to rapid urbanization by Afrikaners during the first three decades of the twentieth century. By 1900, less than 10 percent of the Afrikaners lived in cities and towns, by 1926 this figure had risen to 41 percent.[11] The number of whites who, in the words of the Carnegie commission of Inquiry into the Poor White question in South Africa, were very poor, rose from 106,000 in 1921 to 300,000 in 1933. They were in fact destitute—people who subsisted largely through the efforts of welfare organizations or who lived in extremely impoverished conditions on farms. The destitute were perhaps as much as one-fourth of the Afrikaner population of just over one million. The income of the remaining three-fourths was not high either and, with some exception, their background history of a deficient diet and education had not been dissimilar.[12]

Poverty was of course widespread in the Western world

10. Davies et al., "Class Struggle," p. 10. The drop in both mining and industrial wages should be seen against the background of decreasing consumer prices. If April 1970 prices are used as a base of 100, the South African consumer price index dropped from 44,8 in 1921 to 32,5 in 1932. Even if this is taken into consideration, wages in 1932 were still somewhat below the 1922 level.

11. F. A. van Jaarsveld, *Stedelike Geskiedenis as Navorsingsveld vir die Suid-Afrikaanse Historikus* (Johannesburg: R.A.U., 1973), p. 16.

12. Verslag van die Carnegie-Kommissie, *Die Armblanke-Vraagstuk in Suid-Afrika*, 5 vols. (Stellenbosch: Pro Ecclesia, 1932). A very useful shortcut to the most important sections of the report is Dian Joubert, *Toe Witmense Arm Was* (Cape Town: Tafelberg, 1972). For a comparison of the structural poverty in which Afrikaners were trapped in the 1930s and that of the Coloureds in the 1970s see S. J. Terreblanche, *Gemeenskapsarmoede* (Cape Town: Tafelberg, 1977).

during the Depression, but in South Africa it was confined to one section of the white population, the Afrikaners, whose lack of proficiency in English was often a barrier to economic advance. It was this context that made Afrikaner poverty such an emotional issue, allowing ethnic mobilizers to hold British imperialism responsible for the condition of their people rather than accepting it as part of the generally painful process of industrialization and of the breakdown of the Western economic order.

In their desire to uplift the underdeveloped Afrikaner population group, the National Party was motivated by both ethnic and class concerns. As poor Afrikaners they were to Hertzog a sad reflection on the group which he considered as the pioneers of civilization in South Africa; indeed they were a constant reminder of the low level of development of the Afrikaner group compared to the English. As members of the proletariat, they constituted a threat to the capitalist order. There was the danger that these unemployed whites would sink into what a parliamentary Select Committee called a "corrupting intercourse with non-Europeans,"[13] spearheading a militant nonracial workers' movement.

Hertzog intervened on behalf of the unskilled poor whites with his civilized labor policy. Under this policy the state employed "civilized" persons in preference to the so-called uncivilized workers. As a result, large numbers of poor Afrikaners in the 1920s and 1930s were absorbed in the public sector, particularly in the railways, where between 1924 and 1933 the proportion of unskilled white workers employed rose from 9.5 to 39.3 percent (an absolute increase of 13,023) while that of Africans fell from 75 to 48.9 percent (an absolute decrease of 15,556). Twenty years later, over 100,000 mainly unskilled and semi-skilled whites were working for the railways, then the biggest single employer of white labor in the country.[14] The state also put pressure on private enterprise to

13. Davies et al., "Class Struggle," p. 10.

14. Lawrence Solomon, "The Economic Background to the Survival of Afrikaner Nationalism," in *Boston University Papers in African History,* ed. Jeffrey Butler (Boston: Boston University Press, 1964), vol. 1, p. 234.

maintain sufficient quotas of civilized labor. Significantly, this did not include mining. In fact, it was tacitly agreed that the mining industry would not be burdened with having to take on unemployed whites, although there was now statutory protection of the existing positions of white miners.

The Depression and particularly the crisis over the gold standard brought Hertzog's National Party and Smuts's South African Party together. Malan's Purified National Party immediately raised the cry that Hertzog had sold out to mining capital and imperialism. In fact, the ruling United Party continued to implement policies that benefited the local steel industry and the Afrikaners as a group. The doubling of the gold price in 1934 and direct taxes on the gold-mining industry, which during Fusion provided a third of the state revenue, enabled the government to do so. In particular, it came to the aid of the Afrikaner-controlled agricultural sector, which had been badly hit by the Depression and the drought of 1933 with income falling by 45 percent between 1927–28 and 1932–33. Between 1927–28 and 1938–39, expenditure on agriculture and irrigation increased by 400 percent—the most rapid increase of all the categories of the state budget.[15] The Hertzog government also aided the farmers by legislation that increased their control over the black labor force. Moreover, control boards, the first of which was established in 1936, not only ensured the orderly marketing of agriculture and stable prices but also favored the cooperatives, which now had the function of pricing taken out of their hands.

Yet the Fusion period gave to different sections of Afrikanerdom, particularly the small businessmen and workers, the impression that they were losing out in a changing economic structure in which secondary industry was overtaking agriculture and mining in its contribution to the gross domestic product.[16] Without the capital resources, connections, and

15. Davies et al., "Class Struggle," pp. 14, 18.

16. Secondary industry encompasses manufacturing, construction, gas, and water. The contribution of secondary industry surpassed agriculture in 1932 and mining in 1942. See Bureau of Statistics, Pretoria, October 11, 1967 document, p. 12. Between 1933 and 1939 the white manufacturing work force

interlocking directorates of big English capital, the small Afrikaner businessman could not compete successfully for a share of the growing economy. The Afrikaner workers who entered industry in the 1920s and 1930s usually found themselves in the lowest paid roles assigned for whites, that of semi-skilled operatives working machines. They were faced with the apprenticeship system guarded by the English-dominated unions, which often acted as an effective barrier against the acquisition of skills. For the relatively few Afrikaner professionals (lawyers, teachers, civil servants, and university professors) it was not so much the economic but the political transformation, that is, Fusion, which posed a threat in the form of stronger competition for the patronage of the state. They, more than any other group, were deeply conscious of the detrimental effects of rapid industrialization on the ethnic outlook of their people.

The financially strongest group of Afrikaners, the farmers, was also in trouble. Despite financial support from the government it took agriculture much longer to recover from the Depression than gold mining and industry. Prices of farm produce dropped relative to those of industrial products. Droughts, debts, and over-capitalization exacerbated the crisis. Even more serious was the shortage of African labor. Paying higher wages, the rapidly expanding mining and industrial sector increasingly drew African labor from the farms. In the depressed condition of agriculture, farmers were unable to pay substantially higher wages. African farm laborers, also struggling to survive, began to resist low wages and barriers to their mobility, such as monetary indebtedness to employers and the pass laws. Relations between farmers and laborers deteriorated. Farmers complained bitterly of a changed relationship: the Africans had "lost their respect" for

---

grew by 77 percent, from 133,000 to 236,000, and the black work force by 88 percent, from 76,000 to 143,000. The value of the gross output grew by 108 percent during this period and a further 116 percent during the war. D. Hobart Houghton, *The South African Economy* (Cape Town: Oxford University Press, 1964), pp. 122–23.

them. World War II and the postwar boom intensified the farmers' crisis. In order to meet the needs of industry and manufacture the government relaxed the existing curbs on the flow of Africans to the cities. During the period 1936 to 1951 white farms and white rural areas contributed nearly half the increase of urban blacks.[17]

Despite the expanding economy, the huge gap in wealth and status not only between black and white but also between Afrikaners and English remained. Various commissions (particularly the Carnegie commission of 1934) reported and the "civilized labor" policy continued unabated but the plight of the Afrikaner poor was unrelieved. In 1939 there were still 298,000 white persons reported to be living in "terrible poverty," all with monthly incomes below £12—an amount considered to be the minimum for the preservation of health. Afrikaners in the cities generally occupied the physically hazardous, low status occupations and were underrepresented in the high prestige, high salary occupations. In 1936, for instance, only 27.5 percent were in white-collar jobs as against 31.3 percent in blue-collar jobs and 41.2 percent in agricultural occupations (see table 2). In business, the turnover of Afrikaans enterprises (excluding agriculture) in 1938–39 was 5 percent of all trade, industry, finance, and mining. C. G. W. Schumann estimated that in 1936 the average annual per capita income of Afrikaans-speakers was £86, compared to £142 for other whites.[18]

During the 1930s members of the Afrikaner cultural and business elite embarked on a strategy of ethnic mobilization to improve the economic position of the Afrikaners. It was a strategy with both a materialist and ethnic appeal. First, mobilization offered to certain sections within Afrikanerdom

17. This section on agriculture is based on two excellent studies, one by M. L. Morris, "The Development of Capitalism in South African Agriculture: Class Struggle in the Country Side," *Economy and Society*, 5, no. 3 (1976), 292–338; the other by Stanley B. Greenberg, "Race and the Rural Economy in South Africa," unpublished paper.

18. Solomon, "Economic Background," p. 235; Du Plessis, *'n Volk staan op*, p. 235.

the prospect of distinct advantages. For businessmen there was a huge potential to be tapped if the Afrikaner community, whose purchasing power by 1939 was estimated to be about £100 million a year, could be persuaded to support and invest in Afrikaans business. For the semi- or un-skilled Afrikaner workers the mobilizers offered racial privilege. At the "Poor White" conference of 1934, Verwoerd clearly stated that it was more economical for the nation that the poor whites should be employed and the nonwhites unemployed. On behalf of the commission Verwoerd declared that where "a particular privilege for the poor white causes a problem—however a solvable problem—for the Non-white, there has been no hesitation in choosing it."[19] For semi-skilled Afrikaner workers the strategy favored by the mobilizers of job color bars and segregation in the work place offered a more extensive protection of their jobs, higher wages, and the prospects of advancement in the racially structured work situation.

Second, ethnic mobilization also appealed to status and psychological needs in providing a greater sense of "belongingness." An important causal factor was the feelings of resentment toward the English for considering the Afrikaners and their culture as inferior. To be accepted as members of the South African business elite, Afrikaners were often expected to shed their ethnic ties and use English as their medium of communication. Ethnic identification offered to these businessmen a greater sense of fulfillment. They could consider themselves as "innovators in the service of their community, creating job opportunities for Afrikaners."[20] At

19. Verwoerd's argument was that blacks should be provided for elsewhere, for instance by taking the place of imported black mine workers or through improved economic development of the reserves. H. F. Verwoerd, "Die Bestryding van Armoede en die Herorganisasie van Welvaartswerk," P. du Toit, comp., *Report of the National Conference on the Poor White Problem* (Cape Town: Nasionale Pers, 1934), p. 31.

20. J. L. Sadie, "Die Ekonomiese Faktor in die Afrikaner-gemeenskap," in *Identiteit en Verandering*, ed. H. W. van der Merwe (Cape Town: Tafelberg, 1975), pp. 96–97.

the same time the idea was propagated among Afrikaner consumers, particularly the civil servants and professionals, that to support the business enterprises of the *volk* was something that added to the moral worth of the individual. Ethnic mobilization also appealed to the status needs of the Afrikaner workers, particularly their sense of racial superiority. As secretary of the Garment Workers Union, a nonracial union comprising mostly Afrikaner women, Solly Sachs was constantly aware of the threat this posed to the class strategy he believed in. He considered the Dutch Reformed clergy as his main adversaries. According to him, they "organised regular visits to clothing factories, ostensibly to hold prayer meetings, but actually to incite the white workers against the non-Europeans. On almost every occasion when such a prayer meeting was held in a clothing factory, relations between white and non-white workers deteriorated."[21]

The spearhead of the movement of ethnic mobilization was the Afrikaner Broederbond whose influence grew rapidly since the early 1930s. It was the Broederbond, through the Federasie van Afrikaanse Kultuurverenigings (Federation of Afrikaner Cultural Associations), that in 1939 called the First Afrikaner Peoples' Economic Congress to review the economic position of the Afrikaner people. The reports of the proceedings of this conference and the journal *Volkshandel* convey the ideological terms in which this "second economic renaissance" of the Afrikaner was launched. The Afrikaners had to capture their "legitimate" place in the economy. To do this they had to be activated to assume collective responsibility for the entire Afrikaner nation: the poor had to be saved from going under, the worker had to be better protected, the businessman had to be supported, the cities had to be captured for the Afrikaners, not only for the wage and salary earners but also for the entrepreneurs in trade, industry, mining, and finance.

The "economic renaissance" was mainly directed at pro-

21. E. S. (Solly) Sachs, *Rebels Daughters* (London: MacGibbon and Kee, 1957), p. 151.

moting Afrikaner capitalism and the interests of the middle class. The congress of 1939 had originally been called to perform a *reddingsdaad* (act of rescue) on behalf of the 300,000 poor whites. From the congress flowed the establishment of the *Reddingsdaadbond* fund. However, only 10 percent of this fund was allocated to poor relief. The rest was devoted to investments in Afrikaner businesses, particularly in Federale Volksbeleggings, a new investment house, which gradually succeeded in winning the confidence of Afrikaner investors. As directors of new enterprises, leading members of cultural organizations, particularly the Afrikaner Broederbond, acquired a considerable influence in Afrikaner business life.[22]

While there were obviously gains in the form of wealth and influence in exploitating the economically backward position of the Afrikaners, it would be a distortion to see the Afrikaner nationalist elite as driven by such motives. There seems to have been a sincerely held conviction among this group that only through a combination of ethnic mobilization and *volkskapitalisme* (people's capitalism) could the position of the poor be fundamentally improved. *Volkskapitalisme* rejected the laissez-faire notion that those who were not able to adjust to the economic struggle should drop to poor-whiteism. But to give the poor alms in a philanthropic manner was to belittle them and separate them from the more affluent members of the *volk*. The aim should rather be, as L. J. du Plessis phrased it at the congress of 1939, to "mobilise the *volk* to conquer the capitalist system and to transform it so that it fits our ethnic nature."[23] *Volkskapitalisme* would entail Afrikaners owning the means of production, investing in and patronizing Afrikaans enterprises, and employing and caring for Afrikaner workers.

Yet the mobilizers knew that *volkskapitalisme* alone was not sufficient. Indeed Albert Hertzog warned the congress that some Afrikaner employers were equally guilty of exploiting

22. T. Dunbar Moodie, *The Rise of Afrikanerdom* (Berkeley: University of California Press, 1975), pp. 204–05.
23. Du Plessis, *'n Volk staan op*, p. 104.

the white worker. The only effective protection for Afrikaner workers was to organize themselves in trade unions that would promote their interests.[24] One of the main objectives of the Broederbond of the 1930s and 1940s was to organize the Afrikaner workers to enhance their bargaining position against the English capitalists. However, at the same time the kind of class consciousness which the socialist unions espoused was to be fought as the greatest danger for ethnic mobilization. When Solly Sachs in 1938 wished to send his Garment Workers to participate in the celebrations of the Voortrekker centenary he was told: "We Afrikaners acknowledge no classes' as you and your satellites are trying to introduce—therefore we do not want the garment workers as a "class" to participate in the celebrations, but all together with us as Boers—the factory girl with the professor's wife. You and Johanna Cornelius, who all day organise and address kaffirs—will you dare to bring them also along to the celebrations? They are your fellow workers and Comrades'."[25]

One of the main objectives of the Reddingsdaadbond was to make the Afrikaans laborer "part and parcel of the national life and to prevent the Afrikaans workers developing as a class distinct from other classes in the Afrikaans national life."[26] From 1944, the Reddingsdaadbond's campaign to "save the Afrikaner workers" was channeled through the *Blankewerkersbeskermingsbond* (White Workers Protection League). Propagating the job color bar and segregation in the work place, it inspired or supported attempts to establish separate Afrikaner trade unions or to take over the leadership of existing unions led by English officials. The mobilizers portrayed themselves as fighting for the cause of "Christianity" and "white civilization," their opponents, the trade union leaders, were not "nationally minded" and their "communis-

24. Louis Naude, *Dr. A. Hertzog, Die Nasionale Party en die Mynwerker* (Pretoria: Nasionale Raad vir Trustees, 1969), pp. 263–64.

25. Sachs, *Rebels Daughters*, p. 138.

26. *Ons Reddingsdaad*, brochure issued by the Head Office of the Reddingsdaadbond, n.d.

tic outlook" was apparent in their support of the principle of legal recognition of trade unions for blacks. The major achievement in this strategy occurred in 1948 when the attempt led by Albert Hertzog to take over the Mine Workers Union succeeded.

The mobilizers in the Afrikaner economic movement realized that ultimately only political power would effectively enhance the Afrikaners' economic position. In 1939, when the Economic Congress was held, the National Party was still a small opposition party far removed from power. Two years later "nationalist Afrikanerdom" and even the Broederbond were hopelessly divided between the National Party and the Ossewa Brandwag. After the election of 1943 the National Party gradually succeeded in presenting itself as the sole political front of nationalist Afrikanerdom. It won in 1948 because it succeeded in selling the image of an all-embracing popular movement that would promote the interests of all the various sections of Afrikanerdom.

After 1948 control of the state would to an important extent shape the Afrikaners' economic advance. Consequently the period 1939 to 1948 is the only one in which the achievements of the "second economic renaissance" of the Afrikaners could be evaluated without taking the factor of political control into account. Unfortunately the economic boom as a result of the war makes such an evaluation problematic. It might be speculated that it was not so much the economic mobilization of the Afrikaners but rather the expanding war economy that largely eliminated the poor white problem. Nonetheless, the Afrikaners had made some real economic progress. Between 1939 and 1950, when the second Economic Congress was held, the Afrikaners' share of the private sector in the entrepreneurial function rose from 5 to 11 percent, the most important advance occurring in trade and commerce as the result of taking over small English and Jewish shops in the rural areas. Largely for the same reason the number of Afrikaner directors and manufacturers rose by 295 percent compared with 8 percent among non-Afrikaners. It was estimated that Afrikaner employers provided incomes for at least 25,000 to 30,000 more whites than 10 years before. In addition the political and educational advance of the Afrikaners compelled English businesses to employ more Afrikaners.[27]

There were also setbacks. Significantly the fund of the Reddingsdaadbond collecting donations from the public received only £183,000 of the projected £2 million. The fund was abolished in 1946. The major achievement, then, of the economic movement was the promotion of Afrikaner enterprises and the opportunities it created for an upcoming business elite.

ECONOMIC ADVANCE
AND NATIONAL PARTY RULE, 1948–76

When the National Party came to power in 1948 the gap in the per capita income between Afrikaners and English in general was still wide (see table 6). For instance, the annual per capita income of Afrikaners in Johannesburg and nine other cities along the Witwatersrand was £162, compared with £349 for English-speaking whites. A similar disparity prevailed in the other main urban areas. Even in Bloemfontein where, (according to the 1951 census), three-quarters of the white population were Afrikaners, the corresponding figures were £180 and £318.[28] Before the war, Afrikaners had comprised 86 percent of the white unskilled laborers in the towns and less than 20 percent of managers, professionals, directors, and manufacturers. However, by 1948 they were dominating the skilled working class occupations as the English moved up to the higher categories of employment.[29] While the civil service had progressively become Afrikanerized in the twentieth century—already in 1936 some 59 percent of white civil servants were Afrikaners—the higher ranks were still predominantly occupied by the English. In 1952 some 80 percent of the

27. For a sympathetic report of achievements see Du Plessis, *'n Volk staan op*, pp. 168–99.

28. Solomon, "Economic Background," p. 235.

29. Welsh, "Political Economy," p. 261.

South African Railways and Harbour personnel were Afrikaans-speaking but 67 percent of those in the income group of £1,000 and higher were English-speaking. While 68 percent of all white Post Office officials were Afrikaners, they occupied only 40 percent of the senior positions.[30]

The National Party of 1948 was primarily an ethnic party, but within the ethnic group its main class bases were the farmers and workers. As Albert Hertzog declared in Parliament in 1953: "We on this side are partly a party of farmers but largely a party of workers."[31] In most sectors of the economy, 1948 did not represent a decisive break with the past. The National Party, for instance rejected Albert Hertzog's plea that the gold mines be nationalized. In the case of the farmers and the workers, however, the party did intervene, offering support and protection. In doing so it greatly increased the scope of state intervention in the economy while fostering Afrikaner economic advance.

The Smuts government (1939–48) had been unwilling to use compulsion to meet the crisis in agriculture. Instead it suggested that farmers improve conditions in order to entice urban blacks back to the farms. Through the agricultural unions the farmers after the war strongly insisted that rural and urban African labor be divided into two separate compartments, thus ensuring a stable farm labor force. However, the government did not act. In the 1948 election the United Party lost all of the 15 Transvaal rural seats; the maize farmers had decisively withdrawn their support.[32]

Soon after it came to power the National Party moved to meet the labor needs of agriculture. It tightened the system of influx control and established labor bureaus. Before any Afri-

30. Sheila Patterson, *The Last Trek: A Study of the Boer People and the Afrikaner Nation* (London: Routledge and Kegan Paul, 1957), p. 58.

31. Cited by Jeff Lever, "White Strategies in a Divided Society: The Development of South African Labour Policy," unpublished paper, p. 21. Lever states that in the late 1930s there were between 40,000 and 60,000 unskilled white workers alone, who together with their families must have accounted for around 200,000 largely Afrikaans-speaking whites.

32. Morris, "The Development of Capitalism in South African Agriculture."

can could leave a rural district, the local labor bureau had to be satisfied that the labor situation in that district was adequate. Here in a new form the National Party implemented its concept of a strong interventionist state resting on an elaborate system of controlling African labor.

Farmers were not only aided by the stabilization of the rural labor force, but also by the favorable prices set by the marketing boards for their produce, by government subsidies, and by massive funding of agricultural research. In the case of maize, the government, in order to encourage production, raised the average price from 21s. 3d. to 30s. between 1949 and 1952. The acute shortages of commodities that were characteristic of the years just before World War II were rapidly replaced by surpluses that were usually exported at a loss. Between the period 1936–39 and 1956–59 the total output of crops increased by 93 percent and that of livestock by 61 percent. The production of maize, to name but one crop, rose from 24.8 million bags over the three years 1946–48, to 57.1 million bags in 1961–63.[33] The economic position of the farmers improved rapidly since the critical years before the outbreak of World War II. Between 1939 and 1955 the price index of all agricultural produce quadrupled while the consumer index only doubled.[34]

At the same time the wages of farm laborers remained low. Undoubtedly substantial capital accumulation occurred as more was produced and earned by a declining number of farmers. (The number of whites active in agriculture, forestry, and fishing declined from 181,409 in 1936 to 117,599 in 1960,[35] 96,000 in 1970 and 82,000 in 1975.) A recent study of agriculture between 1866 and 1966 concludes that cash wages and the general standard of living of black farm laborers in

33. Francis Wilson, "Farming, 1866–1966," in *Oxford History of South Africa,* eds. Monica Wilson and Leonard Thompson (New York and Oxford: Oxford University Press, 1971), pp. 143–44, 163–65.

34. S. S. Brand and F. R. Tomlinson, "Die Plek van Landbou in die Suid-Afrikaanse Volkshuishouding," *The South African Journal of Economics* 34, no. 1 (1966), 46.

35. Brand and Tomlinson, "Die Plek van Landbou," p. 43.

selected areas rose little in that century.[36] They only started to improve in the decade after 1966.

The National Party also proceeded to give better protection to the unskilled and semi-skilled white worker. Predominantly Afrikaans, they were poorly educated, badly paid, and the most exposed to black competition. Unlike members of the craft unions, they could not protect their economic position through restricting the acquisition of skills to whites. In 1957 the government instituted the policy of job reservation that was especially directed at protecting the semi-skilled white workers, particularly in the garment, leather, and engineering industries, and in municipal employment.[37] More informally the white workers were also protected by the government's two cardinal labor principles: whites must not be replaced by blacks in the same job, and blacks must not be appointed in a supervisory position over whites. Through a combination of this protection, an expanding economy, and restricting black opportunities, the income of the white worker rapidly improved. O'Meara has made the following calculation: Using the real earnings of whites and Africans in private manufacturing and construction in 1947–48 as a base of 100, the index of real white wages rose by over 10 percent in the first five years of National Party rule. During the same period those of Africans fell by 5 percent. It was only in 1959–60 that the real industrial earnings for Africans again reached the levels of 1947–48. At this stage the index of real white earnings stood at 130.[38]

The National Party also used the public or semi-state corporations to promote Afrikaner economic progress. Some of these public corporations, such as ISCOR and the Industrial Development Corporation, were established before 1948.

36. Wilson, "Farming," pp. 158–63 and Sadie, personal communication.

37. For perceptive analyses of race and labor policies see Lever, "White Strategies" and Stanley B. Greenberg, "Race and Trade Unionism in South Africa," unpublished paper.

38. Dan O'Meara, "Analysing Afrikaner Nationalism: The 'Christian National' Assault on White Trade Unionism in South Africa, 1934–1948," *African Affairs* 77, no. 306 (1978), 71.

Under National Party rule, however, the dimensions of public corporations have been greatly extended. State capitalism reflects the Afrikaner conception of South African economic development. It attempts to diminish English and foreign control of the economy, especially their virtual monopoly of mine ownership. The state-initiated enterprises have been instrumental in expanding secondary industry, thus making the country less reliant on the gold-mining industry and on private business in certain vital sectors of the economy. Because of government backing in raising funds, projects of strategic or military importance have been launched which private enterprise alone would not have been able to finance. While state corporations were not founded primarily to promote Afrikaner interests, they in effect have greatly aided Afrikaner economic advance. The public corporations at their senior level are almost exclusively manned by Afrikaners. They have provided a training school outside the private sector where Afrikaner scientists and business leaders could acquire technical skills and managerial ability. Besides the various agricultural control boards there exist twenty-two public corporations: for example, ISCOR (iron and steel corporation); ESCOM, which at present supplies 80 percent of the national electricity needs; ARMSCOR, which has made South Africa largely self-sufficient in many armaments; Industrial Development Corporation, which promotes industrial development; NUFKOR (concerned with uranium enrichment); SOEKOR (oil exploration); and SASOL (the production of petrol from coal and a petrochemical industry).[39]

Under National Party rule the public sector's share of the economy nearly doubled.[40] Public sector investment in the period 1946 to 1973 rose ten times from Rand 102 million to Rand 1,120 million (at constant 1963 prices) and investment by public corporations alone jumped from Rand 14 million to

39. For a general discussion see Ruth Weiss, "The Role of the Parastatals in South Africa's politico-economic system," in John Suckling et al., *Foreign Investment in South Africa: The Economic Factor* (Uppsala: Africa Publications Trust, 1975), pp. 56–91.

40. J. L. Sadie, "Assault sydige boek . . . ," *Die Burger*, March 4, 1977.

Rand 286 million. Compared to an average of 6.2 percent in 1946–50, the corporations' ratio of fixed investment in the whole South African economy nearly doubled to 11.5 percent in 1971–73. In the period 1946 to 1973 the share of the private sector declined from 63.5 percent to 53 percent.[41] The South African economy has in recent years increasingly become a state-controlled and -owned economy. This is perhaps most dramatically illustrated by the fact that annual expenditure of the public sector, as a percentage of gross domestic fixed investment, has increased from 36.5 percent in 1946 to 47 percent in 1973 to 53 percent in 1976.[42] This growth of the public sector has provoked great resentment from the English-dominated private sector (see chapter 7).

Since 1948 the personnel of the public sector have progressively become Afrikanerized. It was partly due to economic forces such as the movement of English-speakers to the more remunerative private sector. However, equally important were political factors: the stricter application of bilingualism, which favored Afrikaners, and the deliberate appointment by the government of well-disposed Afrikaners in key positions of the civil service to buttress its political control and ensure proper administration of its policies. By 1968 there were twice as many Afrikaners in government jobs than before the election of 1948.[43] In 1976, some 60 percent of the white labor force in the public and semi-public sector were Afrikaners. In this year the fully employed labor force totaled 8,470,000 people (English-speaking whites 670,000, Afrikaners 930,000, Coloureds 880,000, Asians 210,000, Africans 5,780,000). Sadie estimates that in 1977 some 30 percent of the whites employed are in the public and semi-public sector. Some 35 percent of all economically active Afrikaners

41. G. Steenkamp and C. H. Swanepoel, "Gross Investment of the Public Sector," *S.A. Reserve Bank Quarterly Bulletin* (December 1974), pp. 20–28; *Financial Mail* (Johannesburg), December 27, 1974, pp. 1167–68.

42. United States Senate, Committee on Foreign Relations: *Report on U.S. Corporate Interests in South Africa, Washington* (U.S. Government Printing Office, 1978), p. 25.

43. Personal communication by J. L. Sadie.

are in this sector against only 25 percent English-speaking whites who occupy less than 10 percent of the top positions.[44]

Finally, the Afrikaners have advanced through the private sector. "The growth of state capitalism in South Africa since 1948," a recent study observes, "has also been the growth of Afrikaner capitalism."[45] According to this view, the Afrikaners have used state power to promote the growth of Nationalist private industry.[46] Another view, which is also strongly entrenched in the literature, is that Afrikaner private business came to wealth purely by exploiting Afrikaner sentiments.[47] State favoritism and Afrikaner sentiment have un-

44. Personal communication, J. L. Sadie and S. J. Terreblanche, November 21, 1977. The Department of Statistics put the total labor force (as distinct from the fully employed work force) at the end of 1977 at 10,210,000 (South African Institute of Race Relations, *Survey*, 1977, p. 212). According to answers in Parliament, (*Financial Mail*, March 24, 1978, p. 920), 1,362,970 were in public sector employment in mid-1977 of which whites and Africans each made up 40 percent of the total, Coloured people 17 percent, and Asians 3 percent. It is interesting how heavily the South African civil service is dependent on blacks participating in their administration. The breakdown of the public sector employment in 1977 looked as follows:

Central government	305,962
Provincial administration	229,726
Bantustan governments	96,000
S.A. Railways & Harbour	262,065
Post office	70,352
Local authorities	223,600
Statutory public bodies	175,265
	1,362,970

The rapidly growing administrative apparatus of Bantustan governments is of particular significance for the emergence of a relatively privileged black bureaucratic bourgeoisie.

45. Alex Collinicos and John Rogers, *Southern Africa After Soweto* (London: Pluto Press, 1977), p. 38.

46. See also Brian Bunting, *The Rise of the South African Reich* (Penguin: Harmondsworth, 1969), p. 388.

47. Patterson, *The Last Trek*, p. 173. For a good structural analysis of the role of the state in the Afrikaner advance in the 1940s and 1950s see Stanley Trapido, "Political Institutions and the Afrikaner Social Structure," *American Political Science Review*, 57 no. 1 (1963), 75–87.

doubtedly aided the Afrikaner advance in the private sector (see table 3). But these two elements hardly make up the full and rather more complex story.

The organizers of the Economic Congress of 1939 discovered that it was difficult to convert enthusiasm for a "second economic renaissance" of the Afrikaners into hard business sense and profits. The Economic Institute, established at this congress, at first conferred public recognition upon firms that identified themselves with the "economic aspirations" of the Afrikaners. It soon had to retract since the system lent itself to abuse, particularly as the public tended to infer that the Institute was guaranteeing the honesty or success of the businesses involved. The Economic Institute was quickly surpassed in importance by the Afrikaanse Handelsinstituut (Commercial Institute), established in 1942, which organized "nationally minded" Afrikaans businessmen on similar lines as the English Associated Chambers of Commerce and the Federated Chambers of Industries. The most important service of the Institute in the 1940s and 1950s was to disseminate information on numerous aspects of business and the South African economy by means of talks, circulars, annual meetings, newsletters, and journals, particularly *Volkshandel.* Though now better organized, Afrikaner businessmen still found it by no means easy to attract Afrikaner support. Sentiment was not enough: Afrikaner businesses had to be competitive. While patriotic Afrikaners have made some effort to "buy Afrikaans," the rank and file have been more interested in prices, quality, design of the article, credit terms, and the location of the business. In recent years, the Institute has been urging members to desist from applying sentiment as a means of attracting custom.[48]

If pure sentiment was not crucial, how is one to account for the Afrikaners' advance in the private sector? Obviously the special relationship since 1948 of the Afrikaner businessman to political control was of great importance. The Handelsinstituut is, for instance, consulted on legislation pertaining

48. Sadie, "The Afrikaner in the S.A. Economy," pp. 49–60.

to economic matters and is represented, along with other interest groups, on government commissions, tender boards, and marketing boards. Afrikaner capital also benefited occasionally from government favoritism through the allocation of fishing quotas and mineral concessions and the award of government contracts and accounts. In 1977, for instance, 98 percent of the Department of Information publishing budget of 3 million dollars went to the Perskor group, an Afrikaans publishing house that had several cabinet ministers, including the Minister for Information, on its board.[49] Afrikaner firms have also been aided by a system of interlocking directorates between the state corporations and Afrikaner private capital.

Yet there are limits to state favoritism if the government wishes to maintain an impartial image and to avoid embarrassing press exposés or the censure of the Auditor-General as happened in the case of the Department of Information. To explain the rise of Afrikaner private capital adequately, a focus on some phenomena in the wider South African social and economic context is necessary. First, all whites benefited from the rapid economic development in South Africa for three decades since 1939. Second, rigorous government control of the African labor force provided abundant cheap labor to Afrikaner and English businessmen alike. Third, one suspects that the capital accumulated in Afrikaner-controlled farming since the 1940s set off a flow of funds through Afrikaner banks to Afrikaner businesses. Lastly, there has been a vast improvement in educational facilities for Afrikaners since 1948. The government established engineering and medical faculties at Afrikaans universities; it also built more secondary, technical, and vocational schools specifically for Afrikaners whose education on all levels had lagged behind the wealthier and more urbanized whites. All these contributed to a general improvement in the position of the Afrikaners in the occupational sphere. In the liberal professions the Afrikaners probably trebled their participation from 1939 to 1964. There was a general movement away from unskilled,

49. *New York Times*, May 10, 1978.

TABLE 2   Percentage of Afrikaners in Broad Categories of
Occupation, 1936–77

Category	1936	1946	1960	1970	1977
Agricultural occupations	41.2	30.3	16.0	9.7	8.1
"Blue collar," & other manual	31.3	40.7	40.5	32.4	26.7
"White collar"	27.5	29.0	43.5	57.9	65.2
	100.0	100.0	100.0	100.0	100.0

Source: J. L. Sadie, "The Afrikaner in the South African Economy," manuscript, January 15, 1966; and personal communication, July 20, 1978.

poorly paid labor to skilled, better paid, usually well-
protected careers. In the case of the Afrikaners this general
trend in industrial economics was accelerated because the
Nationalist government assiduously promoted Afrikaner education. Table 2 indicates the movement.

A key role in the Afrikaner advance in the private sector
has been played by some "new man," Afrikaner entrepreneurs who by inspiring confidence in their business
methods succeeded in attracting Afrikaner capital with which
they established empires with investments in all sectors of the
economy. The most outstanding of these men include C. R.
Louw (chairman of Sanlam and Santam), M. S. Louw (Sanlam), C. H. Brink (Federale Volksbeleggings), Andries Wassenaar (Sanlam), Jan S. Marais (Trust Bank), and Anton
Rupert (Rembrandt). As has been seen above the most important achievement of the Economic Congress of 1939 was
Federale Volksbeleggings which spearheaded the expansion
of the Afrikaner private sector during the past three decades.
Most significant is its establishment of Federale Mynbou in
1953. In 1963 it took over General Mining and Finance Corporation, with assets in gold and uranium mining worth about
Rand 250 million, from Anglo-American Corporation. This
step was seen as a breakthrough for closer business cooperation between Afrikaners and English. In 1976 Federale Mynbou's subsidiary, General Mining, acquired control of Union
Corporation. It was now the third largest of South Africa's

TABLE 3 The Afrikaner's Share in the Private Sector of the South African Economy in the Entrepreneurial Function (in Percentages), 1938–75

Sector	1938–39	1948–49	1954–55	1963–64	1975
Agriculture, forestry, fishing	87	85	84	83	82
Mining	1	1	1	10	18
Manufacturing & construction	3	6	6	10	15
Trade and commerce	8	25	26	24	16
Transportation		9*	14	14	15
Liquor and catering		20*	30	30	35
Professions		16	20	27	38
Finance	5	6	10	21	25

Miscellaneous	27	35	36	45
Aggregate	24.8	25.4	26.9	27.5
Aggregate excluding agriculture	9.6	13.4	18.0	20.8
(% of GDP if 100% of entrepreneurial activity in the public sector is attributed to Afrikaans-speaking whites)	40.3	41.0	43.0	44.7

Source: Survey of the Economic Institute of the F.A.K. 1948–1949; J. L. Sadie, *Die Afrikaner in die Landsekonomie* (South African Broadcasting Corporation, 1957); Bureau of Statistics, *Population Censuses; Balance Sheets and Profit and Loss Accounts of Companies; Censuses of Distribution and Service Establishments 1946–1947, 1952, 1960– 1961;* Afrikaanse Handelsinstituut, direct communication to J. L. Sadie. This table has been prepared by J. L. Sadie. The calculations are based on the private sector's contribution to the gross domestic product.

*These figures, which are no more than guesstimates, are not important in the overall picture.

TABLE 4   Share of Income per Person Employed According to Ethnic Group, 1946–76

(Size of Each Population Group as a Percentage of the Total Population is Given in Parentheses)

Year	1946	1960	1976
Whites	74.0 (21.05)	70.0 (18.56)	63.0 (16.82)
English	44.5 (8.77)	37.0 (7.78)	31.5 (7.04)
Afrikaners	29.5 (12.28)	33.0 (10.78)	31.5 (9.78)
Coloureds	4.6 (7.89)	5.5 (8.98)	7.6 (9.78)
Asians	1.8 (2.63)	2.0 (2.99)	2.7 (2.94)
Africans	19.6 (68.24)	22.5 (69.46)	27.0 (70.45)
Total	100.0 100	100.0 100	100.0 100

mining finance houses, with assets worth Rand 750 million. A secret Afrikaner Broederbond study concluded that after the Federale Mynbou–General Mining takeover of Union Corporation 30 percent of South African gold mines were under Afrikaner control.[50] This study estimates that Afrikaner-controlled companies now crush 24 percent of the country's goldbearing ore. In addition, more than 30 percent of the uranium, 40 percent of the platinum, 35 percent of the coal, 50 percent of the asbestos, and 40 percent of the chrome interests in South Africa are now under Afrikaner control. If Iscor, S.A. Manganese, Armscor, and Sasol are considered as Afrikaner concerns, the overwhelming share of all manganese and iron mines fall under Afrikaner control.

Table 3 indicates that the Afrikaner share in the aggregate private sector has not changed much since 1938 because the importance of Afrikaner-dominated agriculture in the generation of the gross domestic product has been declining over the years. However, in the aggregate excluding agriculture the Afrikaner share shot up from 9.6 in 1948–49 to 20.8 in

50. *Sunday Times*, January 22, 1978.

TABLE 5   Per Capita Income of the Various Ethnic Groups,
1946–76

Year	1946	1960	1976
Whites	389	831	3150
English	561	1050	3587
Afrikaners	266	673	2538
Coloureds	64	135	623
Asians	77	148	737
Africans	32	71	304

Per capita income equals the total Gross Domestic Product divided by the
total population.

1975. In a world perspective this rapid narrowing of the gap
by a less-developed section is perhaps unique.

Tables 4–7 give a further indication how the Afrikaners
have advanced with respect to the English since 1946 while
the gap between them and the various black groups first
widened before that trend was gradually reversed.[51]

From these tables it is clear that the gap between Afrikaner
and English has narrowed rapidly since 1946. The position of

51. These tables were prepared by S. J. Terreblanche of the University of
Stellenbosch. Terreblanche based the tables on a University of Stellenbosch
M.A. dissertation of 1966 by W. Keizer, computations of the Bureau of Market Research of the University of South Africa, and personal communications
of J. L. Sadie. Personal income consists of the remuneration of employers,
income from property (interest and profits), transfer payments of the state
(pension subsidies, etc.). Not including company tax and savings and savings of the public authorities, personal income comprises 87 percent of the
net national income. These tables indicate distribution before tax and government allocations (other than pensions and subsidies). Economists generally accept the percentage share of the various population groups to be more
equal after tax and government allocation. Thus in the case of the Coloureds
their total contribution to the treasury in 1977–78 through tax and company
tax was Rand 190 million. The departments of Housing and Coloured Affairs
and Hospital Services of the C.P.A. in this year spent Rand 457 million on the
Coloured population group.

TABLE 6 Relative Incomes of Ethnic Groups in Terms of per Capita Income of Whites, English, and Afrikaners, Respectively, for the Years 1946, 1960, and 1976

Population Groups	White income = 100			English income = 100			Afrikaner income = 100		
Year	1946	1960	1976	1946	1960	1976	1946	1960	1976
Whites	100	100	100	69	70	88	146	123	124
English	144	126	114	100	100	100	211	156	140
Afrikaners	68	81	82	47	64	71	100	100	100
Coloureds	16	16	20	11	13	17	24	20	25
Asians	20	18	23	14	14	20	30	22	29
Africans	8	9	10	6	7	8	12	11	12

the Coloureds, Asians, and Africans with respect to the Afrikaners declined from 1946 to 1960. Between 1960 and 1976 it improved to a ratio roughly similar to that of 1946. Since 1960 the gap in the overall position of the Coloureds, Asians, and Africans relative to Afrikaners has narrowed slightly. The position of the English declined with respect to the Afrikaners and also relative to the black population groups.

A similar trend toward a slight narrowing of the relative gap between white and black income (with a widening of the absolute difference) is shown by a comparison between average monthly earnings per person employed (see table 8). Be-

TABLE 7 Ratio of Income of Afrikaners to English, 1946-76

Year	Personal income	Per capita income
1946	40:60	100:211
1960	47:53	100:156
1976	50:50	100:141

174

TABLE 8   Average Monthly Earnings per Person Employed in
Rand and Percentage of White Earnings, 1973–76

	1973		1974		1975		1976	
Whites	388		449		510		571	
Coloureds	103	26.6	118	26.3	134	26.3	154	27.0
Asians	111	28.6	128	28.5	153	30.0	183	32.1
Africans	72	18.6	88	19.6	106	20.8	126	22.1

Source: STATS, June 1977, p. 88, as quoted in SAIRR, *A Survey of Race Relations in South Africa, 1977* (Johannesburg, 1977), p. 234.

cause of the strictly enforced reporting of employment income for tax purposes, these statistics are probably more reliable than figures based on market research interviews.

Afrikaner economic advance since 1939 is the result of ethnic mobilization, political control (after 1948), and rapid economic development which South Africa experienced from 1939 to c.1974. For most of the period 1946 to 1976 two or more of these factors worked in tandem with each other, often at the expense of Coloured, Indian, and African economic advance, particularly in the period 1946–60. It will be seen from table 4 that whites in 1960 received 70 percent of the total income although they constituted less than 19 percent of the total population. In recent years, however, a gradual redistribution of wealth has begun with the result that whites in 1976 received 63 percent of the total income. This redistribution has been the result of the vigorous growth of the economy in the late 1960s and early 1970s accompanied by a white concern with promoting greater stability by relieving the depressed economic condition of politically subordinate groups.

A prominent feature of the Afrikaner economic advance has been the role of the state. Its intervention in the strike of 1922 occurred in terms of larger white South African interests. The intervention on behalf of the farmers and semi-skilled workers during the 1950s was concerned largely with promoting Afrikaner nationalist political and economic interests. In this decade the workers and the farmers were the main class bases of the National Party and their interests were predominant. In the late 1970s larger economic concerns prevail. But this does not mean that the business class is dominant. As a result of massive intervention—whether it be to promote Afrikaner interests, to control black labor, or simply to stabilize the economy—the state has during the past half century emerged as a giant apparatus that has spread its tentacles to virtually every sector of the economy. The state no longer only mediates between the other classes of society but often acts as a class of its own, entrenching its dominant position in society and expanding its control over the private sector. Classes such as businessmen, farmers, and white workers, which have benefited greatly from state-intervention, have a decreased ability to challenge the state effectively in terms of their perception of their own interests.[52] The state has been a major support of the Afrikaners' advance to prosperity. It has now become a major constraint as bureaucrats daily decide according to their perceptions and interests how the future fates and fortunes of the peoples of South Africa should be ordered.

52. This is analyzed and documented in detail in a forthcoming study by Stanley B. Greenberg. See also his unpublished paper, "Understanding Race and Class: Preview of a Conclusion," pp. 39–44. I am indebted to Stanley Greenberg for illuminating discussions on the role of the state.

7 Interests behind Afrikaner Power
Heribert Adam

Afrikanerdom has come some way in making up the arrearage in economic power with its former imperial English rival. It has consolidated its political power through a unified nationalist movement. The basis of its success lies in ethnic mobilization. The resulting structural transformation of South African society amounts to an ethnic revolution. It channeled and stimulated rapid industrialization through protectionist and racial legislation. The parallel accumulation of wealth and the acquisition of undivided political control by a formerly disadvantaged out-group resembled the takeover by a new class. In this instance the new "ethnic class" entrenched itself within the existing economic system by ethnic patronage and exclusion.

However, a ruling group is no monolithic block, even in the face of formidable adversaries. White power consists of competing interest groups. If politics constitutes the overt expression of underlying interests, who on the white side are the winners and losers of recent developments? What is the weight and relationship of the various factions? Are new political splits conceivable if certain groups are shortchanged through escalating costs of system maintenance? How can the apparently irrational decisions as well as the contrary pragmatic actions of Afrikaner survival politics be rationally explained? This analysis attempts to explore the decisive realm of intrawhite cleavages with a few tentative hypotheses.

Two groups may be singled out as having increased their political power and influence in the decision making: (1) English and Afrikaner big business, (2) certain sections of the state bureaucracy. The white unions may be discerned as the main losers and to a certain extent farmers also.

The mobilization for a war economy had obviously strengthened the importance of those interests that contribute most to the foreign exchange and can utilize international connections to ward off economic isolation. The mining industry, particularly Anglo-American as well as some Afrikaner multinationals, stand in the forefront of cultivating the essential lifelines to outside loans, markets, and know-how.[1] A progressive English capitalism that realistically calculates the costs of apartheid maintenance and a government that is dependent on growth and stability have moved closer to an understanding of economic essentials. They still differ in political tactics and the rhetoric of their respective constituency. But Harry Oppenheimer, the epitome of foreign-oriented capital and financial backbone of the official apartheid opposition, has his speeches to the corporate establishment abroad occasionally published by the Department of Information as paid advertisements in foreign newspapers. Such use of Oppenheimer's services has not yet given Anglo-American veto power in the Nationalist caucus, but its voice is heard. Nevertheless, how far and how fast racial reforms should be carried out in the specific instance, and under which constitutional formula, remains a serious bone of contention.

The new class of Afrikaner businessmen has deepened the cleavages within the Afrikaner establishment by making common cause with their English counterparts against preindustrial apartheid practices. However, at the same time a greater measure of unity between the English economic elite and Afrikaner political elite has manifested itself. English and

1. According to the *Financial Mail* (December 16, 1977), "Rembrandt still enjoys considerable leeway in bringing overseas profits to account via cash-flush foreign registered pipeline companies. How much comes from where and for what is an international mystery." One could guess that very few of the Third World politicians who make flaming anti-South African boycott demands have the faintest idea that they support sophisticated Afrikaner capitalism when they visit Rothman-sponsored tennis tournaments in their country or consume other Rupert products.

Afrikaner elites are now able to interpenetrate each other. It is one of the more obfuscated facets of South African politics how the very perception of Afrikaner power has led many opponents of apartheid to ingratiate themselves with the authorites in the hope of future favors. This has long been the informal policy of the mining houses. In 1924, for example, English Randlord Lionel Phillips advised his son in Johannesburg not to let personal dislikes interfere with business advantages: "I made it my duty to cultivate the new masters, and, in the end, greatly modified the relations. You and Walters will have to try to get upon good personal terms with Hertzog, Beyers and Co. It is amazing what can be done by discreet action."[2]

With an Afrikaner government in power, it is highly feasible for English-dominated corporations to have influential Afrikaner executives on their boards. The state on the other hand, including the parastatals, increasingly utilizes the economic clout, know-how, and international connections of suitable English speakers. The Afrikaner banker Jan Marais, who in the election of 1977 was wooed by both the Nationalists and Progressives as candidate, symbolizes the interchangeability of business rationality between these political "extremes." While political decision making still takes place within the Afrikaner context and the English have by no means all joined the Nationalists[3] or, for that matter, would be accepted as participants in the Afrikaner power centers, the mutual collaboration of decisive individuals from both camps has increased considerably. To be sure, there are still relics of the old rivalries alive when Afrikaners were considered an "inferior race," and, vice versa, English speakers were viewed as untrustworthy agents of an aggressive imperialism. Many visitors have observed that the Boer War is

2. Maryna Fraser and Alan Jeeves (eds.), *All That Glittered. Selected Correspondence of Lionel Phillips 1890–1924* (Cape Town: Oxford University Press, 1977), p. 355, quoted in *Social Dynamics* 4, no. 1 (1978), 64.

3. In the 1977 general election, 30 percent of the English-speaking voters supported the National Party, compared with close to 80 percent of the Afrikaner voters.

still being fought. The stereotypes affect chances of promotion even in the higher echelons of the civil service. To a lesser degree, the historical relics are cultivated within the English-dominated private business circles. However, the trend clearly moves toward a convergence within a broader white meritocracy. The mergers and joint ventures of Afrikaner and English capital have greatly increased in the 1970s. Afrikaner capital, first accumulated in banking and insurance business, was forced to diversify by the sheer weight of funds. This led to many partnerships. The *Financial Mail* sums up the blurring of the traditional English/Jewish/Afrikaans business cleavage: "Never before has it been more difficult to stamp a tribal tag on to a rand note."[4]

Particularly on the crucial question of white labor policy, the mining industry and the Afrikaner government now see eye to eye, although this too represents no new development. The mining industry has traditionally adapted remarkably well to the racial restrictions on labor while professing its repugnance of apartheid. This is perhaps best illustrated by the attitude of its notorious founder, as richly portrayed in the autobiography of Lewis Sowden.

> Sir Ernest Oppenheimer, last of the great magnates, was then [1957] in his seventy-seventh year, living in a great house in Parktown, Johannesburg. He received me once in a large, beautiful room that was hung with Renoirs, and talked of the Diamond Corporation's new headquarters he was to open in London on his next birthday, and then of the apartheid laws. "They are no trouble to us, you know... I mean on the mines. We have all the native labour we need. You know why? The natives come to us because they know that on the mine they are sheltered. No Pass Law raids. No chivying by the police. We look after them..." As the magnate explained, holding a long-stemmed glass, he spoke, with a shrug and a smile. "The Government's restrictive laws—apartheid and all that—

4. *Financial Mail,* August 25, 1978, p. 685.

don't touch them... So we have no labour problems. That's how it works out for us... That's how it is."[5]

Oppenheimer's son, the present chairman of Anglo-American, declared 20 years later that "most South African companies did not need to be told how to advance the lot of the black worker."[6] The large supply of unskilled migrant labor on which Anglo-American depends has benefited, above all, extractive industries. However, it is a frequently made mistake, particularly in the Marxist literature, to conclude from an analysis of the special conditions of mining economics that the high profit rates in other sectors also result mainly from the restricted labor system. Here South African protectionism, which the mining sector did not favor, also played an important part. The relatively high returns for capital in manufacturing and commerce are only partly due to cheap labor. It is generally accepted that the low hourly wages for blacks in comparison with the white South African standard of living are nevertheless higher than wage rates in significant Third World countries such as India, Brazil, and Korea. The high tariff walls, import restrictions, and import substitution regulations—introduced for strategic reasons and the protection of a fledgling local production—have insulated the South African market from outside competition with cheaper products from economics of scale and contributed to investment returns above the international averages for foreign capital in particular.

With the political pressure for the mobilization of white workers for the achievement of ethnic political power fallen by the wayside, the main losers of recent trends in the South African political economy are the remaining white/Afrikaner unions. However, it is crucial to remember that in the tradi-

5. Lewis Sowden, *Land of the Afternoon* (London: Elek, 1968), pp. 169–70. Most of the recent academic literature on gold mining in South Africa, particularly the studies of Francis Wilson and Frederick A. Johnstone, despite their different emphases and political perspectives, confirm the collaboration thesis of state and mining interests.

6. *South African Digest*, February 2, 1978, p. 2.

tion of Afrikaner decision making by inclusion of all interest groups, the white unions so far still have a certain veto role, despite their dwindling membership and declining overall influence vis-à-vis Afrikaner capital. Job color bars are lifted not because of pressure by industry but only when the unions agree. Only in these sectors where whites have moved out anyway do the unions no longer oppose the removal of job determinations. However, the new threat to white unions expected as a result of the Wiehahn Commission is clearly reflected in Afrikaans press comments on labor relations. While editorials stress the need for organized labor and the government to cooperate, the alternative is also spelled out: "Should he [the Minister of Labour] be forced to do so through unreason, he may act on his own in the interest of the country."[7]

The justification for such unilateral anti- (white) union action, unthinkable in the 1950s and 1960s, is found in survival politics: "There are things which our country simply must do in order to be able to look the world in the eye and to defend itself. May worker and Government leader continue to follow this road."[8] In the name of national survival intraethnic class cleavages are relegated to secondary importance. But this time such indoctrination of a stubborn Afrikaner union relic is not directed against English foreign capitalists on behalf of a nascent Afrikaner capital through ethnic mobilization. Rather, a mature Afrikaner bourgeoisie in full control of state power has now identified itself once more with the laissez-faire labor policies of English capitalists with whom it shares similar interests of curbing the historical monopoly of expensive white labor. An editorial in *Die Vaderland* succinctly sums up the new thinking on labor policy:

But an unskilled and unmotivated worker's labour is also expensive because it is insufficiently productive. In practice this means that three or four people have to be employed to

7. *Die Transvaler*, February 22, 1978.
8. Ibid.

do the work of one. It also means that the white man is overburdened with the responsibility of providing skilled labour which places too great a demand on him, as well as putting him in an unhealthy bargaining position *vis-a-vis* the employer. Count up the cost of all this and it should be evident that we have for many decades been running our economy with the handbrake on.[9]

The influential Afrikaanse Handelsinstituut in its proposals to the Wiehahn Commission suggests that closed shops be outlawed. It also wants a legal prohibition against employers deducting trade union dues. On the other hand, the Instituut now backs the admission of urban Africans to registered trade unions, although unionizing the other half of black labor, the migrant workers, is considered "neither desirable nor possible."[10] These proposals aim at subjecting bargaining of all groups to heavy control from the top. A labor court is envisaged to arbitrate in job reservation disputes and enforce the "national interest" against the bargaining power of all unions. Although the government's Bantu Labour Relations Regulation Amendment Act of 1977 makes for the first time in South Africa's labor history provisions for Africans to negotiate binding wage agreements, it allows only for factory-level not for industrywide bargaining. It is only within the existing structure of works, and even less adequate liaison–committees, that binding wage negotiations can take place. Cases of frequent intimidation and reprisals against African union organizers, despite their legal activity within this system, abound.[11] When faced with threats to strike by white miners, Anglo-American can now hope, as in 1922, for government intervention, despite union charges of ethnic betrayal and a "sell out to Anglo-Jewish capitalists." As *The Star* put the South African version of the General

9. *Die Vaderland,* January 31, 1978.

10. *Financial Mail,* March 1978, p. 824.

11. For documentation see the *South Africa Labor Bulletin,* a relatively unknown but highly informative journal, published by the Durban Institute of Industrial Education.

Motors slogan: "In South Africa's present economic predicament the interest of the mining houses becomes almost synonymous with the interest of the country."[12] Yes, indeed, one would have to conclude, considering that the rise of each dollar in the gold price amount to $20 million additional foreign exchange for South Africa annually. The government earned over 40 percent of its total hard currency in 1975 from the sale of gold.

Farmers may be considered the other organized interest group whose influence has begun to decline. The farmers have greatly benefited from the state's regimentation of black labor and the elaborate system of subsidies. However, through the marketing boards the state now has almost full control over the fixing of prices of farm produce. To be sure, farming interests still command disproportionate political power. As a result, a third of the Nationalist members of parliament indicate farming as their main occupation. But since the 1970s the government has succeeded in imposing decisions against the explicit opposition of organized agriculture. Those state interventions included the permission to sell yellow margarine, to tax agricultural cooperatives, and to curb overstocking. Commenting on the latter decision, *Die Burger* wrote: "The prosecution of farmers who overstock their farms underlines the drastic change the approach to farming has gradually undergone in South Africa. Not so long ago such interference on the part of the authorities would have caused a rebellion among farmers. But these days are gone forever."[13]

Simultaneously, the dependency of farmers on the state for the provision of sufficient labor has decreased. As in other industrial societies, farming in South Africa has become a highly mechanized and specialized agribusiness. The number of tractors per farm rose from 0.2 in 1946 to 2.0 in 1970. Combine harvesters increased sixfold in 15 years. Weed sprays in particular affected the former labor intensive operations. Es-

12. *The Star*, April 1, 1978, p. 12.
13. *Die Burger*, January 27, 1972.

timates are that in 1981 only 4.3 percent of the economically active whites will be employed in agriculture. The number of all persons employed in this sector outside the Bantustans dropped from 1.2 million in 1970 to 0.95 in 1976.[14]

In an important new study Stanley Greenberg has demonstrated how in the judgment of the more progressive farmers, the previous tenant and squatter system became dysfunctional.[15] Unmotivated workers are being replaced with skilled and better paid loyal employees. The potential damage that a disgruntled squatter could afflict on a sophisticated farming process exceeds the profits from his otherwise cheap labor. Labor relations on the farms have become a security matter. As the Minister of the Interior remarked in a speech in which he called for a thorough investigation into the wages and living conditions of farm labor: "In these days we have to relate labour to security. A black labour force which is well trained and cared for is not only a smaller security risk but could become a good ally if domestic conditions become more difficult."[16] New developments on the farms only mirror similar processes in manufacturing. The tragic consequences for the displaced African farm laborers who can now neither eke out a living in the overcrowded Bantustans nor find employment on the mines is well known.

The Greenberg study highlights the important insight that the coercive state apparatus of apartheid laws emerged in response to demands from specific constituencies. However, the labor bureaus and mobility restrictions that forced the African farm labor into medieval relations of *Leibeigenschaft* are now becoming superfluous. But what is the fate of, and function of, those who man the administrative machinery that has outlived its purpose?

This consideration leads to the second main interest group that has extended its power under National Party rule. The vast state bureaucracy—both of state capitalism and more

14. SAIRR, Annual Survey 1977, pp. 255, 254.
15. Stanley Greenberg, *Race, Class and the State,* forthcoming.
16. *Rapport,* July 2, 1978, editorial.

particularly the specific apartheid administration—has developed a vested interest in perpetuating superfluous functions. A key to the understanding of South African political immobility lies in comprehending the civil-service structure. To the sociology of organizations from Parkinson to Peter Blau one would have to add, in South Africa, the specific mentality of guarding an outdated doctrine. Because the apartheid laws cannot be formally scrapped for fear of endangering Afrikaner unity, an eager bureaucracy is ready to implement the regulations, although they may in fact now go against the new interests of those who created them in the first place. A reified apparatus, whose very status and existence depend on traditional apartheid, has acquired considerable power not only to guard its realm in the name of sacred legal principles but frequently to extend its scope to new activities.

The ensuing conflicts manifest themselves in three partly overlapping intrawhite cleavages: (1) the contradictions between state capitalist activities and an entrenched private sector, (2) the conflicts between an expanding social welfare state as crisis management at the expense of private interests, and (3) the cleavages between traditional apartheid bureaucracy and business interests, which suffer lost opportunities and bear new costs.

To begin with the third cleavage, it is obvious that private business in South Africa has long happily adjusted to, if not instigated, the state apparatus of black labor control. Particularly the nascent and weak Afrikaner capital has looked to state protection against more competitive outsiders and labor threats alike. As a journalist aptly commented: "Ironically, organised commerce, industry and agriculture, which in theory should be the main pillars of the free economy, are among the worst culprits. Their congresses are riddled with resolutions calling for government intervention."[17] These groups needed the state to elaborate and back up restrictions.

17. Leon Kok, "Capitalism or Philanthropic Socialism," *Financial Gazette*, September 23, 1977.

The state met these expectations and went beyond them. State intervention eroded the independence of increasingly more confident business interests which lost out in their previous ability to impose at will their particularistic perceptions on their patron.

The state's elaboration of the racial order has brought in its wake new costs and lost opportunities. Manufacturing and commercial interests demand more trained black labor, need greater political stability, a larger domestic market, and better export opportunities. The racial order militates against all these imperatives. Above all, it can no longer guarantee relatively peaceful labor relations. Business is divided as to whether recognized industrywide African unions, plant-based organizations, or traditional police repression can best confine disputes. Tactics and real possibilities between large and small enterprises diverge on these issues. Big corporations favor more readily an integrative policy of bargaining with recognized unions, better social security systems, and higher minimum wages. This puts smaller firms, among which Afrikaners are still overrepresented, at a competitive disadvantage.

Intra-Afrikaner rivalry, usually expressed as a political North-South split between progressive Kaapenaars and conservative Transvalers, relates to the second controversy between an expanding social welfare state at the expense of private interests. In reverse directions, the cleavage resembles the different outlooks between the old and more sophisticated capital of the New England regions in the United States and the new-rich coalition of oil, real estate, and farming interests of the U.S. Southern belt. Whereas in the North the bureaucratic strata predominate in Afrikaner life, the salient feature of the South is the more established Afrikaner bourgeoisie of the Cape, based, more characteristically, on private wealth or professional qualifications. While united in the earlier stages of its ethnic revolution against English economic dominance, its ascendancy to state power has led to a latent divergence in Afrikanerdom, not only on the question of how the Coloureds should be treated. In this vein, one must explain the ironic spectacle of an impeccable pillar of the Afrikaner establishment, A. D. Wassenaar, chairman of Sanlam, the second largest conglomerate in the country (after Anglo-American), attacking the government in a best-selling book for an "Assault on Private Enterprise."[18] Vorster in turn sharply rebuked the author for ascribing communist tendencies to his spreading bureaucracy. Wassenaar was motivated, it is rumored, not only by personal anger of an old-style capitalist about stifling bureaucrats but by a real threat to Sanlam's most crucial activity. This none of Wassenaar's adversaries in the North mentioned by name. But it is fairly certain that the menace for Sanlam meant the planned introduction of a government pension scheme. Such a state-backed insurance corporation with compulsory membership for all employees along the lines of Western European social welfare states would cut severely into the private life insurance business of Sanlam. How far the power of the state bureaucracy should go in regulating economic competition and mediating market forces in the interest of an overall crisis management lies at the heart of the dispute.[19]

Another contentious issue is likely to become who should be allowed to tap the vast consumer market in the African townships. A newly emerging competition between an African middle class and expansionary white entrepreneurs is reflected in the controversial regulations regarding commer-

18. A. D. Wassenaar, *Assault on Private Enterprise* (Cape Town: Juta, 1976).

19. The trend away from partnership to competitors in Afrikaner business houses was further accelerated by the rearrangement of Sanlam and Volkskas relationships in 1977. After differences about who should take over Jan Marais' Trust Bank, which had overextended itself in the declining real estate market, Sanlam offloaded most of its 28 percent share in Volkskas onto the Rembrandt empire of Rupert. This parting of the ways made it possible for Volkskas to launch its own merchant and industrial banks in competition with Sanlam's Senbank and Kredietbank. Since the much smaller Volkskas nevertheless is considered to have closer government connections, the hint that Wassenaar's book could hurt Sanlam's business meant no idle threat and Sanlam's board quickly stressed that *Assault on Private Enterprise* by no means represented corporate opinion but the personal views of its chairman in whom they had full confidence.

cial township development. Past government policy of keeping white business out of Soweto is now strongly supported by black middle-class organizations such as the National African Federated Chamber of Commerce and the Soweto Trader's Association. White business is prevented from tapping directly the potentially lucrative African market by the government's policy of restricting the townships to essential services and it had to be satisfied by purchases in the white central business district.[20] However, in complete reversal of earlier policy to keep the black dormitories as bleak as possible one can now read: "There is a great need for business complexes in Soweto . . . If white capital on an agency basis or otherwise is needed, the blacks should also have the opportunity to have a say in it."[21]

Such interest in potential lucrative profits tie in neatly with the traditional liberal political strategy of an alliance with an emerging African bourgeoisie that is now also advocated by sections of Afrikanerdom as suitable for the defense of

20. Figures for retail spending reveal the consumer power of Africans. Of the R434 million that was spent in the central business district of Johannesburg in 1975, half accounted for African purchases. Only R23 million, roughly 10 percent of total African spending, was spent in Soweto itself (*Financial Mail*, September 30, 1977). Another reliable indicator for the growing purchasing power of an emerging black middle class is the expenditure on racial advertising. While in the past confined to beer, cigarettes, and "skinlightners," it now includes clothing, furniture, and toiletries. Some 60 African models of John McKendrick, the largest agency in the country, earn R20 an hour. Expenditure on black advertising is reported to have grown from R8.5 million in 1970 to R22 million in 1977 (*Financial Mail*, October 14, 1977, p. 116). A study of the black consumer market by the Johannesburg stockbrokers firm Pollack & Freemantle concluded that real increases in earnings by blacks between 1970 and 1976 was 51.3 percent, compared with 3.8 percent for whites (*The Star*, December 17, 1977). The survey expects the total wage bill of blacks to grow at an average annual rate of 15 percent in real terms. As a result, and taking the age structure and population growth into account, the authors stress that "Black consumer spending would be one of the most important future aspects on the South African commercial world." If blacks, like Afrikaners in the 1930s, were to mobilize this purchasing power for political gains (an "Inkatha Reddingsdaadbond"), the effects could be considerable.

21. *Die Transvaler*, February 20, 1978.

capitalism. Thus *Beeld* links opposition to the admission of black undergraduates to Stellenbosch, desegregation of the Pretoria Opera, and equal pay of black and white academics and calls them "outdated standpoints." "The Afrikaner cannot, by those means, succeed in making himself a focal point in the growing movement aimed at consolidating the middle class as a bastion against the attack on our free capitalist way of life."[22] Even before Soweto, the Graduate School of Business at Stellenbosch warned in special public seminars that "the country, including the homelands, will continue to drift towards socialism" if the government would not, "in addition to creating work opportunities for job-seekers" also "deliberately encourage members of all races to become independent entrepreneurs, i.e. job-creators."[23]

In commending the West Rand Administration Board for its intention to provide better houses for blacks in higher income brackets, *Die Vaderland* recommends long before the 1976 unrest: "There would be little sense in building more luxurious houses in Soweto among the sub-economic four-roomed dwellings. What the Black city needs is better residential areas for its economically better-off classes. In other words, Soweto should also have its Houghtons and its Parktowns."[24] Such unreal visions nevertheless indicate a backlash against traditional government interference into the market, including the black labor market. In the name of classical economic liberalism, prominent Afrikaner economists, such as Lombard, assail the government for overplanning and undermining of risk-taking and entrepreneurial spirit.[25] These tendencies undoubtedly reflect the mood of a self-

22. *Die Beeld*, February 2, 1978.

23. See full-page advertisement in *Financial Mail*, April 15, 1976.

24. *Die Vaderland*, April 15, 1978.

25. For a typical statement of orthodox, elitist liberalism with emphasis on entrenched constitutional rights but little concern for economic equality, despite the authors discipline in economics, see W. H. Hutt, "South Africa's Salvation in Classic Liberalism," in *Studies in Economics and Economic History*, ed. Marcelle Kooy (Johannesburg: Macmillan, 1966), pp. 103–25. It is interesting to note how many of the author's suggestions of the mid-1960s the government has implemented in the meantime.

confident Afrikaner business class that no longer needs to rely on state protection as in the past. It is big business and not the small and struggling Afrikaner enterprise that now sets the tone. Among the confirming incidents for this view, for example, the dilution of the controversial antimonopoly legislation stands out. An initially proposed mergers tribunal was scrapped upon representation from interested parties, leading the *Financial Mail* to the unusual triumphant headline: "Pretoria has listened."[26]

In this context, a third smouldering strain, namely that between the Afrikaner-controlled public corporations and the private conglomerates, deserves attention. In the early 1970s, when the public sector aggressively expanded, the mouthpiece of the English-dominated private sector plaintively asked whether the government "really believe in the private enterprise system which handsomely rewards those who meet the community's needs most effectively. Or has it already changed South Africa in a centrally controlled and planned economy where Pretoria knows best and state ownership and direction needs no apology?" It quoted Harry Oppenheimer who stressed the competitive advantages of public enterprise, free of the constraints of profitability or bankruptcy and therefore able to take higher risks with little accountability: "And since these corporations are virtually uncontrolled by Parliament, and since they are not answerable to any body of private shareholders, they are left free to develop policies which, in fact, amount to nationalisation of a substantial part of the SA economy. Moreover, since they operate with public money, they are able to carry on their operations with a large measure of freedom from the normal economic sanctions which impose discipline on businessmen managing their own or their shareholder's money."[27]

In 1974, the government for the first time acknowledged certain limits to the state's role in the economy. The Prime Minister's Economic Advisory Council agreed with a

26. *Financial Mail*, June 2, 1978.
27. *Financial Mail*, June 2, 1972.

memorandum stating that "public corporations should be managed in accordance with business principles; that they should as far as possible avoid competition with the private sector." The Minister of Economic Affairs declared that a committee will "review continually the governments' activities in regard to manufacturing in general in order to eliminate clashes of interests as far as possible and to serve as encouragement for the private sector to progress to full development."[28] Whether the government will in fact put an end to the expansion of the state sector remains to be seen.

Little research has been undertaken on the internal functioning and conflicts within the parastatals. The state bureaucracy as a whole seems to have largely escaped the critical examination of social scientists. Since the white public bureaucracy comprises such heterogeneous interests and individual backgrounds, its common denominator would seem to be an ethnically motivated service to the state. Susceptibility to calls for loyalty, particularly allegiance to a strong Afrikaner political leadership, can be expected from this group more than any other section of the *volk*. Such an outlook would explain why relatively modest pay increases have not caused much overt opposition, let alone mobilization for strike action. "The national interest certainly demands restraint," comments the SABC in a manner hardly different from the expressions of gratefulness by the spokesmen of the Civil Service Association. "It is apparent from the balanced reaction to the 5 percent rise that they are prepared to go on playing the game," remarks the radio commentator.[29]

With such an outlook, the crucially important civil service seems relatively well-equipped for obedient crisis management, even against opposing interests in its own ethnic group. John Kenneth Galbraith has lucidly described the difference in the collective attitudes between private entrepreneurs and corporate bureaucrats: "Capitalists, no one needs to be reminded, were a socially indigestible force—

28. *Financial Mail*, December 27, 1974, pp. 1,167–68.
29. SABC, *Current Affairs*, December 8, 1977.

individualistic, uncompromising, power-hungry, often rapacious, always ready for a fight. Modern corporate bureaucrats, in contrast, are faceless, cautious, courteous, predictable and given to compromise."[30] This description of private management applies even more to public bureaucracies. With such a technocratic mentality of the numerically and politically dominant section of the ruling group, speculations about an imminent split in the Afrikaner oligarchy in terms of a fundamental realignment of political forces seem farfetched indeed. None of the cleavages investigated would justify such predictions. And even if by some miracle political power would fall into the hands of a more progressive, color-blind opposition party, a continuing Afrikaner civil service could ensure that new policies are implemented quite differently. The Weimar Republic collapsed under the hostility of its unfaithful servants. More than any other group, it would seem that the vested interests of the powerful administrators of apartheid represent at present the main stumbling block for a fast and radical change.

A telling example of reified bureaucratic power was the attempt by the Department of Community Development to apply rigidly historical blueprints of business segregation in 1978. The removal of Indian traders from Transvaal city centers to the outskirts was no longer backed by public opinion. Afrikaans papers attacked the costly scheme in the name of a changed taxpayer sentiment. "What difference does it make if businessmen compete shoulder to shoulder or a few metres away from each other?"[31] "That whites in their thousands should be able to drive to Laudium to buy from Indian traders there but that it is undesirable for the Indian trader to buy or hire a shop in Pretoria's Church Street, is an argument that will no longer stick."[32] Why then does the Group Areas bureaucracy stall on the establishment of color-neutral areas? Obviously this civil-service sector would

30. John Kenneth Galbraith, "A Case For Capitalism," *New York Review of Books*, April 20, 1978.
31. *Rapport*, June 4, 1978.
32. *Die Beeld*, June 5, 1978.

lose status at the least, and make itself superfluous at the worst, if the purpose of its existence fell into oblivion. The zeal with which the squatter camps of the Cape were cleared despite the negative image effects testifies also to the power of a semi-autonomous machinery. So do numerous "unexplainable" decisions from pass raids to beach segregation.

Decentralized administration according to widely differing local conditions is blocked by an inherited top-heavy centralized structure. Deracialization in South Africa, therefore, also presupposes large-scale debureaucratization in the sense of an organizational restructuring of administrative purposes.[33] Since the rationale of a section of the bureaucracy lies in the inherited racial legislation, a reform of the civil service would in turn presuppose a formal abolition or, at least, an officially enforced benign neglect of the legal relics. As long as threatened bureaucrats can invoke their sanctimonious duty of merely carrying out the law against those who apply common sense, neither morality nor pragmatism is likely to have much of a chance.

This specific South African predicament is compounded by the involvement of the departmental apparatuses in the inner-Afrikaner rivalry of their political heads. They depend largely on the support of their senior civil servants who can destroy or make a minister. In the corporate politics of ingroup image cultivation, the minister then frequently utilizes his loyal apparatus to score points against political rivals. But within an extraordinarily wide network of intricate laws they can decide which aspects should be activated at which particular moment and which provisions should remain dormant. The frequently noted trend toward rule by executive order in South Africa has its roots in the wide framework of laws open for utilization when the minister deems it necessary. Frequently, factional and personal expediency rather than pragmatic national interest guides such decision making.

33. The option of abolition, radical retraining, or quick attrition of an existing civil service with long-term contractual rights would be difficult to achieve.

The seemingly irrational actions of "unnecessary" repression in terms of overall white self-interest would seem to result from such rational intragroup power politics.

Such a conceptualization of Afrikaner decision making can explain both the modernized pragmatic as well as the "irrational" traditional versions of specific actions. This perspective avoids assuming a fictitious technocratic mastermind behind Afrikaner politics as well as the equally false notion of stubborn obsession with racism. Instead it traces decisions to the specific interplay of competing forces and personalities within the corporate attitudes and organizational structures of Afrikanerdom. These remain so far intact, despite the latent cleavages.

8   Afrikaner Politics: How the System Works   Hermann Giliomee

> *Maar die man wat sy deelname weier*
> *is die man wat sy nasie vermoor.*
> (But the man who does not play his part
> stabs his nation to the heart.)
> —I. D. du Plessis, *Vaderlandse Verse* (trans. Anthony
> Delius)

> *The draconian racial and security laws of the last 30 years*
> *were made for one purpose and one only, and that was to*
> *ensure the security and survival of Afrikanerdom.*—Alan
> Paton, *Sunday Times*, October 1, 1978

One of the ironies of the South African political scene is that
both the staunchest supporters and the fiercest opponents of
Afrikaner nationalism regard it as a monolithic monument
that mysteriously produces an unchallengeable *volkswil*, an
ethnic consensus of opinion. In contrast, my perspective will
highlight the pluralistic nature of Afrikanerdom and analyze
the independent role and influence of the constituent parts of
the ethnic movement which have often found themselves in
conflict with one another. It will also attempt to assess to
what extent each of these parts gained or lost influence since
1934 and how this influence has been exercised. In that year
the National Party in its present form came into existence,
and in the years that followed the party, the Afrikaner
Broederbond, the Afrikaans press, writers, businessmen,
schools, universities, and even the church all attempted to
foster the consciousness among the Afrikaners of an exclusive

political identity. After winning power in 1948 the National Party had to operate in a much larger context but it still succeeded in keeping its ethnic base intact and in overcoming cleavages within Afrikanerdom. This chapter endeavors to investigate how this system operates.

It is a daunting subject, one that has been neglected by political scientists and one that any historian in ordinary times will be well advised to leave alone until more distinct patterns form in the layers of time. This analysis is nothing more than a preliminary and exploratory survey based on the few published sources and conducted interviews.[1]

THE NATIONAL PARTY

In some respects the party has changed remarkably little since the 1930s when it was a small opposition party and merely one of the constituent parts of the Afrikaner ethnic movement (*volksbeweging*) till the present when it rules South Africa and stands as the guarantor of ethnic interests. It has always been a well-disciplined party in which the decisions are made by a small elite while at the same time allowing members the free-

1. Four outstanding recent contributions to the study of Afrikaner nationalism are the two complementary essays by André du Toit and F. van Zyl Slabbert in Leonard Thompson and Jeffrey Butler, eds., *Change in Contemporary South Africa* (Berkeley and Los Angeles: University of California Press, 1975), pp. 3–50; a class analysis by Dan O'Meara, "White Trade Unionism, Political Power and Afrikaner Nationalism," *South African Labour Bulletin*, I, no. 10 (1975), 31–51; and T. Dunbar Moodie, *The Rise of Afrikanerdom* (Berkeley: University of California Press, 1975), the standard work on Afrikaner ideology in the 1930s and 1940s. A major problem, common to all history writing but acute in this instance, is that almost all sources are or were insiders who told their story in terms of their own ideological commitments or material interests. In some cases there was little opportunity to verify their evidence. The advantage of an insider may be stated in Kipling's dictum that "it is good to be back among one's countrymen because one knows when they are lying." Even so, it should be kept in mind that ideology, myths, and image-making constantly color the perceptions of those who are cited and will undoubtedly have crept into my analysis as well.

dom to express opinions and dissent within the party structures. The organizational framework has remained basically
the same. It is a decentralized party in which each province
has its own constitution, party machine, and annual congress. Each constituency is organized in several branches that
compete with one another in the raising of funds and the
enrollment of new members. In the continual demands it
makes on its members, the National Party is a "standing"
political party rather than one that is resurrected for each
election. A large proportion of Nationalist supporters are
card-carrying members of the party. In 1966, for instance, the
Cape Province had 166,390 enrolled members while its estimated total strength in the election of that year was 274,678.
In the Transvaal the corresponding figures were about
300,000 and 516,000.[2] Candidates for Parliament and the Provincial Councils are nominated by the branch committees of
the constituencies and approved by the provincial leadership.
In general, branches favor as candidates the staunch party
supporters known for their orthodox views rather than independent minds from the business and professional world
who usually stand aloof from the party machine.

In policy-making the party has remained elitist. According
to the constitution, the highest authority on party policy in a
province is the provincial congress, which must de jure ratify
all policy changes of the party before it becomes the official
policy of that province. However, provincial congresses do
not have the power to make final decisions on the party's
program of principles. They can discuss proposals and submit them to the Federal Council, the supreme body on which
the various provinces enjoy equal representation. Since the
leaders of the party in parliament are strongly represented on
the Federal Council, they are able to block resolutions approved by a congress or submit proposals to the various congresses. During the past forty years all the proposals by the
Federal Council have been accepted by the congresses with-

2. William A. Kleynhans, *Political Parties in South Africa* (Pretoria: University of South Africa, 1973), p. 104; Kenneth A. Heard, *General Elections in
South Africa* (London: Oxford University Press, 1974), p. 73.

out much opposition. The party leaders have also bypassed the congresses in major policy changes. Without consulting the congresses, Verwoerd in 1959 committed the party to self-government for the various homelands and the abolition of African parliamentary representation. In 1967 Vorster similarly decided to establish diplomatic relations with black states without consulting the congresses. In practice, the annual party congresses of the four provinces are forums where policy and party matters are discussed and where cabinet ministers can explain and justify decisions made in the preceding year. Even in ideologically sensitive matters such as the "multinational" sport policy introduced in the early 1970s, congresses, after expressing some reservations, almost unanimously gave their approval to new policies initiated by the cabinet.[3]

The caucus, comprising National Party representatives in the House of Assembly and the Senate, chooses the party leader. In its functioning the caucus reflects the party's character of an elitist body that at the same time maintains a democratic form. The caucus is not a policy-making body but one that determines the strategy of the party during a parliamentary session. Ministers can be asked to explain decisions or statements, but the cabinet is not obliged to lay everything before the caucus. Verwoerd, for instance, in 1959 announced the government's decision to abolish African representation in Parliament before consulting the caucus. Challenged in the caucus, Verwoerd admitted that bills ordinarily should be presented to caucus at an early stage since it was a "combat unit which must know beforehand what is going on and then have to decide about the manner in which the struggle will have to be conducted in Parliament." Conceding this, Verwoerd at the same time clearly stated that the caucus

3. Kleynhans, *Political Parties in South Africa*; Jan J. van Rooyen, *Die Nasionale Party: Sy Opkoms en Oorwinning—Kaapland se aandeel* (Cape Town: Nasionale Handelsdrukkery, 1956), pp. 177–85. For an analysis of the decision-making process in the National Party see R. A. Schrire, "The Formulation of Public Policy," unpublished paper, 1978. Schrire first used the term "chairman of the board" to describe Vorster's prime ministerial style.

did not have the competence to reject measures the cabinet had decided on. If members of the caucus expressed objections, the cabinet did have to discuss them since "it would be foolish for cabinet to insist on things knowing that it cannot take its own people along on an issue."[4]

This statement touches on an important feature of the decision-making process during the past two decades. Decisions are taken in neither an authoritarian nor a democratic way. The first step in the process is the establishment of consensus on important matters in the cabinet before they are taken to the caucus. The caucus is not the place where cabinet ministers express their differences about ideology or strategy with their colleagues. Several cabinet ministers were adamant about this in personal interviews: "The Prime Minister will never take a divided cabinet to the caucus; and ministers will never attack each other in caucus." Once a cabinet decision has been taken all ministers are bound by it. Their task is now to win the support of the caucus for the cabinet decision.

The caucus generally ratifies cabinet decisions without serious objections. The system works smoothly except in the case of crucial policy shifts. To resolve differences within the cabinet, prime ministers in these instances have used the device of appointing a cabinet committee to produce a general agreement that is then submitted to the full cabinet.[5] In the cabinet's deliberations the caucus is important in an indirect way: Its members embody *die volk daarbuite* ("the people outside"). Ultimately a cabinet decision rests on an evaluation of whether it will "play" in the caucus and by extension in the

4. See B. M. Schoeman, *Van Malan tot Verwoerd* (Cape Town: Human and Rousseau, 1973), pp. 65, 173–75. Based on the diary of Albert Hertzog, this book and its sequel, *Vorster se 1000 dae* (Cape Town: Human and Rousseau, 1974), are valuable sources of information on struggles behind the scenes in the party. Despite his obvious conservative and racial bias, Schoeman seems intent on telling the story as he received it from his sources. The main problem is to establish whether his sources were intent on telling the truth. In this case, the evidence is corroborated by the personal notes of Japie Basson, a caucus member who at this occasion clashed with Verwoerd and was eventually expelled. I wish to thank Basson for permission to consult his notes.

5. Personal interview with a close confidant of Verwoerd and Vorster.

provincial congresses.[6] However, once the cabinet has reached a fair measure of consensus neither the caucus nor the congresses are in a position to deflect it from its course. The system has been described by a cabinet minister as follows: "Both cabinet and caucus operate within the confines of trust and obligation. The caucus has faith that the cabinet with its access to superior information will act in the general interests of the Afrikaner people; the cabinet trusts the caucus members to fulfill their obligation to defend unpopular decisions to the people at large." If that breaks down there is still the very rigid caucus discipline. Those who flaunt it are sure to be expelled from the caucus and the party. Only very rarely are members allowed to speak and vote in Parliament in a way that deviates from the party line. For any member hoping to gain promotion the conformity pressures are enormous.

Virtually the sole impetus in the decision-making process thus comes from the cabinet either guided by its assessment of the situation or influenced by the top bureaucrats. In such context the composition of the cabinet is of crucial importance. The prime minister does not in practice have a free hand in forming a cabinet. With the party becoming increasingly bureaucratized, it has in recent years also come to resent technocrats or business leaders being brought in from the outside and quickly promoted to the cabinet. Also for the sake of party unity, the prime minister is obliged to appoint the provincial leaders of the party who are chosen by the respective congresses. To make the call for white unity credible he has to appoint an English-speaking minister or two. He is also under pressure to balance his cabinet in such a way

6. Schoeman in *Van Malan tot Verwoerd,* pp. 62–75, records an instance when the minority faction in Malan's cabinet took the matter to the caucus where it tried to get a decision on the Coloured vote that would be binding on the cabinet. Leading this faction, which favored a more intransigent line, Strijdom proposed that the cabinet should consider the matter but that the caucus would not be bound by its decision. It was accepted with two or three dissenting votes. One could envisage a similar scenario if the cabinet is seriously divided on some future issue.

that it reflects the different intraethnic divisions. Verwoerd is reported as having said that he sometimes found it difficult to reconcile the divergent interests and views of the various members of his cabinet. For him the task of the prime minister was "to keep your team together and unite the *volk* behind you."[7] While also subscribing to this strategy, Vorster's cabinets reflected the shifting class and ideological base of Afrikanerdom. With the sacking of Albert Hertzog in the late 1960s, the representation of the Afrikaner working class distinctly weakened in the cabinet, which became more oriented toward the interests of business.

Verwoerd and Vorster differed in terms of their personal involvement in the process of decision-making. After he had established his undisputed authority in the party, Verwoerd became an authoritarian leader who forced through major changes. A towering personality, he overruled ministers on departmental matters and in general created the impression that he alone was making all the decisions. This impression was not far from wrong. When Vorster became prime minister he is reported to have stated at his first cabinet meeting: "Verwoerd was an intellectual giant. He thought for every one of us. I am not capable of being a second Verwoerd. From now on each of us will have to know his own field, immerse himself in it and control it."[8] In departmental matters Vorster allowed a large measure of autonomy to ministers. Insiders in the party consider Vorster as a man who in general policy matters was more a chairman of the board whose government did not run unless there was a great measure of consensus. It was a process of accumulating accord through patient listening, persuasion, and building of support. Unlike the years of Verwoerd when decisions were made in accordance with an all-embracing master plan, Vorster's deliberations were pragmatic, experimental, and tentative. If serious divisions arose, the issue was shelved or delaying tactics were employed as far as possible. The overriding concern in the

7. Schoeman, *Van Malan tot Verwoerd*, pp. 214–15, 253–54.
8. Schoeman, *Vorster se 1000 dae*, p. 14.

decision-making process was always the maintenance of unity.

The rise to power of P. W. Botha illustrates some significant trends in the party. First, it reflects the rise of the professional politician and the increasing bureaucratization of the party. To take the party in the Cape Province as a case study: In the 1930s and 1940s the party organization on the local level was largely in the hands of volunteers. In 1936 the party appointed three full-time divisional organizers, one of whom was P. W. Botha, to assist the chief secretary in promoting the interests of the party and the Nasionale Pers (the nationalist publishing house in Cape Town). These organizers struggled to win respect for their office, being often referred to contemptuously as "paid agents," because they were paid a salary. When Botha in 1946 resigned as assistant secretary to become propaganda officer of the Federal Council he found it necessary to express his gratitude to the Cape head-committee for the fact "that every member has always made me feel like a comrade—which I want to be—and not a paid agent who only seeks to make a living."[9]

During the 1950s party organizers were often criticized for interfering too much in the nomination of party candidates or using their office to promote their own political career. Only after Botha became Cape leader in 1966 were these differences resolved. Under him the Cape party ran as a smooth and efficient machine. By 1978 there were sixteen full-time organizers under the chief secretary who in a very professional way orchestrated party activities throughout the province. Opposition to the nomination of party organizers for political offices had all but disappeared. The number of Cape parliamentarians who had started their career as full-time party organizers rose from three (one of whom was P. W. Botha) in 1948 to eleven in 1978 out of a total of fifty-five. More important is the fact that Botha through the party machine has been able to influence the general pattern of the

9. Jan J. van Rooyen, *P. W. Botha: 40 Jaar* (Cape Town: Cape Province National Party, 1976), p. 32.

nomination process in the province. Unlike the former Transvaal leader Mulder who had encouraged the recruitment of professional men as candidates, Botha in the Cape favored party stalwarts whom he tied to him through bonds of personal obligation and loyalty. This played a major role in the election of Vorster's successor. While some of Mulder's "professional men" defected to R. F. (Pik) Botha and ultimately to P. W. Botha, his "party men" backed him to the hilt. It is estimated that only three or four Cape members did not vote for him.

Botha's accession to national leader also indicated the weakening of ideological divisions within the party. Power has come to rest increasingly on a provincial rather than an ideological base. The provincial parties have become the personal fiefdoms of the respective leaders with enormous patronage, including cabinet posts, at their disposal as well as the power to protect followers. It was different in 1958, the previous occasion on which an election had to be held to appoint a national leader (Vorster was appointed unanimously in 1966.) Then a decisive number of Cape parliamentarians supported Verwoerd, the ideological hardliner, instead of Dönges, the moderate Cape leader. However, in the 1978 election, Koornhof, the most enlightened cabinet minister, proposed as national leader Mulder, who was the least enlightened candidate but his provincial leader. Mulder is known to have protected Koornhof in the past when he was under fire in the cabinet for his deviant views.

Because Transvaal is so strongly represented in the caucus (80 votes against 55 of the Cape, 24 of the Orange Free State, and 13 of Natal) Mulder could still have won despite the loss of those who defected to R. F. Botha. However, on the eve of the election Schlebush, the Free State leader, stated "that 20 and possibly 21 Free State members of the caucus would support P. W. Botha and tip the scale in his favour." With the votes Pik Botha and Schlebush delivered, P. W. Botha was able to clinch the election by 98 votes against 74. In terms of ideology, the Free State has traditionally been much closer to the Transvaal than to the Cape. Both in 1954 and 1958 it supported the Transvaal candidate in the election of a national leader. This time, however, the Transvaal candidate was vulnerable because of the scandal surrounding the Department of Information of which he was the head. Another factor was the competition between the two large Afrikaans press groups, the southern Nasionale Pers (with P. W. Botha as a director) and the northern Perskor (with Mulder as a director). Nasionale Pers publishes dailies in the Cape, Free State, and Transvaal, while the Perskor dailies are confined to the Transvaal. Explicit provincialism is taboo in Afrikaner politics, but the Nasionale Pers papers contributed to Botha's victory by subtly disseminating the message the Cape represented more "civilised" values and a greater sense of responsibility than the brash and volatile Transvaal.

As Prime Minister, Botha can be expected to build up his national power base on the model of his rise in the Cape party. People will be bound to him through personal loyalty rather than ideological affinity. Whereas Verwoerd bound Afrikaners through ideological mastery and Vorster through the image of a protective strong man, Botha will tie people to him through the commitment to the machine and ultimately to him as its personification. He has much of the dynamism of Verwoerd and like him appears to be moving toward set goals. In Botha's case one of the goals may be the endeavor to bind the Coloureds more closely to the whites. (He has hardly expressed himself on the position of the urban blacks.) However, like Vorster, he is also a pragmatist who believes in making adjustments according to the exigencies of the times rather than set principles. Whereas Vorster desired to achieve the greatest measure of consensus before making a decision,[10] Botha has built up a reputation of an authoritarian leader with a zest for overpowering or eliminating his opponents politically. In some ways he represents Lyndon Johnson in the early years of his Presidency, someone who could work the party machine, who realized the need for faster change, and who seemed destined to grow as a leader

10. *House of Assembly Debates*, April 12, 1978, co. 4552.

provided he was not tempted to enter the wrong war beyond his border.

Since gaining power the National Party has steadily increased its representation in Parliament. After the 1948 election, its majority in alliance with the Afrikaner Party was only 8, and it registered only 37.2 percent of the polled votes compared to the 47.9 percent of the United Party. In the 1966 election it won 126 of the 166 seats, attracting 57.8 percent of the polled votes against the 36.3 percent of the United Party. In 1977's election, it captured 134 of the 164 seats, drawing 64.5 percent of the polled votes.[11]

Against this background two constitutional trends have become manifest in recent years. First, the party has increasingly usurped the functions of Parliament as the link between the electorate and the executive. During the urban upheavals of 1976, arguably the greatest crisis the state has yet faced, Vorster did not recall Parliament but summoned a special meeting of the caucus to discuss the situation and sample the mood of the Nationalist constituency. Parliament still functions according to established procedures, but the debates have little influence on the course of legislation.

The decline of Parliament as a link with the electorate has been accompanied by the growing abandonment of legislative control over the executive. (Judicial control effectively does not exist. South Africa has inherited the British system of the sovereignty of parliament; the courts presently have only a testing right as to the one entrenched clause of the constitution, namely the equal status of the two official languages, and subordinate legislation, for example, municipal ordinances.) During the past two decades the executive has accumulated increasing powers to bring about social, economic, political, and legal changes by administrative fiat. However, no attempt has been made to provide for the necessary supervision of the way these powers are exercised.

11. B. M. Schoeman, *Parlementêre Verkiesings in Suid-Afrika, 1910–1976* (Pretoria: Aktuele Publikasies, 1977), pp. 312–13, 438–49; *South African Foundation News*, December 1977.

According to a leading constitutional expert, South Africa has already moved so far in the direction of executive power that a new constitution providing for a presidential-style chief executive will make little difference in practice.[12] With the party having largely supplanted Parliament and the executive overriding the legislature, the executive can crush extra-parliamentary political opposition to the system, bypassing the courts and Parliament.

The scandal which broke in 1978 over the Department of Information and its misappropriation of secret funds revealed the vast unchecked powers entrusted to officials of the executive branch. It also provided a striking illustration of the extent to which executive power can be used to throw a legal pall of secrecy over government activities and stifle attempts by Parliament, the press, and other independent agencies to expose improper conduct. The heart of the Department of Information affair was the erosion of Parliament's right to control executive spending of public funds. Between 1973 and 1978 the cabinet allocated Rand 64,000,000 in secret funds to the Department of Information in order to counter "the total onslaught on South Africa." Since no statutory authority existed for the provision of such funds to this department the cabinet transferred money from other departments, notably Defence, to the Department of Information. This was an irregularity from a technical, constitutional, and audit point of view. It escaped attention primarily because the Auditor-General, an officer of Parliament, was prevented from auditing any secret funds on the grounds that it was against the interests of national security. When evidence surfaced in 1977 that serious irregularities were occurring in the Department of Information, the cabinet permitted a parliamentary select committee to conduct an investigation, but the department's secret operations were declared outside its scope. Unlike the American Congress, South Africa's legislature is cabinet-controlled and has no comparable powers to initiate investiga-

12. W. H. B. Dean, *Whither the Constitution?* (Cape Town: University of Cape Town, 1975).

tions of executive irregularities. Put simply, the Prime Minister determines who shall investigate what.

This is, broadly speaking, true in all Westminster styles of governments, but in countries such as Britain a measure of control is built into the system in that the government is very sensitive to charges of "corruption in high places," which could easily bring about its fall. In South Africa, in contrast, there is at present no likelihood of the government being voted out of power. Enjoying the trust of the Afrikaner people, it has been able to advance reasons such as "national survival" and "security" for nondisclosure of facts or the refusal to allow investigations by independent agencies such as the judiciary and the press.

In the Department of Information irregularities the Prime Minister appointed various officials of the executive branch in 1977 and 1978 to investigate the abuse of secret funds. It was later revealed that one of those officials, the head of the Bureau for State Security, was an accessary to the irregularities. He used the Official Secrets Act to intimidate newspapers working on the case. On the eve of the election of a new National Party leader he was stopped at the last minute from announcing that his investigation had shown no irregularities in the Department of Information. This would probably have cleared the way for the election of Mulder, the head of the department, who was a party to the irregularities.

That the vast extent of misuse of secret funds was indeed revealed was due to several factors. Powerful elements within the executive used the scandal to discredit Mulder in the succession struggle. In their own interests they favored a limited disclosure, but the government's hand was forced after evidence was given of the irregularities committed by the Department of Information, particularly of state funding of a progovernment newspaper, to a judiciary commission investigating exchange control. The judge published the evidence despite attempts by the new Prime Minister to dissuade him from doing so. The Prime Minister's attempt to prevent publication in the press also failed. It was thus the measure of independence the judiciary and the press do enjoy which thwarted the executive's plans to release the findings in a way that suited it.

It is still too early to establish the broader political and constitutional effects of the Information scandal. Its most immediate consequence is that the government accepted that all secret funds should be audited by the Auditor-General. Also, for the moment at least, cabinet ministers appear more concerned with accountability and the spirit of parliamentary democracy. In general, as a result of the affair the Afrikaner people are much more sceptical of the claims of the executive that their actions are guided by the considerations of "national security" and "survival." As in the Watergate scandal the press has emerged with enhanced credibility and independence. However, in other respects not much has changed. The body of security legislation produced by the fear of an overwhelming threat to the state has created a climate in which unchecked rule by the executive can flourish. Second, while opinion polls published in December 1978 indicate a small loss of support, the National Party is still so strong that there is no need for the executive to accept further curbs on its powers and of the area of government conducted in secrecy to win electoral support. The personal style of the new Prime Minister and not structural reasons will determine whether his promise of clean administration will have any substantial effect on the existing powers of the executive.

Cabinet ministers have used the vast powers at their disposal in removing some of the crudest forms of discrimination and segregation (so-called petty apartheid). Ministers committed to these reforms have evolved a political style that differs distinctly from the 1960s when apartheid legislation was boldly proclaimed and enacted. The assumptions and actions contained in the approach can be summarized as follows. First, it is accepted by the leadership that for the sake of party unity no such reforms should be presented as a break with the past. Second, it is a firm conviction that any public declaration of the intention to institute far-reaching reforms will only harm the cause of reform: To have publicly announced five years ahead that the government was committed to mixed sport on club level, the abolition of job reservation, and the desegregation of theaters countrywide would have raised such an outcry in the party that any reforms would have been suppressed. Third, the ministers have adopted the practice of assembling the leaders in a particular field (sport administrators, trade union officials) in confidential meetings where they argue the case for reform. After consensus has been established, everyone is bound to these decisions. Fourth, the press was persuaded not to publicize the gradual implementation of reforms. This entails the incorporation of new influential elites within the party's decision-making process: a minister who had spelled out the secret agenda of his plan for reform in his field to Afrikaans *and* English journalists remarked afterward, "I talked to them more confidentially than with members of the Broederbond" (personal communication). Fifth, the caucus was confronted with the fait accompli of these reforms but assured that control would continue to be exercized by way of permits. Existing legislation has rarely been repealed: It is the administration, not the law, that has been changed.

While these strategies could be employed for pragmatic adaptations to the separate development blueprint, the proposed new constitution for South Africa is too much of a break with the past, be it only in theory, to be introduced in this way. This constitution provides for (1) three separate parliaments for whites, Coloureds, and Indians, which will have control over their own respective affairs and will make laws on matters of common concern; (2) a state president appointed by an electoral college consisting of 50 members of the white parliament, 25 of the Coloured parliament, and 14 of the Asian parliament (the ratio of representation is fixed according to the present population figures), and (3) a cabinet council consisting of the state president, seven whites, four coloureds, and three Indians.

Some of the more *verligte* government spokesmen argue that this plan provides for discussion by representatives of the three groups about common affairs. On matters of national concern a measure would become law only if passed by all three parliaments. Each of the three parliaments would then have a veto right in respect of every piece of legislation touching on national issues. These spokesmen have publicized this as "consensus politics" and "the sharing of responsibility." At the same time, Vorster had publicly stated that control remains in the hands of the president. He explained that the proposed cabinet council, where consensus will have to be reached before draft legislation is laid before the various parliaments, will function in the same way as the South African cabinet presently does: "even if the majority of cabinet feels that legislation should be introduced, the prime minister can still say in practice that it shall not be introduced. That is how cabinet government operates. If one were to count votes in a cabinet, or if one were to argue in a cabinet until one has reached consensus on every detail, there will be no governing."[13]

The veto of the president could thus block draft legislation the National Party opposes. However, he does not have the power to legislate by decree. Should the party wish to pass new legislation, it may have to secure the consent of the governing parties in the other parliaments. Here the basic dilemma of the party is that the veto right is split among three separate bodies that are rigidly stratified among racial lines. The Progressive Federal Party has tried to resolve this by declaring itself in favor of the principle that groups must be able to form under conditions of free association: all laws enforcing ethnicity would be repealed. The PFP proposals that it would lay before a national convention provide for a federal government responsible for national matters, such as defense and finance, and several self-governing states that will be autonomous in matters such as health and education. The federal assembly would comprise political party representatives elected on a proportional basis within each self-governing state. The cabinet, or federal executive council, will

13. *House of Assembly Debates*, April 12, 1978, cols. 4552.

include representatives of all significant parties in the assembly chosen proportionally in contrast to the winner-takes-all-system in which the majority has a monopoly of power. While budgets and money bills would be decided on a majority vote, most other decisions would be by consensus. A minority of at least 10 to 15 percent will be able to veto a measure in parliament and the cabinet. The hope is that cross-cutting affiliations will develop in such a political dispensation that will remove to a considerable extent the need or inclination to organize groups or parties on an ethnic basis. But if the whites chose to form a racial front they could still protect their interests. (A purely Afrikaner party would, however, be too weak.)

In putting forward their constitutional plan the National Party leadership adopted the following procedure: (1) a cabinet committee was charged with the task of drawing up a draft constitution; (2) it operated in isolation without engaging any sector of public opinion except perhaps the executive council of the Broederbond (see later section) and a few academics; (3) the cabinet's deliberations remained private until it made public its completed recommendation. The editors and senior political correspondents of the Afrikaans newspapers were called in to attend the meeting where it was announced to the caucus and was thus put in a position of trust and corresponding restriction of freedom to report and express opinions on the plan. Commenting on the process whereby the constitutional plans were conceived, Marinus Wiechers aptly observes that it illustrates their very nature: "they are basically guidelines for future party political action aimed at constitutional reform, and do not, in themselves, constitute broad proposals which have to be considered by all interested groups and parties concerned. . . . Instead of being directives for a future development which will affect all the people in the Republic, they represent the outcome of rather parochial party political policies."[14]

14. Marinus Wiechers: "Current Constitutional Proposals," Unpublished paper, February 1978.

The proposed constitution, based as it is on the cornerstones of the apartheid system (population registration, group areas, and so forth) makes it unlikely that the authentic Coloured and Indian leaders, who reject these cornerstones, could be succesfully incorporated in the scheme. The plan has, moreover, been introduced in a climate in which common goodwill and the unity of common purpose are conspicuously absent. Consensus government has been introduced without securing the consent of the participants in the first place. And there is as yet no sign of a political unity emerging among the three groups on which consensus politics can be based.

However, despite all the flaws,[15] the new constitutional plan also has some potential to break new ground in the South African political system, provided that a president emerges who is determined to make the system work, exploiting the considerable scope he has within the party and utilizing the party's strict discipline.[16] At the start of its administration, the Botha cabinet promised a more conciliatory stance on the proposed new constitution. In distinct contrast to the Vorster strategy, the *verligte* elements in this administration referred the proposals to a parliamentary select committee. Its task was defined as also considering alternative proposals, submitted by representatives of all interested parties. Compared with the unilateral decision-making of the past, this procedure indicated a greater desire to appease. However, the question remains whether a prime minister, or state president, heading the National Party as presently constituted, is structurally capable of embarking on fundamental reforms.

There is a complex of reasons for the failure of major reforms to emerge from a party commanding an overwhelming majority and finding itself under strong pressure both internally and externally to introduce fundamental change. In the

15. The lacking preconditions for outside acceptance are described by William J. Foltz, "The Foreign Factor in New Constitutional Provisions for South Africa," unpublished paper, July 1978.

16. G. E. Devenish, "The New Constitutional Proposals: The Politics of Reconciliation or Dictatorial Rule," unpublished paper, February 1978.

213

case of ethnic parties it is particularly important to focus on the hidden cleavages and interests among their supporters. From recent opinion surveys a picture emerges of a whole array of political attitudes prevalent among Afrikaners of whom more than 80 percent nevertheless support the same party that claims to be ideologically cohesive. Drawing on these studies, the following generalizations may be made. In the political field the Afrikaners in the late 1970s are divided equally between those who favor consolidation of the home-lands or radical partition and those who wish to retain the status quo; some 40 percent support a form of qualified franchise within a common political system; less than a tenth support power sharing in a federal state with no group pre-dominant. Two-thirds favor the abolition of the traditional racial privileges in the economic field while a third wish to retain them. A fifth favor the lifting of racial barriers in state schools, marriages, and residential areas, but nearly four-fifths reject such measures.[17] This is hardly a clamor for fun-damental reform. In a Market and Opinion survey conducted in December 1976 and January 1977 in the wake of the Soweto upheaval, National Party supporters responded as follows to the question whether drastic changes were needed in the party's policies in order to solve the problems of the country: 23.7 percent said yes, 53.5 percent said no, and 22.4 percent was uncertain.[18] Thus, there is obviously no clear consensus for change in the party.

However, as outlined earlier, a distinct characteristic of an ethnic party is the large degree of loyalty and trust leaders command. The Freiburg survey found that 60 percent of a sample of Afrikaners interviewed would support the leaders even if they acted in ways they did not understand or ap-prove.[19] This indicates that if the leadership could agree on

17. Lawrence Schlemmer, "Change in South Africa: Processes, Oppor-tunities and Constraints," paper, April 1978, to be published in *Optima*; Theodore Hanf, Heribert Weiland, and Gerda Vierdag, *Südafrika, Friedlicher Wandel?* (Munich: Kaiser, 1978).

18. *Rapport*, February 6, 1977.

19. Hanf et al., *Südafrika, Friedlicher Wandel?*, pp. 421–22.

the nature and direction of change they would be able to take their following with them. On the other hand, any significant split at leadership level would simply be duplicated at lower levels. Assuming for a moment that the leadership is much better informed than the public of the need for change and of escalating pressures—why has it failed to introduce far-reaching reforms?

The answer is that the party leadership does not have the necessary consensus to embark on such a course. In fact, since the early 1970s it has been characterized by what may be called a permanent succession crisis in which most of the internal debate and politicking has been concerned with the prospects of rival claimants to be the successor of Vorster. This in turn leads to the further question whether this kind of infighting is merely a matter of political ambition and rivalry or whether it is indicative of the party's structural condition.

In the National Party there exists in practice no mechanism through which ideological and other conflicts can be resolved except via the leader. Through his disposal of patronage, the power to form the cabinet, his sole responsibility to decide whether legislation should be introduced or not, and his brief to formulate the party will and consensus, he is in the position to influence the pace and direction of change and to resolve conflicts in favor of one side against their ideological rivals. Through all these means Verwoerd propelled the party in the Bantustan direction. Under him there was an ideological cohesiveness, unity of purpose, and little talk of who his successor would be. However, if a leader assumes the chairman of the board approach, as Vorster did, the ideological differences in the party surface at all levels. The result is an almost permanent succession crisis as each ideological faction seeks to prevail over the others by blocking their initiatives and ultimately by winning the struggle to elect the next prime minister. The position of the prime minister remains unchallenged, but within the party's structure several rivals for the succession emerge. Rivalries, of course, also exist in Western parties but are usually only significant when a leader falters or when a new one has to be chosen. In the National Party of the late 1970s, however, there has been a continuous rivalry and jockeying for position in which the issue was not so much a conflict of different ideological approaches as an attempt to outbid rivals in assuring the Afrikaners that their interests are safest in a certain pair of hands. In such circumstances there has been little question of firm political action in the direction of set political goals.

The National Party also differs from traditional Western political parties in the narrowness of its political base and its limited responsiveness to the population at large. In recent decades most large Western parties have spread their support to incorporate, effectively, interests and views across a wide political spectrum. Despite substantial English-speaking support in the 1977 election—some 30 percent of the English-speakers who voted supported the National Party—the National Party is still fundamentally ethnically based and is primarily responsive to ethnic pressures. English-speaking big business, to name but one important interest group within the white section, is not represented in the party. Also underrepresented so far are Afrikaner-based groups that have only recently risen to prominence, such as the military or the state corporations. With rare exceptions, the Afrikaner business, educational, and professional elite do not go to Parliament. Their thinking is only indirectly brought to bear on the caucus or cabinet. And of course the black voice is not heard. Very few caucus members ever talk to middle-class blacks; fewer still are confronted with black anger and frustration. The Minister for "Plural Relations" simply "administers" blacks. His dealings with the black population may conceivably convince him of the need for reform and he may persuade the cabinet or caucus to accept policies that might stabilize the political situation. However, within the structural context he is hardly in a position to get something accepted that will damage his own constituency's interests. Those are and remain firmly within the ambit of white politics. Members of the caucus, as can be expected, are predominantly concerned with policies that would further the interests of the people they represent who can return them to parliament. Suffice to say, the National Party represents an ethnic group that is determined to protect the political power safeguarding its material interests that rest to a large degree on control of the state.

For these complex reasons the party under its present leadership would hardly have been able to introduce far-reaching reforms that went too far beyond the confines of consensus within the party even were they themselves persuaded of the need for it. This brings one back to the original assumption: that the leaders are convinced of the pressing need for major changes. If this may be true of some members of the cabinet, it does not hold for all. Though a greater sense of urgency has crept into ministerial pronouncements in the late 1970s, probably the majority of the cabinet is of the opinion that there is still time to shelve the issues of statutory discrimination and the political accommodation of blacks. Certainly it has less priority than the overriding need to maintain party unity.

What are the main ideological tendencies within the party at present? It has become standard practice to discuss ideological cleavages within the party in terms of the *verlig-verkramp* dichotomy. The term *verlig* is historically related to those Nationalists who during the late 1960s and early 1970s within the party and the other traditional institutions of the ethnic movement advocated greater white unity and "harmonious" race relations through mixed sport and the abolition of petty apartheid measures. *Verkramptes* during the same period championed undiluted Afrikaner domination and racial exclusiveness. While they were still members of the party, they formed the internal opposition within the whole range of Afrikaner institutions against the cautious, more open policy of the leadership.

While these terms still have currency, they have in fact become obsolete as indicators of present cleavages within the party. After the *verkrampte* leadership had been purged and the Herstigte Nasionale Party H.N.P. had split off, the *verkramptes* were considered by the Nationalists to have been excised from the party. In fact, at grass-roots level many remained or returned. Members of the party who still favor undiluted white supremacy and social discrimination consider themselves as the *behoudende* faction, that is, people who wish to retain the status quo.

Verligtes, in the period 1967 to 1974, claimed to work and think within the framework of separate development. During the watershed period of 1974 to 1979 they have begun to see separate development as an instrument rather than a goal. In the words of Gerrit Viljoen, reputed head of the Broederbond, there was a realization that "apartheid's original formula cannot cope with this situation."[20] However, they still insisted on the party as the vehicle for change. Whereas *verligtes* in the late 1960s emphasized the most positive and dynamic aspects of the ideology of separate development, their present role is different: they are now proposing some changes to the economic and social cornerstones of apartheid, for example, the abolition of the Immorality Act, Mixed Marriages Act, and job reservation. Increasingly they are being forced to come to grips with the political dimension. While no longer insisting on statutory racial differentiation or the need for social separation to the same extent, they still reject all forms of power sharing. In most other respects, however, the ideology has been relegated to secondary importance and *verligtes* are increasingly attracted toward the traditional strategies of bourgeois liberals to maintain middle-class interests. What distinguishes them from Progressives in their approach toward effecting constitutional change is their insistence on (1) taking the ethnic group (rather than individuals) as the basis of any new political arrangement, (2) initiating change from the platform of the National Party rather than calling a national convention to work out a new constitutional dispensation, and (3) insisting on the division rather than the sharing of power in a common society.

With one or two exceptions, cabinet ministers and members of Parliament have spurned a *verligte* or *verkrampte* tag. While the present impasse exists in the party, most ministers

20. Interview of Gerrit Viljoen with Helen Zille, *Rand Daily Mail,* August 1, 1978.

have tried to build up a centrist image, speaking *verlig* on some issues and *verkramp* on others. The leadership is not so much guided by an enlightened vision or moral concerns but reacts mainly to political and economic imperatives. At the moment the main imperatives confronting the leadership are (1) the need to strengthen South Africa against any assault from the outside, (2) the need to promote economic growth to accommodate some of the growing numbers of unemployed blacks, (3) the need to reach an accommodation with the Coloureds and Indians as possible allies, and (4) the need to prevent black unrest, above all another Soweto, which could lead to escalating demands for sanctions.

Within the party at large the following approaches to meet these needs can be discerned: (1) *Ideological hardliners*. They favor the implementation of separate development as an end in itself. The various subordinate groups can exercise authority only through their separate homeland structures, and all blacks who are not essential for the "white" economy should be settled in the homelands. Racial equality in the job market and further sharing of public facilities are opposed. (2) *The pragmatists*. Separate development is only a means to the end of political stability. They wish to create a stable black middle-class with common capitalist interests and a stake in containing black unrest. This they hope to achieve mainly by the rapid abolition of job reservation and the promotion of economic growth. In the social field they insist for the immediate future on the "identity component" of their policy with separate state schools and residential areas as the keystones, but they favor the improvement of public facilities, living conditions, and business opportunities in the black group areas.

In the political field serious disagreement exists about the strategies that should be adopted toward the various non-white groups and how to achieve a greater measure of stability. The unresolved problem is that the government still considers the various homeland structures as the major black decision-making units, which is rejected by the majority of urban blacks. Three tactics are advocated: (1)*Paternalistic con-*

219

sultation: On a basis of seniority, whites should consult with black leaders but black political rights should be restricted to responsibility for their own communal affairs in the homelands or black townships. (2) *Indirect rule:* The various non-white groups (first the Coloureds and Indians and later also the urban blacks) should have a right of say in their own communal and certain common affairs. However, white sovereignty in white affairs and almost the entire field of common affairs must remain under white control. (3) *Medeseggenskap:* (The Afrikaans word is ambivalent: it could mean only also having a "right of say" or it could refer to common decision-making.) Those who attach the latter meaning to the word favor a gradual evolution toward power-sharing, most probably in a consociational system in which various ethnic groups will participate and make decisions on the basis of consensus.

The new constitutional plan has been represented by the right wing of the party as indirect rule and by the left wing as an approach that implicitly entails common decision-making. To win acceptance for this plan, the party finds itself in a classic double bind. Only if a new dispensation provides for real power-sharing will authentic Coloured and Indian leaders be persuaded to participate in attempts to negotiate. However, if a new dispensation does involve power-sharing, the right wing of the party threatens to break away, raising the specter of a divided ethnic group.

It is possible that chronic instability may prompt a faction to explore strategies for genuine power-sharing or even a form of supraethnic class rule, which, of course, is largely the antithesis of what the Afrikaner ethnic movement embarked upon. For the present, however, the main significance of the proposed new constitutional dispensation is that the government has conceded the unacceptability of the status quo at least insofar as the Coloureds and Indians are concerned. With regard to the urban blacks, who are still excluded from any proposals for constitutional reform, it is difficult to predict how the party will respond to pressures to accommodate them in a common political system. As has been pointed out above, the elitist nature of the party and its loyal following make it possible for the leadership to introduce changes provided unity is not their prime concern. But it is impossible to anticipate the specific configuration of events that would permit the emergence of a leader who would be willing to embark on fundamental reforms of the apartheid structure as it relates to the blacks.

THE APARTHEID BUREAUCRACY

The swollen apartheid bureaucracy is the stronghold of the defenders of the Verwoerdian ideology. Here separate development has assumed tangible form in the apartheid structures of the state—the departments of Bantu Administration (Plural Relations), Coloured Affairs, Indian Affairs, Community Development, and so forth. The ongoing efforts to structure South Africa further along separate lines come from these departments, which guard against the demolition of the existing structures.

In its relationship with the officials who administer the racial order, the National Party has come almost full circle. When the party assumed power in 1948, Native Affairs and several other state departments were headed by more liberal-minded incumbents, opposed to the incoming government's apartheid policies. Soon members of the National Party caucus became convinced that these officials were using every opportunity to delay or thwart the implementation of the apartheid policy. It was alleged that Native Affairs officials burdened the Minister of Native Affairs, E. G. Jansen, with minor decisions with the result that he was unable to devote his attention to the broader aspects of policy. When Jansen failed to remove obstructive officials in key positions, the Native Affairs group in the party caucus attempted to force him into action or alternatively have him replaced as minister. The government, against the will of the Public Service Commission, then appointed W. W. M. Eiselen, one of the architects of the policy of apartheid, as Secretary for Na-

221

tive Affairs and in 1950 Verwoerd as minister. Together they imposed their will and policy on the department. Only much later was it sensed that the government succeeded in implementing key aspects of its policy such as more rigorous influx control and the removal of some of the vested rights of urban blacks.[21]

Verwoerd embarked on the elaboration of the apartheid policy and the creation of a vast bureaucratic structure. Just before he became prime minister in 1958 he was under fire within the party for creating "an empire of unprecedented scale out of his own department—a state within a state."[22] Verwoerd more than any other prime minister before or after him imbued the bureaucracy with his particular political vision. "He attracted not pliable servants but like-minded ideologues," a top bureaucrat who had worked in close association with him would later recount (personal interview). Today the apartheid bureaucracy is staffed mainly by men dedicated to the ideology of separate development. They form the resident opposition in the National Party to any attempts at reforms of the Verwoerdian blueprint. Marinus Wiechers, a constitutional expert and legal advisor to the Bophuthatswana government, observed: "However optimistic or pessimistic you are about the willingness of politicians to change in South Africa, it is virtually impossible for them to break through the bureaucratic barrier. We have created a vast 'plural administration' to prove the fact that we are a plural society. In the long run this administration, which should be the servant of society, has become its master."[23]

The strength of the bureaucracy lies first in the maze of laws, rules, and regulations that governs South Africa. For instance, about 4,000 laws and 6,000 regulations affect the private sector alone.[24] Cabinet ministers have to rely greatly on the bureaucrats for guidance on how the complex system

21. Schoeman, *Van Malan tot Verwoerd*, p. 21.

22. Heard, *General Elections*, p. 72.

23. Cited in Ivor Wilkins, "A Nation of Bureaucrats," *Sunday Times*, July 16, 1978.

24. Ibid.

really works and what is possible within the legal framework. If a minister and his officials are of one mind, the department runs smoothly; if not, serious problems arise. A cabinet minister explained in a personal interview:

> A minister can never know all the laws and is dependent on his senior civil servants for guidance. If they come into conflict with each other on personal or policy issues they can complicate his task enormously. They can slow down the implementation of policy initiatives they dislike. By supplying the minister with wrong or inadequate information they can cause him to make errors which can have a disastrous effect on his image. It is like driving a car with the handbrake on.

The option of sacking obstructionist civil servants is virtually closed to ministers. Civil servants enjoy entrenched rights and can only be dismissed on specified grounds and according to a set procedure of investigation where they are allowed legal representation. Ministers do have some limited scope to transfer obstructionist civil servants to other departments, but this could damage their image or unleash ideological conflicts within the party, something that most of them would rather not risk.

The bureaucrats are further strengthened by the system of recruitment of cabinet ministers. With some notable exceptions they are appointed to the cabinet because of service to the party and political legwork rather than their technocratic skills. Small-town lawyers and party organizers by profession rise, after some years in Parliament, to positions of power where they are subject to intense pressure since all lobbying in South Africa is directed at ministers. They suddenly have to make delicate decisions on a myriad of intricate matters. In the apartheid bureaucracies they have to devise ways of coping with the elaborate legal web of racial legislation that has been spun during the past two or three decades. (According to a computation of the Institute of Race Relations, 353 acts specifically affect the lives of Africans.) In such circumstances the recommendations of the top bureaucrats have a significant effect on the policy decisions cabinet ministers have to make in the daily administration of the country.

An academic who has worked with several departments sums up their position and role:

I am convinced that the higher echelons of the civil service exercise a definite influence on policy. More than 80 percent of the white civil servants are Afrikaners. The present civil service has grown up with the traditional policy of apartheid which it has been administering for thirty years. Senior civil servants have gained their positions because they were acquainted with, and faithfully carried out, the existing policies. I am convinced (in fact, I have experienced it myself) that when legislation is prepared the civil servants simply proceed to interpret the policy. Ministers who dare to deviate from the existing policy would definitely encounter stiff resistance in the civil service. Civil servants who have promotion in mind will of course not act contrary to National Party policy and a minister who is dependent on the loyalty and co-operation of his civil servants will in turn not challenge their interpretation of these policies. I am convinced that civil servants can make or break a minister (Personal communication)

Another source of the bureaucrats' power lies in the unwillingness of the cabinet to challenge squarely the Verwoerdian blueprint. This enables the bureaucracies, who have a direct interest in the maintenance of the apartheid structures, to legitimize their interests and actions in terms of the ideology. Their power is bolstered by the cabinet's style of "reform by permit," that is, using permits to desegregate, to circumvent its own laws, as it were. Another academic who has had intensive discussions with several senior civil servants in various departments describes their role in the power structure as follows:

You should always remember the bureaucrats are the most loyal supporters of the party. The ideology underpins their

job and status in the apartheid structures of the bureaucracy. They have acquired enormous power through the
permit system. The pragmatism of the leadership ultimately means that it realizes that separate development in
its present form cannot work, but it is not prepared to relax
control. Concessions may be made through permits; however, when these concessions are abused or become politically costly the permits can be revoked. The concession to
non-whites to trade in the central business districts is a
good case in point. A top bureaucrat said to me: "We will
issue these permits but the policy of separate development
stays: it is like a sjambok on the wall. When concessions are
abused we can resort to the sjambok." Because cabinet
ministers are too busy it is often left to the bureaucrats to
decide whether to issue a permit. It is difficult to overestimate their power. It is obvious that the bureaucracy is
strongest where the minister is weakest. But even strong
ministers have privately despaired of overriding the resistance of a bureaucracy who thinks and acts in the Verwoerdian ideological mould. (Personal interview)

It may be useful to illustrate the way in which the interests
and actions of the bureaucracy intrude upon the political process by means of five specific case studies: (1) Coloured Affairs, (2) Bantu Administration, (3) Urban leaseholds, (4)
Namibia, and (5) Bophutatswana independence.

Coloured Affairs

Government commissions are often considered the only
compromise for a cabinet that is unwilling to challenge
squarely the apartheid heritage and to free itself of some of its
ideological and bureaucratic shackles. The apartheid bureaucracy sees commissions that recommend moving away from
the principles of separate development as an attack on itself
and on the ideology. And because the cabinet does not have
an embracing conceptual alternative to separate development, the bureaucracy is often successful in sinking the recommendations of commissions.

The fate of the Theron Commission appointed to investigate the condition of the Coloured people illustrates this. The report of the commission effectively challenged the existence of the Department of Coloured Affairs, which is par excellence a creation of the ideology of separate development. The Commission recommended that the University of Western Cape and the Peninsula College for Advanced Technical Education be transferred from the Department of Coloured Affairs to the Department of National Education; the Coloured Development Corporation to the Department of Economic Affairs; Coloured sport to the Department of Sport; Coloured cultural affairs to the Department of National Education; agricultural affairs to Agriculture; and welfare services to the Department of Social Welfare and Pensions. If all these recommendations were implemented, only Coloured school education and the (interracial) public relations committees would have remained under Coloured Affairs. In all other respects their affairs and those of the whites would have been administered by the same departments.

For the Department of Coloured Affairs such recommendations meant transfers of civil servants to other departments and possible loss of seniority or promotion. Initially the government responded cautiously but not unfavorably to the report of the Theron commission. Eight months later the White Paper, drawn up by the Department of Coloured Affairs and the other state departments involved, was tabled. In the White Paper those departments came out strongly against the findings and recommendations of the commission. In the end only a minor recommendation for the transfers mentioned above was accepted: Coloured library services were transferred to the Department of National Education. In most other instances the bureaucracy and the ideology it served remained intact.

The bureaucrats were of course not in the position to reject these recommendations simply because they threatened their own interests. However, they could conduct the fight on an ideological level and were successful primarily because the government was unwilling to break with the Verwoerdian blueprint. They were also aided by the fact that a relatively weak minister assumed control of the Department of Coloured Affairs. Moreover, both the Theron commission and the cabinet were split on the most important recommendations. In such a context the bureaucrats' vested interests were virtually unassailable.

Bantu Administration (Plural Relations)

It is in this department that bureaucratic interests and ideological commitment are most acute. During the past twenty-five years officials of the vast Bantu Administration empire have acquired a vested interest in the status quo. Through their control over township housing they exercise authority over the occupants. If full property rights were granted not only would they lose the accompanying status but several of their jobs would become redundant. Also, if the townships were to be run by black councils, the administrative machinery would increasingly become Africanized. The result would be that even more white officials would lose their present jobs. Understandably the bureaucracy of Bantu Administration is strongly cast in the ideological mould that blacks are temporary sojourners without vested rights in "white" South Africa and that the administration of the townships should rest with the bureaucracy. With the help of M. C. Botha, the responsible minister, the Bantu Administration bureaucrats effectively killed the Urban Bantu Councils for which enabling legislation was passed in the early 1960s. Only after the Soweto upheavals did this matter again recieve government attention.

Urban Leasehold

The role of the bureaucracy is highlighted by the struggle that ensued in the evolution of a more satisfactory form of tenure and home ownership for urban blacks.[25] In the wake of the 1976 upheavals the govenment announced as part of its new deal for urban blacks that it would grant them a meaningful form of security in the townships. When the Urban Foundation was established at the beginning of 1977 with the objective of improving the quality of life in urban communities,

25. This section is based on personal interviews.

one of the priorities was to give meaning and content to this undertaking by the government. Time and again it articulated the importance of home ownership for blacks that was of a lengthy duration and capable of being freely transferred and bequeathed.

Although the government had set its face against the granting of freehold title, it had indicated a willingness to implement a scheme along these lines. The bureaucracy of the Bantu Administration Department, however, resisted this and worked to introduce as limited a scheme as could be enacted. It prevaricated on the drafting of legislation and first submitted a draft that only provided for a lease of limited duration that contained none of the essentials for private sector participation in the financing process. Only determined efforts on the part of the Urban Foundation and the Association of Building Societies, stimulated by an appreciation on the part of the political leadership that private sector resources could be made available to assist the state in eliminating the housing backlog for urban blacks, made the evolution of a new scheme possible. Ultimately a scheme was enacted that provided for 99-year leasehold tenure for qualified urban blacks, capable of transfer and bequest to others who also qualify for permanent rights in the urban areas. While some black leaders privately accepted the leasehold scheme as a major advance that could ultimately be converted into freehold, it was rejected by others such as Dr. Motlana of the Soweto Committee of Ten who insisted that the principle of freehold title be accepted. At the time of writing it is still not yet a reality because the regulations that are necessary to give it content have not yet been promulgated.

Independence for South West Africa/Namibia

In March 1978 the newspaper *Die Republikein* reported on the friction caused by civil servants in the northern territories of the country who persisted in implementing the homelands policy despite black resistance and the fact that this was in conflict with South Africa's agreement with the Western Five. The civil servants claimed that the homelands policy for

South West Africa had not been officially discarded by the Department of Bantu Administration (Plural Relations).[26]

Bophuthatswana Independence

The role of the Bantu Administration bureaucrats might be illustrated by giving the record of an interview with a participant in the negotiations between the South African and Bophuthatswana governments on that territory's independence. (It is published here with a minimum of editing.)

The main thing that has come out of these negotiations is that homeland independence is something for the officials. They have lived with this for so many years and everything that may stand in the way—lack of consolidation, black administrative know-how, etc.—is just going to be bulldozed, they are going to carry it out to its final conclusion and deprive these people of their South African citizenship and give them independence, in whatever size or condition this homeland may be. They have got their standard agreements, they want everyone to adhere to them and they don't want much resistance in this negotiation process.

Once the Bophuthatswana cabinet had decided to opt for independence the whole thing was steamrolled in an incredible way. The two main contentious issues, the retention of South African citizenship and consolidation of the homelands, were played down in the working committee all the time by Bantu Administration officials who persuaded the Bophuthatswana representatives first to pass all the various agreements, about sixty of them. It was remarkable the dexterity of the officials. If something cropped up; if the Tswana representatives would question something, e.g. consolidation, they would say: let's refer it back and carry on. The whole process of independence was so highly geared that the blacks were just being pulled along all the time. On consolidation, the Tswanas were

26. *Die Republikein* (Windhok), March 22, 1978.

unhappy all the time; they were battling, they were trying this and the other thing but it was just all the time promised the final plans will come up. Until right up to the end when it was said: these are the final consolidation plans, we can after independence negotiate on other lands. Everything, the plans for consolidation etc. were drawn up by the department and proposed to them.

On citizenship the Bophuthatswana government was very adamant that they don't want to deprive their people of their "birthright" which is South African citizenship and in the negotiations it was more or less agreed that the Tswanas will have a free choice to decide whether they will revoke their Tswana citizenship and retain South African citizenship or the other way round. It was put to them that it was the same if a man acquires also German or American citizenship, that he then can decide to relinquish his South African citizenship. This was agreed to by the Tswanas but what they did not realise, until they finally saw the Status Act, was that at the date of independence they would lose their South African citizenship. The fact is that it has never been explained to the Tswanas in the process of negotiation that this is not negotiable: at the time of independence you lose your South African citizenship. The attitude of the officials in the negotiation was just to bulldoze the issue.

When the Bophuthatswana representatives realized that there was no way to retain their South African citizenship they concentrated on other things: the rights of ex-South African citizens living in South Africa; that they would retain all their rights and privileges. The Tswanas and even the South African Prime Minister were shocked when the officials at a very late stage during the negotiations acknowledged that the legal position was that Tswanas living in the republic after independence would have the status of a prohibited immigrant. Eventually the Tswanas got an agreement that they would maintain their rights (section 10, representation in community councils, everything) and that these would even be extended after independence.

We also asked for an agreement that if any disputes arise from this agreement then they would be referred to a tri-

bunal, consisting of three judges. This was met with considerable resistance from the officials. It was resented, it
was resisted by the officials right to the end. I got the impression all the way that independence was going to be
worked out in accordance with set principles: the deprivation of citizenship and agreements which the blacks will be
presented with and that the officials are not going to depart
from that. Everything that cropped up from the other side
was met with considerable resentment from the officials.
These negotiations, e.g. on citizenship are done in an extremely paternalistic way, according to set ideas on the
grounds on which blacks will get independence. It is very
difficult for the blacks in this negotiating process to stand
up and say: this is what we want.

When the government in June 1978 published the bill
enacting its 99-year leasehold plan for urban blacks it became clear that the children of Africans who qualify for the
leasehold would not inherit this right if their parents were
citizens of an independent homeland and they were born
after the day of independence. The Bophuthatswana government objected to this bill depriving their children's descendants of leasehold. After negotiations it was agreed by
the South African government, in terms of their own
agreement that citizens of independent homelands would
not be worse off in any way than before his homeland
became independent, that children's descendants can have
leasehold rights and would qualify under section 10 for
permanency in the urban areas. On 13 June 1978 Mulder,
the Minister for Plural Relations moved an amendment to
the bill which stipulated that all future generations of urban
blacks who qualified for the leasehold plan would also have
a right to leasehold.

Question: Did Mulder move the amendment because he
did not realise what the bill provided for?

That is so astonishing if he has really realised what was
agreed upon in the negotiations with the Tswanas. I cannot
understand how on earth they could have introduced a bill

like that. It must have been drawn up by the officials and the Minister must have been asked to put this before Parliament.

Question: Does the Minister have much to do with that or does he simply take what he gets from the bureaucrats?

My impression is that the Minister in these technical matters has very little to say and that he leaves it to his officials. He takes the bill as he gets it to Parliament, often without having had the time to study it carefully. All he has is a memorandum the officials have drawn up to explain it to Parliament. My impression is in these instances the officials have a very clear interpretation of what constitutes policy. The officials draw up the legislation and they decide what to put in and it is very difficult, unless the Minister is very knowledgeable, to say I won't take this and this is the way you are going to draw it up. Bantu Administration officials are very knowledgeable. They draw up legislation the way they want it and according to their very set ideology.

THE NATIONALIST AFRIKAANS PRESS

If the apartheid bureaucrats are the resident opposition to the breaking down of the structure of separate development, the present Afrikaans daily newspapers, all of which support the National Party, constitute the most important institutional pressure within the Afrikaner community against the too rigid application of this policy. This is a relatively new role for the Nationalist press. In the 1930s and 1940s it crusaded on behalf of the ethnic movement, moving in step with the party. Between 1948 and 1968 it acted as publicity agents for the policies of apartheid and separate development. The exception was the daily, *Die Burger*, published by Nasionale Pers in Cape Town. After the power base in the party had shifted to the north in the 1950s, *Die Burger* proceeded to articulate a distinct "Cape voice" in the party. In 1965 the

Cape-based Nasionale Pers established a national Sunday newspaper, *Die Beeld*, in Johannesburg. This was part of the ongoing economic battle between the northern and southern Afrikaans publishing houses, but it was also a determined attempt by Nasionale Pers to carry the Cape voice to the Transvaal. A senior executive of Nasionale Pers gave the following account of the line of thinking:

> We in the Nasionale Pers thought that there would not be another Cape Prime Minister. Consequently we decided in the 1950s that alternative ways would have to be sought to ensure that the Cape voice continue to make an impact on the party and the people. What is the Cape voice? Nationalists in the Cape have firstly stood for the principle that the Coloureds should be treated differently from the Bantu. Secondly we believed that segregation and discrimination should not be ends in themselves but that those aspects of the policy which stressed communal development and fulfillment should carry equal weight. In general we favoured a softer, more liberal implementation of apartheid. This was anathema to the Transvaal nationalists. When told of Nasionale Pers plans to expand to the North, Strijdom, who was then Prime Minister, said immediately: this will split the party in two! In 1965, Verwoerd ordered a boycott of *Die Beeld* even before it appeared.

The appearance of *Die Beeld* in 1965 under the editorship of Schalk Pienaar did precipitate the *verkramp-verlig* split in the party. *Die Beeld* heralded the "new Afrikaans journalism," characterized by a much greater sense of independence of Nationalist newspapers, and it was followed by other Afrikaans papers. This greater sense of independence was directly related to historical developments within the ethnic movement, which by the 1960s had achieved most of its political ideals. The party no longer feared defeat at the polls and criticism was no longer considered dangerous. At this time too the Afrikaners were enjoying greatly increased material prosperity. The growing self-confidence of the Afrikaners was reflected in the press where professional journalists from successful publishing houses were not prepared to be "paid parrots" of the party. The greatly respected Schalk Pienaar, pioneer of the independent Nationalist journalism, first sensed the growing gap between the existing realities and the past assumptions on which the policy was based. Without challenging the basic structure of white domination, Pienaar and some other independent Nationalist journalists in the late 1960s began to stress the need for properly recognizing the human dignity of blacks and the removal of "bottlenecks" that caused group conflict and were unnecessary to policy implementation. In the 1970s they championed economic reforms that would increase productivity and black mobility, the rights of blacks to home ownership in the urban areas, and a new political deal for the Coloureds and Indians. These calls had been made much earlier by the English press in South Africa; but it did so as "external critics" while the Afrikaans journalists spoke as partisans and a "loyal opposition."[27]

In assessing the role of the Afrikaans press, Gerrit Viljoen in 1974 remarked: "We have to realize that lately extremely strong, independent and influential leaders among our newspaper editors have come to the fore, taking their place in their own right next to—and I think in some instances even ahead of—our acknowledged leaders. Increasingly these journalistic leaders set the pace, take the initiative and determine the aims."[28] Since the watershed events of 1974 to 1977, the accent of press comments on National Party policies has shifted. Before 1974 the press was concerned with moderating the way in which separate development was implemented, criticizing the application of policy when it was too expensive, harsh, or detrimental for the party's image. The present

27. For an overview of the South African press in the 1960s see Elaine Potter, *The Press as Opposition: The Political Role of the South African Newspapers* (London: Chatto and Windus, 1975).

28. "Redakteurs gee die pas en toon aan," *Beeld*, October 4, 1974.

leading opinion makers among the press—*Die Transvaler*, *Beeld*, and *Rapport*—have now begun to question the fundamental principle of the policy that there should be no political rights for blacks outside the homeland framework. Unlike the party, these papers have been much more ready to acknowledge that the new constitutional plan does in effect entail some power sharing with Coloureds and Indians. In general there has been an acceptance that alternatives to separate development should be explored. This was articulated as follows by W. J. de Klerk who is at present the most prominent Afrikaans editor:

The old long-term theory of evolutionary development of the black and Coloured man towards political maturity has got stuck.... The attitude of no power sharing is unacceptable to both black and Coloured.... Discrimination is too interwoven in our policy for us to move away from it according to the old model of the policy.[29]

While the Nationalist press insists on its right to criticize the party's representatives and some of its policies, it does not oppose the party that it considers to be the only vehicle that can promote ethnic interests in the political sphere. The Nationalist press willingly accepts the confines of what Schalk Pienaar has called "independence-in-commitment,"[30]

29. *Rapport*, April 4, 1976.
30. Schalk Pienaar, "Die Afrikaner en sy Koerant," *Standpunte*, 108, August 1973, pp. 1–5. Dirk Richard, editor of *Die Vaderland*, formulated the role of the Afrikaans press as follows: "The Afrikaans Press does not forget the reason for its political existence. It is there to promote the cause of Afrikaner Nationalism and the Government's policy of separate development. It must temper its natural right and inclination to criticise with this unalterable condition: the criticism must also take a positive attitude towards Nationalism and South Africa.... The party, on the other hand,... must not grudge the Press its position of independence and status as a critical ally. The old master-servant relationship has gone for ever... [Afrikaans newspaper editors] will not allow themselves to be deprived of the right to speak out when they believe that silence would be harmful to the Nationalist cause." (*Die Vaderland*, November 29, 1976).

striving to maintain credibility on two levels: as newspapers and as Nationalist organs. As newspapers they have the obligation to publicize party blunders and bureaucratic bungling: "to expose in order to rectify what is wrong."[31] Failing this, they would simply lose readers to their rivals, particularly the English press. But they must also retain credibility as Nationalist newspapers. As part of the establishment the press is playing fundamentally on the same team. Persistent criticism would entail the loss of that measure of influence a newspaper has on the party and Afrikaner elite in general who would write it off as an echo of the English press. Consequently, every Afrikaans newspaper is obliged to make a frequent bow to the party's program and leaders and to launch an occasional attack on the English press or opposition party even in instances where they work toward the same goal of reform. As a result, the pleas for reform in the Afrikaans press come across mutedly. Ethnic fears and suspicions, the demands of the vicious circulation battle in the North (where there are five Afrikaans dailies with a market for perhaps only two), and the desire to please the political establishment vie with enlightened sentiments in a message that is lacking in consistency and often fails to carry conviction and transmit a sense of urgency.

The following instances of the ambivalence of various Afrikaans newspapers can be cited: While championing mixed sport *Die Vaderland* published several exposés of mixed nightclubs calling them "dens of immorality" and virtually forcing a massive police crackdown on these clubs. *Die Burger* was for a long period editorially the most independent of the Afrikaans newspapers. However, it has rarely criticized any issue on which the National Party of the Cape Province has taken a specific stand, for instance the removal of the Africans from the Western Cape and the demolition of the squatter camps. On the issue of these camps its reporting varied between the objective and the blatantly partisan while its editorials

31. Schalk Pienaar in *Rapport*, November 30, 1975.

showed no attempts to see both sides of the case. It went further, criticizing those opposed to squatter demolition, the paper persisted in imputing ulterior motives to them. (It should be added that a new editor in 1977 took over from Piet Cillie, one of the giants of Afrikaner journalism.) *Beeld*, which usually takes a reformist line, sided against *Die Transvaler* when it attacked crude racist sentiments emanating from the Natal National Party congress in August 1978. Trailing 16,000 copies behind *Die Transvaler* in a bitter circulation battle that puts a heavy financial burden on the rivalling publishing houses, *Beeld* has adopted the strategy of accepting the role of mouth piece of the party in the Transvaal. *Die Transvaler* of the Perskor group again attempted to whitewash Eschel Rhoodie and the Department of Information scandals at a time when the Nasionale Pers newspapers had withdrawn all support. This paper formed part of the Department of Information-SABC-Perskor "axis" existing at the time.[32]

Both the Afrikaans and English press—the first with its accent on ethnic interests, the second on capitalist growth—remain within the framework of white power and are part of the political and social system of South Africa. They want to build more stable structures of domination without interfering with the substance of power and the distribution of wealth. In varying degrees both criticize the executive's style of wielding power without wishing to transform the present order radically. The government tends to dismiss criticism of the English press as "unpatriotic" and is often much more irritated by strictures which appear in Afrikaans newspapers. However, it accepts, albeit reluctantly, the new role of the Afrikaans press as an independent ally, perhaps because it realizes that a credible Afrikaans press in a legitimacy crisis is a better support than the South African Broadcasting Corpo-

32. The SABC alone adhered to the government's request not to publicize revelations by Justice Mostert in the scandal of the Department of Information.

ration, which still remains an echoing chamber for govern-ment views.[33]

The Afrikaans press had played an important role in educating the Afrikaner public, in combatting racist beliefs and crude racist practices. The question that arises, however, is whether it has adequately prepared the Afrikaners for the more fundamental changes that may await them in the future? While the more "open" Afrikaans newspapers during the past decade have constantly been compelled to maintain their credibility as Nationalist organs, their main challenge in the future would be to remain reliable sources of information on the South African political situation.

Over the past twenty-five years the areas of permissible reporting has been steadily reduced by legislation aimed not at the press in the first instance, but at other agencies.[34] It has become increasingly difficult, for instance, to report adequately on prison conditions because of the restrictive na-ture of the law (the Prisons Act) and uncertainties about the precise meaning and interpretation of some of the provisions. The Defence Act, too, contains restraints, including a censor-ship clause, which makes full reporting of defense matters impossible. Similar considerations apply to the Official Se-crets Act and other security legislation. Another area where newspapers have to tread warily because of the difficulty of knowing just what the legislature meant, is in the field of human relations, where "engendering feelings of hostility be-tween the races" is a crime. In addition, the Internal Security Act (previously the Suppression of Communism Act) pre-vents newspapers from propagating Communism or any of its aims and from quoting anyone listed as a Communist or who has been banned in terms of the Act. In the final resort, of course, the State has the power through the Internal Secu-

33. A recent survey has shown that 81 percent of political news of the TV service has centered on government or National Party officials. Cited by Ivor Wilkins, "Nats get 80 per cent of TV coverage," *Sunday Times* (Johannesburg), July 16, 1978.

34. For a full discussion of such publication restraints see Kelsey Stuart, *Newspaperman's Guide to the Law* (Durban: Butterworth, 1978).

rity Act to ban newspapers by proclamation, as it did in the case of the English papers *The World* (a daily), *The Weekend World* (a weekly), and *Pro Veritate* (a monthly) in October 1977.

This legal situation has produced a great reluctance to cover sensitive areas with the result that a South African abroad, reading the reports of foreign journalists based in South Africa, is sometimes better informed than his compatriots at home. Apart from this publication restraint there is also what can be called benign self-censorship. Afrikaans and English newspapers for a long period refrained from drawing attention to the racial integration of sport (particularly cricket) at the private club level and of Catholic schools that were quietly tolerated by the government. The press, which favored these developments, did not publish reports on this, fearing that publicity would simply lead to a police clampdown on mixed sport or integrated schools. The question is whether they should not rather have informed the public, spelling out the goals and principles of reform.[35]

Lastly, the Afrikaans press has failed to report adequately on the hopes and aspirations, suffering and frustrations of the black community. This has taken its toll in business terms. With the exception of *Die Burger*, which has 127,000 Coloured readers and 204,000 whites, the Afrikaans dailies have an almost exclusively white readership at a time when the white newspaper market has very nearly reached the saturation point.[36] The political cost of an uninformed public may be considerably higher.

The growing influence of the press during the past fifteen years has been accompanied by a corresponding decline in the influence of other traditionally influential Afrikaner institutions, particularly the church and the universities and also the Broederbond in which the elite of these institutions is incorpo-

35. See the perceptive article on this by H. Pakendorff, "Praat hardop oor nuwe wendinge," *Oggendblad*, March 31, 1978.

36. The Sunday newspaper *Rapport* has more Coloured readers than the *Sunday Times*, see C. A. Giffard, "Media Trends in South Africa," unpublished paper, The Road Ahead Conference, July 1978.

rated. A review of these organizations will conclude with an analysis of the Security Apparatus.

THE CHURCH

While the small Reformed (Dopper) Church based in Potchefstroom has recently articulated a distinct, Calvinistic voice in its *Woord en Daad* journal, the Afrikaans church is, for all practical purposes, the Dutch Reformed Church. Some 40 percent of the white population and 70 percent of the Afrikaner people belong to it, including the overwhelming majority of cabinet ministers. In all but name it is the established church, sometimes disdainfully referred to by outsiders as "the National Party in prayer."

Together with the party and the Broederbond, the church in the 1940s and 1950s played a key role in winning general acceptance among its members for the view that there is no fundamental contradiction between Christian principles and the apartheid program. However, tensions still existed on the level of the church elite, while a few influential theologians resisted attempts to justify apartheid in church and state on biblical grounds. A series of ecumenical conferences in the 1950s created theological fluidity. This was a decade in which the Afrikaans clergy were among the leading opinion-makers while many waited for the church to reach a clear position on the burning issues of the day. This happened early in the 1960s. After the shootings at Sharpeville in which 69 Africans died, followed by the declaration of a state of emergency, the World Council of Churches took the initiative of convening an interchurch conference on race relations in South Africa. At the conference held at Cottesloe, Johannesburg, in December 1960 the delegates of the Dutch Reformed Church associated themselves with the resolutions stating that urban blacks could not be denied home ownership and participation in the government, that migrant labor had a disintegrating effect on the family life of Africans, that Coloureds could not be denied direct representation in Parliament, that no biblical grounds existed for the prohibtition of mixed marriages, and that no one may be excluded from any church on grounds of color or race. Verwoerd immediately appealed over the heads of Dutch Reformed delegates to the church at large, demanding in effect that a choice be made between the sentiments of these delegates and party policy. Shortly afterward the church leadership repudiated the Cottesloe resolutions and in so doing made the decision for the average layman.[37]

In recent years a slight theological shift has taken place. Apartheid in church and state is being justified less on strictly biblical grounds and more on practical considerations. At the same time there has been an even more pronounced identification with the party's policies. In 1965 the Cape synod described migrant labor as a cancer in South African society. But in 1974 the attempt by the Landman commission to express a critical note was stifled when the general synod voted to take cognizance of but not to accept passages criticizing the conditions under which Africans had to live and work, as well as passages saying that these conditions were un-Christian.[38] If Edward Munger was correct in stating in 1957 that "The Dutch Reformed Churches are in no position to oppose the National Party—and the National Party is in no position to oppose the *Kerk*,"[39] the latter part of the statement is certainly no longer true. Even in the field of public morality, in which the church has traditionally claimed to be an arbitrator, the needs of state prevail. Despite the strong opposition of the church to a state lottery, the government in 1977 went ahead with its scheme to raise money for defense purposes in a similar manner. In a matter such as censorship the church exercises a strong influence, but here too the state plays a mediating role, ultimately defining moral standards in a censorship system that steers between the church's precepts of morality and the demands of the secularized public. The trend is toward the state increasingly assuming an indepen-

37. A. H. Luckhoff, *Cottesloe* (Cape Town: Tafelberg, 1978).
38. *The Argus,* October 23, 1974.
39. Cited by William Henry Vatcher, *White Laager: The Rise of Afrikaner Nationalism,* (New York: Praeger, 1965), p. 114.

dent role in the moral sphere. The church still has some political influence but mainly as a brake on reform rather than as an innovating force.

The declining role of the church is due to several factors. At the elite level there has been a tendency to avoid at almost any price a confrontation with the party. At the lay level there has been the ongoing process of secularization. Church attendance remains high, one reason being that it is important as a status requirement. However, the Afrikaner of the 1970s is much less inclined to look to the Church for guidance. The teaching of the church has hardly transformed the political values of its members. The studies of Cornie Alant in the early 1970s show that the most regular churchgoers are those with the greatest prejudice.[40] Here developments in the church correspond to those in comparable societies, particularly the American South.[41] They also confirm D. W. Howe's observation that over the past three centuries the growth of affluence within Calvinist groups has universally weakened the dynamic and prophetic voice of Calvinism, although it could regain strength when the group's existence became threatened.[42] Recently indeed a small but influential number of theologians and ministers has begun to argue that the true response of the church in the political crisis should be the practical implementation of the gospel of Christian brotherhood. Within the (white) Dutch Reformed Church they are still in a small minority and are unable to challenge the conservative leadership effectively. However, some of them play an important role in the brown and black Dutch Reformed churches that are now challenging squarely the white "mother" church on the issue of apartheid and the

40. Cornie Alant, "Die rol van die kerk in die moderne Afrikanersamelewing," in H. W. van der Merwe, ed., *Identiteit en Verandering* (Cape Town: Tafelberg, 1975), pp. 102–13 and the interview with him in Piet Meiring, *Die Kerk op pad na 2000* (Cape Town: Tafelberg, 1977).

41. I have elaborated on this in "The Malady of American Racism: A South African Perspective," *The Canadian Review of American Studies*, Vol. 2 (Fall 1974), pp. 202–09.

42. D. W. Howe, "The Decline of Calvinism," *Comparative Studies in Society and History*, June 1972, p. 320.

security legislation. Contributing some 70 percent of the budgets of these churches, the mother church at the 1978 synod firmly rejected calls for a joint synod and the integration of the various Dutch Reformed churches. Reformist theologians and ministers nevertheless are making some headway among the younger generation of Afrikaners who are growing impatient with the strong pietistic character of the church. With reference to the demolition of nearby squatter camps, the Stellenbosch student newspaper recently remarked: "Our Christian charity goes as far as ministering to the spiritual needs of blacks while people in our vicinity . . . are driven from their homes in winter time."[43]

THE UNIVERSITIES

Two phases can be discerned in the involvement of the Afrikaans universities with the ethnic movement: (1) During the first two or three decades of the movement the university of Stellenbosch in particular played a pioneering role in the ultimate rejection of the hegemonic ideology of British imperialism. (2) Since 1948 the Afrikaans universities have elaborated the value system and political ideology of the Afrikaner ruling group, regarding themselves as intimately linked with the ethnic group they serve. H. B. Thom, the former Rector of Stellenbosch, acknowledged a tension between the universalistic commitments of a university and ethnic interests, but to him it was the duty of the university to resolve this by performing in such a way that it wins the trust of the *volk*.[44] In a similar vein Gerrit Viljoen, Rector of Rand Afrikaans University, observed: "We have to take into account the reasonable norms and prejudices of the community without becoming slavishly conformist."[45]

Properly socialized at an early stage in a white community

43. *Die Matie*, August 25, 1978, editorial.

44. H. B. Thom, *Universiteit en Maatskappy* (Stellenbosch: University of Stellenbosch, 1965).

45. Gerrit Viljoen, *New Nation*, July 1972, p. 13.

characterized by *verzuiling* (separate ethnic schools, churches, and youth organizations), Afrikaner students arrive at ethnic universities that are well integrated in the Afrikaner communal life and do not manifest a strongly critical stance toward the political and social system.[46] As a result no study has as yet shown that university attendance brings about a lessening in racial prejudice in the sense of social distance.[47] A recent survey of Stellenbosch students has found that 77 percent of a sample of Afrikaans students uncritically accept the status quo.[48] Among students who are more critically inclined there is the belief that their proper role is not to consider political alternatives but to exercise the greatest measure of influence on future development by remaining acceptable to their own community.[49] The style has thus been to stay carefully within the confines of the political consensus prevailing at the time.[50] Only when important elements in the party veered toward *verligtheid* did any meaningful *verligte* movement develop at the university. In recent years the stirrings in the party about racial legislation such as the Mixed Marriages and the Immorality Act also had reverberations on the campuses. However, the national Afrikaans student movement, the ASB, rejected a call for the repeal of this legislation at its 1978 congress. It is difficult to see a reversal of the general trend of students following the lead of the party as long as the present pattern of political socialization remains the same.

46. See the relevant essays in H. W. van der Merwe and David Welsh, eds., *The Future of the University in Southern Africa* (Cape Town: David Philip, 1977).

47. J. P. Groenewald, *Sosiale Afstand by Afrikaanssprekendes: Verdere toeligting met'n streekproef van studente* (Cape Town: Sentrum vir Intergroepstudies, 1975); Louwrens Pretorius, "Partyvoorkeure van Studente: Stellenbosch, 1970–1974," Master's dissertation, University of Stellenbosch, 1977.

48. *Die Matie*, "Politieke Profiel van die Stellenbosse Student," August 11, 1978, p. 17.

49. See M. le Roux, "The New Afrikaner," in H. W. van der Merwe and D. Welse, eds., *Student Perspectives on South Africa* (Cape Town: David Philip, 1972), pp. 90–91.

50. See Willem Adriaan (pseudonym), "Stellenbosch: Wat gaan aan? Gaan daar iets aan?" *Deurbraak*, February 1973, pp. 10–11, 17.

The influence of intellectuals on the policy-making process has waned considerably since the first decade of National Party rule. With its weak political base the party was keen not to alienate any well-disposed intellectuals in the 1950s. It paid considerable attention to the research and recommendations of university-based organizations such as the South African Bureau for Racial Affairs (SABRA). While pointing out the impracticality of some recommendations, it encouraged "Nationalist-minded" intellectuals to play an innovating role in formulating the political goals of apartheid and in suggesting means to implement the policy. Strijdom told some Stellenbosch professors that as long as they acted in good faith they should be the advance guard of the *volk*.[51] Academics played a key role in the Tomlinson commission (1951–55), which suggested the development of reserved African areas as black homelands. A leading academic, W. W. M. Eiselen, was appointed Secretary of Native Affairs, to give substance to the concept of separate cultures.

Significantly, the party chose a former academic, H. F. Verwoerd, as prime minister at a time when it was elaborating its apartheid policy. Ironically, it was Verwoerd who largely demolished the independent role of the intellectuals. Verwoerd could expound the ideology of separate development better than any academic could. He was in fact the master of the ideology. He appropriated some of the ideas of certain SABRA intellectuals for the ideology and discarded those that did not fit into his grand scheme such as direct representation for Coloureds in Parliament and large government spending on and private investment in the Bantustans. Sometimes he gave the impression that he alone thought for the *volk*. After his death, one of his most persistent critics, declared: "He convinced the Nationalists that their policy of apartheid was ethical and not based on naked racism. The breakthrough for him was being able to convince the Afrikaner academics of this. Without them the policy would not have been able to survive."[52] This is an exaggera-

51. Cited by Thom, *Universiteit en Maatskappy*, p. 14.
52. Helen Suzman, cited in "Some Hated Me," *The Argus*, July 14, 1977.

tion of Verwoerd's personal role and underestimates the dynamic of the increased bureaucratization of apartheid. What Verwoerd did was to impose rigorous ideological discipline upon Afrikaner intellectuals, in which he was undoubtedly aided by a body such as the Afrikaner Broederbond. Dissidents were driven out and isolated politically. SABRA became a subservient intellectual arm of the party, serving mainly to imbue the youth with the Verwoerdian vision of separate development and conceiving even grander Verwoerdian schemes such as consolidated homelands and large scale rapid transit for black migrants to the homelands.

Only in the 1970s, when the party became aware of the defects of separate development, did it start to incorporate academics again in the political process. Five of the twelve white members of the Theron commission, appointed to investigate the condition of the Coloured population, were academics. Some of them played a key role in formulating the majority report that emphasized the structure of political impotence and material deprivation in which the Coloured people were trapped by this policy.[53] Afterward a member of the commission remarked: "It appears as if we now need a generation of Nationalist-minded academics to whom it is not granted to build (as we would have liked to) but to break down, with the proper measure of love and compassion, the ballast which the Nationalist Afrikaner establishment has accumulated in its long years of political power and privilege."[54] With the dimensions of the South African political crisis becoming ever clearer, a few Nationalist academics are now more prepared to challenge the official policy and ideology while still taking the party as the only viable base for reform.[55] The predominant style, however, is that of "ex-

53. For an analysis by a member of this commission, see S. J. Terreblanche, *Gemeenskapsarmoede* (Cape Town: Tafelberg, 1977).

54. S. J. Terreblanche, "Die Akademikus en die Politiek," *Woord en Daad*, July 1977, p. 6.

55. Lack of space does not permit a discussion of Afrikaner intellectuals outside the party and excluded from the Broederbond but who still identify with the ethnic group. They are sometimes called *verlore* (lost) Afrikaners.

pressing concern in closed meetings." Here the Afrikaner Broederbond plays an important role.

THE BROEDERBOND

The Broederbond was founded in 1918 to promote Afrikaner interests and the Afrikaans language. In 1928 it became a secret organization that restricted its membership to male Afrikaners. Desired recruits were described as those who strove for the ideal of an everlasting and separate Afrikaner nation, who would give preference to Afrikaners and other sympathetic persons and firms in economic, public, and professional life, who *were of sound financial standing* (my italics), and who were in every respect trustworthy. The stated aim was the creation of a consciousness among Afrikaners concerning their language, religion, traditions, country, and *volk*, and the promotion of the interests of the Afrikaner nation.[56]

In the 1930s and 1940s key figures in the political, cultural, and economic elite of the Afrikaners were enlisted. During this period the Bond operated in various spheres. Economically it was the driving force behind the movement to promote Afrikaner private capital and combat the influence of socialist trade unions.[57] Culturally it championed mother-tongue instruction in single medium schools. Politically it campaigned against British imperialism and worked for unity among the Afrikaners. During the war years, the Bond was unable to heal the breach within Nationalist Afrikanerdom between the National Party and the parapolitical Ossewa Brandwag movement, but it was apparently instrumental in bringing about the coalition between Malan's National Party and Havenga's Afrikaner Party, which many Ossewa Brandwag members had joined. It was this coalition that was

56. This is based on the constitution published in Brian M. du Toit, *Configurations of Cultural Continuity* (Rotterdam: Balkema, 1976), pp. 134–38.

57. See the article by Dan O'Meara, "The Afrikaner Broederbond, 1927–1948: Class Vanguard of Afrikaner Nationalism," *Journal of Southern African Studies* 3, no. 2 (1977), 156–86.

victorious in the election of 1948 and put the Nationalists in power.

Although overlapping membership existed, considerable problems arose after 1948 in establishing a sound relationship between the Bond and the party. Strijdom was adamant that the Bond should not interfere with political policy. Apart from consolidating Afrikaner unity, he saw it as the Bond's task to capture for the Afrikaners a greater share of commerce and the professions.[58] Toward the end of the 1950s the Bond was reinvigorated by its campaign to persuade the Afrikaner people at large that the time was ripe for the establishment of a Republic. Under Verwoerd there was a marked convergence of the Bond and the party. The Bond now served first as the disseminator of the ideology of separate development and, second, as he put it in a letter, "a closed debating forum for rational reflection on the best interests of the Afrikaner people" (personal interview with confidant). Less concerned now with economic goals, the Bond became specifically concerned with politics and ideological coherence. Toward the end of the 1960s tension again arose between the Bond and the party. Influential *verkrampte* elements in the Bond resisted the slight modification of the policy of separate development, sniping at the Nasionale Pers newspapers and indirectly at Vorster. They had a considerable braking effect until the HNP members were purged in the early 1970s. The Bond now lost much of its political influence above all to the bureaucrats who were in a strategic position to block reforms put forward by the Bond.[59]

Over the years the Bond's membership has grown steadily. In 1952 the organization consisted of 3,500 members of whom 2,039 were teachers, 905 farmers, 357 clergymen, 159 lawyers, and 60 members of Parliament, including the prime minister

58. Schoeman, *Van Malan tot Verwoerd*, p. 120.

59. J. H. P. Serfontein, a journalist who in the late 1960s had wide access to Bond documents, argues that in terms of independent political influence the Bond was the main loser and the Afrikaans press the main winner in the *verkramp-verlig* struggle of the time. See his *Die Verkrampte Aanslag* (Cape Town: Human and Rousseau, 1970), pp. 231–36.

and six cabinet ministers. According to a 1978 disclosure there were 11,190 members of whom the most numerous subgroup (20.4 percent) were described as educators. After the 2,424 educators come farmers (2,240), pensioners (1,124), businessmen (1,096), churchmen (848), public servants (518), lawyers (390), bankers (309), municipal employees (198), agriculturists (265), policemen (212), railwaymen (201), politicians (186), and employees of parastate organization (165). In addition, a junior affiliate of the Broederbond, the "Ruiterwag" ("Mounted Guard"), is estimated to have several thousand members.

Broederbond membership is elitist. In 1972 politicians who were members included the prime minister, virtually the entire cabinet, three-quarters of the National Party members of Parliament, 28 senators, 69 members of the provincial council, and 13 party organizers. Among the educators were 24 rectors of universities and teachers' training colleges—in practice this means almost every Afrikaans rector—the directors of education of the four provinces, the chairman of the national Educational Advisory Council, and the head of the Council for Social Research. Besides these educators there were also 171 university professors, 176 lecturers, 468 headmasters, 121 schoolmasters, and 647 teachers. Roughly half the total number of Afrikaans headmasters and inspectors were members. In the newspaper world, 16 managers of newspaper groups and all the Nationalist editors, with the possible exception of 2, belonged to the organization, but only 3 ordinary journalists were members. With a few exceptions the heads of all the civil service departments were Broeders. Nearly 40 percent of white Dutch Reformed Church ministers were estimated to be members in 1978.[60]

The impetus of the movement comes mainly from the Executive Council, consisting of twelve members, and the secretariat in Johannesburg. From here emanate the newsletters

60. The above two paragraphs are based on disclosures published in the *Sunday Times,* September 24; October 5, 8, and 15; and November 19, 1972; January 28 and February 4, 1973, and January 20, 1978.

that are discussed at the monthly meetings of the roughly 800 branches across the country. Through its "public arm," the Federasie van Afrikaanse Kultuurverenigings (F.A.K.), the Bond lays down broad guidelines and coordinates overall strategy for the more than 200 cultural, religious, and youth bodies affiliated with the F.A.K. The local branches are not passive recipients of head office circulars. They are invited to comment on these circulars and can exercise their prerogative to forward to the head office criticisms and suggestions with respect to the conduct of national affairs. These in turn can be circulated by the head office in subsequent newsletters. Drawn from leaders in various walks of life, branches also play an important role in local affairs. They act as a counter to dissident Afrikaners and to supranational organizations such as Lions International; and, if they wish, they can influence the composition of school committees, the appointment of important vacancies on the staff, and the election of local government bodies, particularly in rural areas. (These often occur on an informal basis and without instructions from the head office.) Local branches also nominate emerging young leaders in their district as members of the Bond.[61]

While the Bond still has a considerable impact as an "ethnic adhesive," its present political significance is usually misinterpreted by the press. It is incorrect to consider it as "the secret body which rules South Africa," manipulating the political process. At most, it imbues its members with a sense of ethnic discipline while the government tries to reach consensus on political issues. A Bond member who served on the Executive Council explained it as follows in an interview: "Its function is to prevent too wide a range of *public* dissent. We debate issues vigorously in private and then communicate our reflections to the head office. It helps the leadership to feel the pulse of the people and get some indication of the di-

61. To Afrikaners who are not members of the Bond it is a perennial question whether men rise to positions of power and influence because they are members of the Bond. The answer seems to be that a Nationalist-minded Afrikaner has to show some potential as a leader to become a member. His membership in turn is a boon to his career chances.

rection it should be moving." But with the gradual loss of ideological coherence, the Bond is finding it increasingly difficult to establish a national consensus, composed as it is of Verwoerdian ideologues, "pragmatic realists," and "radical" *verligtes*. In 1972, Schalk Pienaar, a member himself, remarked "Until recently the Bond could succeed in being a debating community (*gespreksgemeenskap*) which could contain the divergent views in the political life of the Afrikaner and enable collective action to take place. Obviously it is no longer the case."[62] Another newspaper editor declared: "The same quarrels, differences of opinion and gradual division which Afrikanerdom is experiencing in public has also permeated the Afrikaner Broederbond."[63]

In the present decision-making process the Bond acts as a secret communication channel between the government and the Afrikaner elite. It is both a generator of ideas suggested to the political leadership and a sounding board of government initiatives. These roles can be illustrated by reference to two recent political shifts. In the early 1970s when the party began to move toward a new sports policy the Bond brought members serving in sports-controlling bodies from all over the country together for a secret top-level discussion. The propositions emanating from this meeting were discussed by the Executive Council and submitted to the political leadership. With consensus being established among the leading sports administrators, the cabinet could move ahead more boldly; in the meantime, all Bond members were assured that the formulations of the Executive Council "will be reflected in official Government statements."[64] When the government announced in 1976 that it was exploring a constitutional alternative to the Westminster system of government, the Executive Council submitted a memorandum that drew on the political expertise of leading academics. After the proposals

62. Schalk Pienaar, "Broederbond: Vrae en Bedenkinge," *Rapport*, September 24, 1972.

63. Dirk Richard, "Na my mening," *Dagbreek en Sondagnuus*, September 13, 1970.

64. *Sunday Times*, September 24, 1972.

for a new constitution were announced, the Executive Council notified members that the "contents of our memorandum are in many respects reflected in the new dispensation for Coloureds and Indians."[65]

It should be stressed that the final decision rests with the cabinet, which, of course, can reject or ignore the suggestions of the Bond. Vorster mainly used it as a communication channel. He informed the Executive Council about the progress of the negotiations between South Africa and the West on Rhodesia. The council in turn assured members in a circular that the interests of South Africa are used as the only yardstick in the negotiations. He also kept the Executive Council informed of developments during the 1975–76 incursion into Angola. Whether P. W. Botha will make similar use of the Bond is not yet clear. A spate of disclosures of the Bond's activities—there are at the moment three books on the Bond in the press, one of which publishes some 6,000 names of members, or nearly 60 percent of the membership—has greatly diminished its value as a secret communication channel. On issues such as political rights for urban blacks, disagreements within the Bond are so deep-seated that it is unable to offer a firm suggestion. Here its present strategy is to hold wide-ranging discussions (called *dinkskrums*, "think tanks") initiating a process from which some consensus could emerge. There has been one such meeting between Broederbond leaders with the Chairman of the Soweto Committee of Ten and several discussions with Coloured leaders. By instilling into its members a sense of trust in the political leadership and as an agency that can legitimize government actions, the Bond is an important asset to the leadership. However, the Bond at large can clearly no longer produce an ethnic consensus on the complex and controversial issues of appropriate strategies for the maintenance of Afrikaner interests. As in the case of the party and the church, a decisive move to the left or the right will almost certainly precipitate an institutional split. However, such a move is unlikely in the im-

65. *Sunday Times*, January 20, 1978.

mediate future. In the meantime the bureaucracy guards over the apartheid structures.

THE SECURITY APPARATUS

As the assault on white rule in South Africa gathered force, the security apparatus of the state expanded. Once the preserve of English-speakers, the defense force has become predominantly Afrikaans. In 1974, 85 percent of the Army's permanent force staff consisted of Afrikaners while the corresponding figures for the Air Force and Navy were 75 percent and 50 percent respectively.[66] In the 1970s the military embarked on a recruiting campaign among the English. At the same time the exclusive racial character of the military began to change as Coloured, Indian, and African units were established. Committed to equal pay and status, the force is gradually becoming one of the most important nonracial institutions in the country.

So far the military has remained subservient to the civilian leadership. Its perceptions and priorities are brought to bear on the political leadership only through the Minister of Defence. Until now the military has avoided any direct political involvement. However, in public pronouncements top generals have constantly warned that the struggle cannot be won by military means alone. The recurring theme is that the "antirevolutionary struggle is 80 percent socio-economic and 20 percent military. If South Africa lost the socio-economic struggle we need not bother to fight the military one. The objective is no longer territory but the hearts and minds of men."[67]

Having embarked on a total strategy to win a predomi-

66. *The Star*, December 13, 1974, cited in P. A. Nel, "The Role of Technology, Organizational Culture and Ethnic Recruitment in the South African Forces—An Input for Change in South Africa," unpublished paper, July 1978.

67. See for instance the speech of General Boshoff, *Cape Times*, August 23, 1975.

nantly political war, the military's dilemma is that the political leadership has not yet clearly formulated the defensible political goals that such a strategy requires.[68] The military is also handicapped by the ad hoc style of the cabinet and the bureaucracy, which make decisions on a day-to-day basis without reviewing their implications for national security. There is no cabinet secretariat or national security council in which the important agencies of the executive branch could formulate their collective advice on the integration of domestic, foreign, and military policies in any manner touching the national security.

Until recently the military has exercised its influence mainly in pressing for clearer formulation of political goals and the establishment of a consultative body where strategic priorities can be decided. In this they have not been successful, but they have undoubtedly greatly gained influence under P. W. Botha.[69] This was dramatically illustrated when General Magnus Malan, Chief of the Defence Force, on October 16, 1978 joined the Prime Minister, the Minister of Foreign Affairs, and the Secretary for Foreign Affairs in the negotiations on Namibia with the five Western foreign ministers. In domestic matters the South African military is regarded as well to the left of the National Party parliamentary caucus or the cabinet. However, in certain matters such as withdrawal from Namibia and the consolidation of Zululand they are reported to be insisting on the paramountcy of strategic considerations. In other words, while some politicians favor a consolidated and enlarged Zululand as a sound move "to buy Buthelezi off," the military would see this as a military risk, endangering access to the strategic port of Durban. The military and P. W. Botha have enjoyed a harmonious relationship and it can be expected that as prime minister he will articulate much more effective military and strategic

68. See the interview with General Magnus Malan, Chief of the Defence Force, in the *Sunday Times*, January 1978.

69. At the time of the Angolan War a rudimentary security council, consisting of the prime minister and his closest military and intelligence advisers, apparently functioned but met only rarely afterward, under Vorster.

priorities. While this is the case, any speculation that the military will directly intervene in politics is farfetched.

Afrikaner politics have come a long way since the 1930s and 1940s, when the small National party movement struggled to make headway among a divided Afrikaner people, and the 1950s and 1960s, when political power consolidated the ethnic movement until the late 1970s, when cleavages again began to appear. The most important developments have been the rise of the party as the embodiment of ethnic interests and the growing power of the apartheid bureaucracy as the guardians of the apartheid framework. The class nature of the party has also changed. Based primarily on the farming and working class, the party became more oriented toward general business interests during the late 1960s. With manufacturing and commerce in 1975 contributing nearly half the national income and twice as much as farming and mining,[70] Afrikaner and English-speaking business are insisting on changes in the official policy to allow for higher productivity and faster economic development (see chapter 7). However, the party is not a party of the bourgeoisie but an ethnic party. It eschews reforms that will alienate classes within the group because it sees a united Afrikanerdom as a more effective bastion for survival than divided ranks. Unlike the English whose wealth is based on private capital, the Afrikaners' material position depends largely on control of the public sector, which employs 45 percent of the Afrikaners. The party will thus not harm their vested interests by policies that aim at the Africanization of the public sector at the expense of the present incumbents. Lastly, the party represents a minority group haunted by a history of humiliation, deprivation, and defeat and by the realization that once it loses power it will never regain it.

National Party rule has seen the ascendancy of the political

70. On the eve of World War II, agriculture (13.5%) and mining (21%) still contributed more to the national income than manufacturing (15.2%) and commerce (13.7%). In 1975 the contributions were: agriculture, 7.2%; mining, 15%; manufacturing, 22.1%; commerce, 23.8%; others, 40.2%.

executive defined as the broad administrative, legal, bureau-cratic, and coercive systems that structure relations within so-ciety. By and large the political executive has demanded that it rule in terms of party-political priorities and within the constraints of party unity. It has resisted demands from the business class to give primacy to other considerations. When ASSOCOM, representing English business interests, after the upheavals of 1976 called for the restructuring of the racial order the prime minister immediately warned the organiza-tion against any proposals for "a new socio-economic or-der."[71] Neither has the government complied with requests by the military to formulate clearly defensible political goals to assist it in an antirevolutionary war.

There are several reasons why the political executive has not moved more purposefully in terms of broader socio-economic and strategic considerations during the 1970s. First, there are the growth of bureaucratic empires and the increase of "departmentalism." No longer could one man clearly assert his authority; it became necessary to embark on the cumbersome process of establishing consensus and re-conciling divergent interests. Ministers committed to reform have opted for low-profile adaptations rather than boldly spelling out the need and principles of reform. Secondly, there is the power factor. While the hostility to apartheid externally and internally has slowed down economic growth and slightly weakened the South African military arm, the opposition at home and abroad has not yet seriously challenged the autonomy of the South African state. Before this happens the political leadership considers the dangers of faster reform as greater than those of a political split of Af-rikanerdom. In its view, a split may place at risk everything

71. See Stanley Greenberg, "The Political Economy of Change: Problems of Hegemony in Contemporary South Africa," unpublished paper, August 1978. Greenberg argues that it is only after businessmen have established their own hegemony and organized their political interests that they may follow the lead of black resistance and insist on changes in the state structure and prevailing ideology.

the ethnic movement has achieved. Similarly, the costs of the present political order are not yet so high that these two emerging power factors in the white state, the military and the businessmen, will consider a showdown with the political executive.

9   The Failure of Political Liberalism
Heribert Adam

That is why I hold in contempt those young White radicals who sneer at liberals and liberalism. Who were their mentors? If it had not been for the Jabavus, Marquards, Hoernles, they would have been in darkness until now. One cannot measure past labours in terms of present demands. One expects Black power to sneer at White liberals. After all White power has done it for generations. But if Black power meets White power in head-long confrontation, and there are no Black liberals and White liberals around, then God help South Africa. Liberalism is more than politics. It is humanity, tolerance and love of justice. South Africa has no future without them, least of all White South Africa.—Alan Paton, *On Turning* 70

THE CHANGING FACE OF LIBERALISM

White and black nationalists alike deeply resent South African liberals. Afrikaner militants view universalistic notions of civil rights and common franchise of all citizens as suicidal for white minority existence. Its few proponents are considered naive "promoters of communism" in the guise of majority rule. Contemporary African political activists dismiss as irrelevant the liberal insistence on nonviolent, evolutionary constitutional reforms of a system that, by definition, excludes the majority from meaningful political participation at their places of birth or permanent residence. Blacks no longer plead for admission into a white system by demonstrating their "civilized standards" at liberal tea parties, which have ceased to take place.

258

This chapter confines itself to a brief sketch of *political* liberalism without addressing itself in any detail to the complex problem of *economic* liberty as a precondition of liberal democracy. The political history of liberal and radical alternatives in South Africa sheds light on the political success of the antiliberal nationalist forces.

South African political liberalism has traditionally become associated with the idea of a single South Africa in which all its citizens regardless of race enjoy political rights based on universal suffrage. Legal equality of opportunities would be supplemented by social security systems for the weaker, noncompetitive citizens. A comprehensive program of education and social welfare would attempt to compensate for the effects of past discrimination. An independent judiciary and a bill of rights would protect individuals, not groups. The use of the law is recommended to outlaw racially discriminatory practices. Liberals attribute overriding importance to the rule of law; freedom from arbitrary arrest; due process; and free speech, assembly, and association.

Indeed, the classic liberal tenet of at least legal political equality and a promise of equality of opportunities under the protection of a universal bill of rights has never existed in South Africa. The little support there was for this creed among the white section has steadily declined since Union in 1910. Despite an initial nonracial franchise in the Cape, this provision soon became eroded under the pressure of the other provinces with a different tradition and different constellation of interest groups.[1] From the first challenge to the "natives'" constitutional rights to stand for Parliament in the Cape to the rise of franchise qualifications and the manipulation of voting procedures (abolition of plumping in 1883),

1. For a good overview of this period see Phyllis Lewsen, "The Cape Liberal Tradition—Myth or Reality?" in London Institute of Commonwealth Studies, *Collected Seminar Papers* 1, no. 10 (1970), 72–88. An analysis with a focus on the unique class relationships in the Cape Colony in conjunction with the need to restore stability and the British authority through enfranchisement is provided by Stanley Trapido, "Liberalism in the Cape in the 19th and 20th Centuries," in London Institute of Commonwealth Studies, *Collected Seminar Papers*, 4, no. 17 (1974), 53–66.

there was a continuing trend toward the removal of Africans and Coloureds from the common roll: Africans in 1936 and Coloureds in 1955. Finally, their symbolic four white liberal representatives were abolished in 1960 and 1968 respectively.[2]

The emergence of an interracial Liberal Party from 1953 to 1968 with a policy of universal franchise does not contradict this trend. In its heyday in the early 1960s, the party had approximately 5,000 members, half of whom were Africans. Nonetheless, the party of the "left" white but moderate black spectrum at the time had never won a seat in the all-white election or more than a fifth of the white votes in its most successful constituency. Though led by some of the most respected men of letters that South Africa has produced, there were divisions about the universal franchise policy in the liberal camp as well as the commitment to extraparliamentary activity after Sharpeville in 1960. With permanent persecution, harrassment, and exile of leading liberals, particularly after a few party members became involved in acts of sabotage, organized political liberalism in South Africa was long a marginal phenomenon before new legislation in 1968 made interracial political organizations illegal and led the Liberal Party to formally dissolve itself.

What continues as the liberal spirit in South Africa today represents either a diluted version of traditional liberalism or is sufficiently adjusted and patriotic to be tolerated by an ever more powerful Afrikaner nationalism. Pragmatic realism of leading liberals in the 1970s moved much closer to core policies of the Nationalists.[3] They in turn adopted some of the

2. At no point did the exotic liberal import from Britain into the Cape threaten the existing racial power structure. Nevertheless, the voting behavior of the Cape blacks served as a constant reminder to the Afrikaner nationalists of their political rejection as well as the potential force of a liberal English/African/Coloured alliance.

3. As early as 1971, Alan Paton found himself "hoping that all our people who are not white will make the fullest use of these instruments of power which are being put into their hands by the architects of separate development, no matter how feeble they may be." [Alan Paton, *Knocking on the Door* (Cape Town: David Philip, 1975), p. 231.] In the same speech to the alumni of Harvard where he had received an honorary doctorate, he declared that "I

liberal principles (abolition of social racism, greater economic freedom for the brown and Indian middle class) so that some of the pronouncements on both sides are no longer so far apart. Harry Oppenheimer, for example, not a traditional liberal in the narrow South African sense but the financial backbone of the "progressive" apartheid opposition, cannot conceive "a surer recipe for disaster" than one-man one-vote, but asserts that "power-sharing has to come."

While a few dedicated individuals continue their liberal stance, it would be fair to say that under the pressure of an overwhelming reality many former liberals have quietly jettisoned earlier idealistic principles in favor of the politics of survival. This change seems particularly evident in the universities. The English-speaking white students have, on the whole, tended to an apolitical, individual career orientation. Their organization, the National Union of South African Students (NUSAS) has frequently been overrated in its influence and radicalness by both government and its critics. NUSAS, under the constant pressure of harrassment by the authorities and rejection by apolitical or conservative students, has now confined itself more to service activities than to politics, especially since blacks split off to form their own Black Consciousness groups. Similar trends have developed among faculty with a high turnover through emigration since the early 1960s. The once outspoken liberal consensus of faculty and administration at the English campuses has faded into the annual ritual of freedom speeches, reconciling a privileged, segregated existence by celebrating morality. The genuine liberal faculty who care about the daily violation of basic freedoms through their public behavior are few and isolated now.

Other honored institutions that hold up the liberal spirit, such as the Institute of Race Relations, the Black Sash, and

stand not for the withdrawal of American investment but for its dramatic improvement on salaries and benefits." Paton also now urges the U.S. government not "to pressure our rulers to the point they become psychologically impotent to make any changes at all." (Quoted in *South African Outlook,* May, 1977).

some church groups have undergone similar predicaments. C. W. de Kiewiet, one of the more perspicacious observers of the liberal school, had recognized this tendency long ago with the remark: "When the intellectual leaders of a country become demoralised and perplexed or feel repudiated, they can become, despite themselves, even without knowing it themselves, converts to the heresies they have battled."[4]

In short, thirty years of Nationalist policy have created a segmented society—both as an objective as well as subjective reality—from which the perception of its foremost critics could not escape. The conservative implications of the remaining liberal recipe are apparent in the new core formula which holds that forced separation cannot be undone by forced integration, but only by allowing personal choice. Thus, Paton now declares in direct reversal of earlier Liberal Party policy: "Universal suffrage and a unitary state imposed from without is not—for me—compatible with the liberal ideal."[5] Given the safely predictable outcome of personal choices of white South Africans regarding the maintenance of their core privileges at the expense of the underprivileged, the consequences of this classic unequal freedom are apparent: an existing distribution of power and privilege will be protected by the choices of its beneficiaries; the choices of challengers have little institutionalized effective way to counteract them.

Without the political clout of a decisive franchise to decide competing interests over scarce resources only two outcomes are conceivable: (1) the status quo (save some surface modifications) remains on the basis of superior coercion and/or (2) ever more costly extraparliamentary escalation and

4. C. W. de Kiewiet, "Loneliness in the Beloved Country," *Foreign Affairs* (April 1964), 413–27.

5. Alan Paton, *Reality*, September, 1977. In a subsequent controversy a fellow liberal, John Aitchison, challenged Paton publicly to "admit that you no longer stand for what the Liberal Party stood for." Paton replied: "I no longer stand for majority rule in a unitary state in our present circumstances, but for majority rule in a federal state." See *Reality* (September 1978), 6–7.

confrontation ensue in the absence of accepted mechanisms for the institutionalized regulation of vital conflicts. The failure of political liberalism can be defined by the increasingly entrenched allocation of unequal life-chances according to inherited group membership rather than individual merit in the absence of institutionalized redress.

In this predicament of polarized camps, the liberal voice of reason is caught through no fault of its own. It would hardly do justice to these persons to blame them for the absence of radical reformist policies when such a stance would mean political suicide or mere assertion of purist principles with diminishing support. The key to an understanding of the hopeless minority position of South African liberals lies in a structural analysis of their specific limitations in South Africa.

INTERPRETATIONS OF FAILURE

The decisive question, namely, why did political liberalism fail in South Africa when at the same time it had been so successfully exported into other British settler colonies (North America, Australia, and New Zealand) needs to be more fully answered. Moreover, why has formal democracy, a proven regulator of class conflict, not emerged when powerful economic interest groups would obviously have benefited from a stable color-blind arrangement with unrestricted labor supplies and collaborating trade unions instead of overpaid white labour, an artificially restricted domestic market, and international isolation with the prospects of potentially costly future risks? If it was possible to transplant a liberal system of government from abroad into the nineteenth-century Cape colony, why could similar pressure not succeed 150 years later when the missionaries and philanthropes of London or the "friends of the natives" in South Africa have been joined by much more powerful color-blind profit interests? In short, how can the paradox be explained that the American Carter/Mondale administration is now advocating, at least rhetorically, a one-man one-vote system for South Africa with hardly a single prominent white South African supporting such a demand?

A closer analysis of the South African Liberal Party with all its human complexities of personal heroism, decency, fallacies, and shortsightedness may shed light on these questions. Without falling into the frequent trap of personalizing historical forces, eight explanations for the failure of South African liberalism will be explored. These eight, partly overlapping reasons can be weighted according to crude disciplinary labels that distinguish their focus of analysis. In order of rough explanatory value, starting with the least insightful reasons, these are (1) religious, (2) biological, (3) philosophical, (4) demographic, (5) political, (6) psychological, (7) economic, and (8) historical factors.

(1) The least adequate explanation for the resilience of apartheid against the liberal attack of rationality invokes religious barriers of a unique Calvinism. Chapter 2 pointed out that the Calvinist two-class distinction of the elect and the damned might have been used for justification, but it cannot explain the exclusion of the "children of Ham." Notions of the "chosen people" with a "challenge of destiny" that sanctified a collective mentality with a "religious utopianism" did not exist in English South Africa. And yet it evolved similar segregation practices. David Welsh concludes his thorough investigation into the colonial policy of early Natal with the statement that "it is a myth that apartheid is the exclusive product of Afrikaner nationalism."[6] Some contemporary observers on the other hand have pointed out that the broad liberal self-concept of English-speaking South Africa so far has not been tested: "Under the umbrella of Afrikaner control, the conservative colonial settler tradition can be preserved while at the same time the utopia of a future egalitarian South Africa of all races can be cherished and preached."[7] Given the

6. David Welsh, *The Roots of Segregation: Native Policy in Colonial Natal,* 1845–1919 (Cape Town: Oxford University Press, 1971), p. 322.

7. Theodor Hanf et al., *Südfrika: Friedlicher Wandel?* (Munich: Kaiser, 1978), p. 95. This survey is cited as the "Freiburg study."

history of Natal and Rhodesia, one does not need religious explanations to predict the sympathies of English South Africa in a crunch situation.

(2) Pierre van den Berghe has asserted that "there must be a biological basis to our 'gut reactions'" in order to explain the persistence and ferociousness with which communal strife is carried out everywhere beyond any rational cause.[8] Sociobiologists stress the evolutionary principle of "kin selection" as the basis for the ethnocentric preference for one's own kind. Real or invidious badges of group membership are considered to establish putative "blood" ties with the endurance of close kinship bonds. Against such sociobiological fibers liberal notions of fraternity, regardless of ethnic differences, would have, indeed, no chance. And so would the equally universalistic creeds of socialism with its emphasis on cross-cutting working-class solidarity or Christianity with its focus on the God-given fate of all creatures with a soul. Not only the history of South Africa but communal strife almost everywhere, from Northern Ireland to Lebanon and many Third World countries, would seem to confirm the biological pessimism.

And yet what seems more valid is the fact that the mutual resentment always needs to be activated and mobilized. Propagandists of ethnocentric communal organizations benefit from it, and their victims react to it with countermobilization. Without such indoctrination from outside, people do not rise in senseless hate of "others," save in defense of perceived legitimate rights. What accounts for the common appeal of the agitator is not a biological but a cultural factor. It lies in the common socialization experience of members of a distinct culture. In times of anxiety and conflict, this bond offers relief and security, against which the liberal or socialist brotherhood with the stranger on the other side remains a doubtful promise.

8. Pierre L. van den Berghe, "The Impossibility of a Liberal Solution in South Africa," in *Apartheid and Intellectuals: Essays in Honor of Leo Kuper*, ed., P. L. van den Berghe (forthcoming). See also his paper "Race and Ethnicity: A Sociobiological Look," manuscript, 1978.

(3) The success of communalism and nationalism reveals a philosophical bias of liberalism as expressed in its static and unproven assumption about human nature. Perhaps due to the positivistic tradition of its origin, liberalism views human nature as "given" and absolute. Dickie-Clark has perceptively described this built-in bias: "Thus the liberal has tended to assume that too much of the world out there is fixed, amenable to logic, fundamentally rational and open to persuasion. Moreover, that there are certain truths about people, e.g. that they love and strive after freedom under all circumstances, which are eternal and absolute."[9] Like their doctrinaire Marxist opponents, liberals incorporate little cultural relativism in their assumptions about human nature and fail to take into account that these definitions differ according to specific historical circumstances. To dismiss these divergent ideas about good and evil as false consciousness, changes nothing of their reality status, as the ethnomethodologists have rightly stressed.

In the final analysis, the liberal belief in the power of persuasion rests on the idealistic assumption that people will abandon their particularistic group interests in favor of a universal truth, morality, or humanity. However, there is little ground to hope for the success of the individualistic appeal when this group membership guarantees material benefits of power and privilege. This is particularly the case when ethnic chauvinism is reinforced by high degrees of anxiety about fictitious or, as in South Africa, real losses of security, esteem, and general life-chances, linked with ethnocentrism. In this case, ethnic exclusivism is rewarded with the psychological comforts of belonging, reinforced by strong conformity pressures and ostracism of dissenters. In sum, in the liberal belief system, conflicts are caused by prejudice, they exist only in the mind, not as antagonistic, incompatible forces.[10] All con-

9. Hamish Dickie-Clark, "On the Liberal Definition of the South African Situation," in *Apartheid and Intellectuals: Essays in Honor of Leo Kuper*, ed. P. L. van den Berghe (forthcoming).

10. See on this point in particular two instructive essays. Martin Legassick, "The Rise of Modern South African Liberalism: Its Assumptions and its

flicts appear reconcilable by proper reasoning and a universally shared common rationality, which implies the awareness of enlightened self-interest. Leo Kuper contrasts the state of polarization with "the possibility of understanding, of dialogue, of *adjustments of interests.*"[11] Progress means the gradual merging of mere particularisms into a common good, the market of humankind. But what if certain groups progress much faster because they do so at the expense of other sections and precisely because their strategy involves the rejection of the liberal notion of the free exercise of individual energy in the marketplace in favor of much more rewarding ethnic monopoly? For such a constellation, the liberal perspective is not equipped with an explanatory antenna, save the view of a deplorable aberration of mankind.

(4) Obvious demographic factors militate against the acceptance of the liberal principle in South Africa. Unlike in the United States, the dominant group is in fact correct in its tireless admonition that it would lose political power by granting equal rights to a numerically four-times stronger majority. This applies in particular to the Afrikaner subgroup with its relatively recent nationalism and development of a distinct language against the imminent danger of Anglicization. The realistic fear of "becoming a minority in South Africa as helpless as Jews were in Germany"—as one of their leading writers has put it[12]—allowed for the constant successful reinforcement of a corporate identity. The liberals recognized this decisive, immovable obstacle in their path but prescribed a generally unconvincing cure for what they considered a mere Afrikaner paranoia: Rather than surrender itself forcibly later, Afrikaner nationalism ought to bury itself voluntarily now. It is indeed naive to expect a ruling group for

Social Base," (unpublished paper); and Paul Rich, "Liberalism and Ethnicity in South African Politics, 1921–1948," *African Studies* 35, no. 3–4 (1976), 229–51.

11. Leo Kuper, *The Pity of It All: Polarization of Racial and Ethnic Relations* (London: Duckworth, 1977), p. 9.

12. N. P. van Wyk Louw, *Liberale Nasionalisme* (Cape Town: Nasionale Boekhandel, 1958).

moral reasons alone to embrace the liberal principle of self-abdication when it can continue to dominate, albeit as an outcast of a distant humanity.

(5) The moralistic approach, in a polarized contest of power with high stakes, points to the political reasons for the failure of liberalism. That the "Liberal Party of South Africa works for a 'change of heart', on both moral and practical grounds"[13] was indicative of its hardly having come to grips with the nature of politics. Nor had the liberals adequately understood their opposing nationalist foe, as the terminology reveals. The rise of Afrikanerdom is seen in terms of "a great historical drama" that could turn into a "tragedy." The fatal sinners fall because of character deficiencies: "Their own arrogance," which mystically traps them in darkness instead of allowing enlightened compromise.[14]

A leading African member of the Liberal Party, Jordan K. Ngubane, even explains the root of apartheid as an instinctive habit with a specific birthdate: "The present crisis in South Africa has its origins in the whites' desire to dominate the Africans. This sinister inclination has been predominant among the whites since the formation of the Union of South Africa in 1910."[15] Political persecutions are denounced as the actions of a "power-mad government in a state of utter panic,"[16] whereas the moves are clearly planned and weighted for their impact. In short, the partial rationality of a calculating government is underrated. The better-educated English upper-class liberals tended to apply their stereotyped caricature of the Afrikaner as inept, clumsy, fumbling idiots, particularly to the lower-class policemen. In the words of Donald Woods: So many members of the security police seem to be so underequipped to evaluate real subversion that a great deal of time is spent barking up the wrong trees.[17]

13. Alan Paton, *Hope for South Africa* (London: Pall Mall, 1958), p. 5.

14. Paton, *Reality,* September, 1977.

15. Jordan K. Ngubane, "The Road to and from Soweto." *Journal of Southern African Affairs,* 2, no. 2 (April 1977), 167–82.

16. Joel Mervis, *Star Weekly,* October 22, 1977.

17. Donald Woods, *New York Times,* January 8, 1978.

This culturally nurtured underestimation of the rulers' intelligence would seem one of the more important reasons for the failure of many attempts of resistance in South Africa, carried out frequently with innocuous amateurishness by radical liberals in the early 1960s.[18]

The smug disdain of some members of a world culture for the parochialism of an unenlightened adversary is frequently accompanied by an almost masochistic glorification of "creative suffering"; as if martyrdom would prove the truth of a conviction instead of the victory of the superior power. "I cannot even conceive that life could have meaning without suffering," writes Paton for an American magazine. Creative suffering "changed no laws, it softened no customs, but it made the country a better place to live in."[19] No wonder then that the effectiveness of political action generally ranks lower than the affirmation of principle. It would seem that the thorough Christian strain in South African liberalism above all accounts for this unpolitical approach to a political problem. At the same time it was this very moral conviction that equipped leading liberals with an initial staying power and individual courage against all odds that persons with mere pragmatic perspectives could hardly muster.

(6) One of the more important reasons for the failure of nonracial liberalism relates to the psychological obstacles of an interracial alliance in a racially ordered society. Though there have been frequent examples of impressive African/white resistance and common victimization,[20] at the end such unequal cooperation proved stifling for black militancy. White liberals failed to understand that for blacks a period of separation from their well-meaning common brotherhood

18. A revealing analysis by an activist of the failure of the ANC and PAC campaign of armed resistance with emphasis on the elitist nature of sabotage and the unpreparedness of the movement for superior police techniques is Ben Turok, "South Africa: The Search for a Strategy," *Socialist Register 1973* (London: Merlin, 1974).

19. Paton, *Knocking on the Door*, p. 212.

20. Janet Robertson, *Liberalism in South Africa* 1948–63 (London: Oxford University Press, 1971), pp. 161–83.

was essential for the emergence of an independent and self-confident black movement, just as it proved for the later civil rights struggles in the United States or for that matter, the feminist movement nowadays. Only by cutting the bonds from an overpowering mentor can subordinates reach the stage of genuine subjective equality that is a precondition for truly color-blind interaction. Such relationships cannot be decreed or imposed from above by self-appointed allies who do not share the structural inequities, despite all their attempts to identify with their underprivileged counterparts.

From the perspective of a black writer, Ezekiel Mphahlele, who returned to South Africa after two decades of exile, has perhaps best characterized the limitation of white liberal identification with blacks:

> The liberal white writers like Alan Paton and Nadine Gordimer, who are English-speaking, try to portray African life and character faithfully. But because there is a physical barrier between us, they still have to strain the literary imagination and rely for the most part on their compassion and perception. Somehow along the line African life and character eludes them and they take refuge behind symbolic portrayal. . . . The liberal white still cannot shake off the shackles of history by which he is kept prisoner in his own position of exclusive privilege.[21]

Of course there was always a psychological payoff for the white liberal, despite or because of his minority position in the white political culture. The pleasure of belonging to the elite was vicariously balanced by his support for the underdog. This thrilling experience enhanced his self-image almost like an adventurous tourist who has discovered an exotic new world: "For many members of the Party, inter-racial association has meant entering into a new country, exciting, dangerous and beautiful."[22] Being pampered and celebrated for cou-

21. Ezekiel Mphahlele, "South Africa: Two Communities and the Struggle for a Birthright," *Journal of African Studies*, 4, no. 4 (Spring 1977), 49.

22. Paton, *Hope for South Africa*, p. 62.

rageousness in supporting the underprivileged, whose elite extended their warm hospitality to the rare guest from the other side, the white liberal enjoyed the benefits of both worlds and could feel good about his unselfish openmindedness. By accepting such identification, subordinates merely perpetuate their psychologically crippled existence.

By going it alone, the colonized have entered a necessary phase of emancipation. It is they who now have defined the situation. Though the results may well be identical, the effects of the process are essentially different from an integrated struggle: The subordinates have acquired a new identity and shed the internalized inferiority perception. This would seem the crucial difference between the new generation of SASO students and the earlier black resistance in the Congress movement, which despite all its militant rhetoric was ideologically integrated into a liberal value system. The baffled NUSAS students have now learned this lesson from the Black Consciousness movement; but it is doubtful whether the liberal suspicions about "racist rejections" have been dispelled. It would seem the ultimate tragedy for white liberals that despite their genuine identification with the black cause and even common suffering, they are most likely to be marginal or even to be excluded from a victory celebration in Azania, if ever there was to be one in their lifetime.

(7) A class analysis of South African liberalism and the economic basis of its supporters can shed further light on its fate. Unlike their predecessors in Europe, South African liberals never enjoyed the unambiguous support of the mining and business sections in South Africa, who in the 1960s supported the more cautious and paternalistic policies of the official opposition parties instead. That relegated the "pure" liberals to "a party of the intelligentsia" with mainly employed or independent professionals as the decisive supporters and policymakers.[23] These teachers, clergymen, lawyers, journalists, and university lecturers could, so to speak, afford to be liberals, because they were the least threatened with economic losses or replacement by an African takeover, as many

23. van den Berghe, "The Impossibility of a Liberal Solution."

observers have remarked. Moreover, an important reference group for them was the world community of intellectuals with whom they interacted and whose suspicions they had to dispel with proof of their uncorrupted worthiness. This *Weltbürgertum* of nonparochial intellectuals, engaging in "reasoned interracial appeals"[24] and tempered discourse, was far removed from the labor problems of white farmers, the profit calculations of businessmen, or the racial sentiments of the bulk of the blue- and white-collar voters. Elitist philosophizing about human dignity on the other hand could hardly appeal to a white worker, farmer, or housewife whose own dignity was based on having a dependent servant to push around at will.

One shortcoming of South African liberals then would seem that they never transcended the abstract realm of humanity and individual charity to a concrete articulation of economic and political alternatives that would have attempted to reconcile the divergent black and white interests in a specific blueprint with broad appeal. Such efforts emerged only in the 1970s in the form of the SPROCAS Reports. But by then the racial polarization together with the decline and political realignment of the English apartheid opposition posed different problems for the survival of the relics of liberal principles in South Africa.

(8) The absence of political alternatives for divided societies, besides the Westminster model, reveals perhaps the most decisive historical reason for the failure of liberalism. Historical, in the sense that decisive preconditions for political liberalism were present in the culturally more homogeneous societies of Western Europe but absent in the plural colonial societies of which South Africa represents a prime example. As the most profound analyst of liberalism in South Africa had already pointed out in the 1930s, the classic representatives of liberalism, as a by-product of the evolution of modern capitalism, "were dealing with social groups the members of which were, substantially, homogeneous in race

24. Leo Kuper, *Race, Class and Power* (Chicago: Aldine, 1975), p. 274.

and culture . . . they assumed European models to be capable of export and transfer . . . even to European colonies in which Whites and non-Whites met and clashed and fought for survival and supremacy."[25] This assumption proved incorrect as Hoernle suspected, but his liberal colleagues never admitted it.

The fundamental difference between Western political democracy and political procedures in ethnically plural states is the understanding in the former that political power can change from one party to another according to election results. A defeat is accepted by the incumbent group because its basic rights and privileges are not affected by four years opposition before the next attempt at regaining power is due. This interchangeability of ruling groups presupposes in other words a relative equality in life-chances not fundamentally threatened by the opponent's ascendancy to power. Only because the power holder respects the rules of the game does the defeated party succumb temporarily.

In contrast, politics between hostile ethnic segments in so-called divided or plural societies usually acquire the status of indefinite dominance and permanent subjugation. This is the explicit policy and most important end of the incumbent ruler. The logic of the situation precludes rotation in office. The rulers unilaterally dictate how much they wish to accede to demands of the subordinates and only their bargaining power in conjunction with objective exigencies will influence this process.

This situation has developed not because of evil intentions, stubborn prejudices, or similar unique attitudes of ruling groups in power in ethnically heterogeneous societies but because of a set of structural factors not present in Western democracies. These are: The long history of domination together with the accumulation of wealth at the expense of the subordinate group have created a high degree of group cohesion on both sides, but particularly on the part of the superordinate group. Few cross-cutting allegiances exist that

25. R. F. Alfred Hoernle, *South African Native Policy and the Liberal Spirit* (Cape Town: University of Cape Town, 1939), pp. 135–36.

would transcend the ethnic boundaries according to common interests. In a hypothetical election based on a common voters' roll, the numerically strongest ethnic group would, therefore, most likely come out on top. Given the massive privileges that a minority ruling group enjoys, together with the fear of revenge, displacement, and the loss of security generally, the minority clings to power with all its might. This accurate mutual perception in turn reinforces the group cohesion of each antagonist and makes a Western system of political decision-making at the most an intragroup affair but hardly a mechanism for the regulation of intergroup relations. At the heart of the predicament lies the gross inequality of the competing groups which has to be rectified first before majority rule based on the Westminster model of shifting party allegiance is likely to function. And yet, paradoxically, this very model of majority rule is seen as the only just and effective way to achieve the goal of greater equality of life-chances for all citizens.

COMPETING RADICAL STRATEGIES

Thus far the liberal forces have been evaluated in comparison with the Afrikaner appeals on the political right. The assessment of political liberalism, however, would be incomplete without at least a brief reference to the strategies of the left. Since black politics is not the topic of this study, it may be justifiable to subsume black underground resistance since the mid-1960s under this label for the sake of brevity. Up to Luthuli, and including Buthelezi with his powerful Inkatha movement nowadays, black protest stands decisively in the liberal tradition of evolutionary improvements of an existing economic structure. Measured on the basis of the growing support for Inkatha, black liberalism remains astonishingly strong in light of its history of failure. This is confirmed by opinion surveys. In the 1977 sample of 1,020 urban Africans of the Freiburg study, 65 percent still expect improvements "through patient negotiations between white and black leaders" and an equally high number favors private (African) ownership of production over state control. Such "liberal" attitudes, however, are increasingly rejected by the polticized urban youth.

Among the apartheid opponents left of the liberal critics, a variety of long established radical positions exist, which outline a transformation of South Africa into an alternative socioeconomic system. These perspectives of different tinges of socialism disagree sharply with each other about revolutionary strategies as well as short-term goals. Such bitter recrimination among the left continues a long tradition of infighting and power struggles but in the South African case also flows from an astonishing discrepancy in the assessment of an apartheid reality, not just allegiance to different ideological mentors.

Four distinct radical perceptions of change in South Africa can be discerned according to priorities of strategies and delineation of villains among other apartheid opponents. These four positions may be labeled (1) black power, (2) ANC/SACP, (3) "Marxist-Leninist," and (4) Trotskyite. Their differences are not confined to ideological quibbles about purity and compromise in solidarity against a common enemy but sometimes lead to such serious charges as criminal behavior, adventurism, and betrayal. A brief description can attempt to unravel the main contentious issues in the world of committed revolutionaries. Neither detailed evaluation of the realism of the described perspectives nor an analysis of their origins can be given here.[26]

26. Apart from the many writings by the main actors themselves, the most comprehensive collection on black politics is the four volumes *From Protest to Challenge: A Documentary History of African Politics in South Africa 1882—1964,* ed. Thomas G. Karis and Gwendolen M. Carter (Stanford, Calif.: Hoover Institution Press, 1972, 1973, and 1977). In the same vein the informative evaluations of African Nationalism by other authors such as Leo Kuper, Peter Walshe, Mary Benson, and Fatima Meer all deal with the pre-Black Consciousness phase only. The publicity surrounding the assassination of Biko has sparked a number of books (among them a volume by Donald Woods) that, however, represent more reportage than critical analyses. Prior to the Soweto uprisings of 1976 a South African political scientist, D. A. Kotze,

The black power position, as elaborated in SASO and Black Consciousness publications, stresses, above all, the racial humiliation of blacks, including Coloureds, and Indians as members of collectively discriminated groups. In this respect the Black Consciousness spokesmen differ from earlier PAC tactics that were aimed at the inclusion of Africans only. Contrary to assertions that ANC or PAC had organized the township upheavals of 1976–77, Soweto students maintain that the demonstrations originated from a new political awareness among South Africa's youth. This youth rebellion differed from earlier protests and from the industrial action of 1973. In Soweto, the urban proletariat was mobilized successfully in two brief solidarity strikes, but this time it did not push stay-at-home actions because of economic grievances. On the contrary, the economic recession and high unemployment seem to have hampered strike willingness later and facilitated friction between migrants and permanent city dwellers. Policy cleavages deepened between urban students and rural Africans partly as a result of exploitation by the authorities. Inkatha ensured that Natal did not follow the national pattern of uprising despite the earlier strike militancy in Durban.

The ANC/Communist perspective vacillates in its approach

published a study, *African Politics in South Africa 1964—1974* (London: C. Hurst, 1975), for which Gatsha Buthelezi wrote a reluctant and critical foreword. Gail M. Gerhart, *Black Power in South Africa. The Evolution of an Ideology* (Berkeley: University of California Press, 1978), is a first cautious attempt at a balanced assessment of Black Consciousness in light of historical predecessors of similar ideological resistance. But only two out of her nine chapters deal with the 1970s. In the tradition of much of the earlier writing on the topic, Gerhart too describes more well-known events and focuses on policy pronouncements rather than on analyzing the reality behind the rhetoric.

Despite numerous publications by the various banned organizations, including an official history of the South African Communist Party (A. Lerumo, pseud. of M. Harmel, *Fifty Fighting Years*, London: Inkululeko Publ., 1971), there is at present no systematic treatment of South African politics in exile. A perceptive article by John Marcum in *Southern Africa in Perspective*, eds., Christian P. Potholm and Richard Dale (New York: Free Press, 1972), pp. 262–75, and a partisan, PAC-oriented study by Richard Gibson, *African Liberation Movements* (London: Oxford University Press, 1972) are the only exceptions.

to Buthelezi and the African rural bourgeoisie because it defines the South African conflict as a special kind of colonialism.[27] In this internal colonialism, national liberation is said to be the goal of the first stage, a socialist revolution to be followed only after bourgeois democracy is established. The emerging black bourgeoisie, or for that matter all "progressive forces" regardless of race, is seen as an ally in this struggle, because of existing racial restrictions on its advancement. In contrast to the mass solidarity demonstrations of the students, the ANC/SACP leadership now favors tight underground organization and outside training in preparation for guerrilla war and the elimination of collaborators. Alfred Nzo, Secretary-General of the ANC, states laconically: "A number of enemy agents and spies have been eliminated. Some of those eliminated are former members of our revolutionary movement."[28] How such escalation directly threatens unaffiliated liberals who abhor violence has been demonstrated by the unresolved assassination of Rick Turner, a gentle political scientist in Durban, who was in his fifth year of banning in January 1978.[29] A short while after Stephen Mtshali, a former ANC member, working with the security police, had been wounded by unidentified gunmen, Turner was fatally shot at his home. While the police denied any links between the two incidents in the same town, most liberals were convinced that the killing of Turner constituted

27. For a Communist Party assessment of Inkatha see Ngacambaza Khumalo, "The Compromising Role of Inkatha," *The African Communist*, no. 74 (1978), 94–99. The author's main fear is that the alliance would be "offering to take part in an internal settlement as an alternative to the liberation movement."

28. Alfred Nzo, "The Spirit of Lisbon," *Sechaba*, 12, 3rd q. (1978), 31–38. The secret elimination without trial of dissidents was one of the contentious issues in the 1976 split between the official (London based) ANC under Oliver Tambo and a so-called African nationalist faction that was dissatisfied with the Moscow-oriented leadership. The orthodox line refers to its opponents summarily as "A polyglot assemblage of Trotskyists, ultra-left splinter sects, dissident and expelled ex-Communists and ex-ANC men," *The African Communist*, no. 72 (1978), 19.

29. Elegies to Turner appeared in *Reality*, March 1978 and *South African Outlook*, June 1978.

one of the many "right-wing" attacks on public antiapartheid activists. Although an escalation of unofficial revenge against prominent opposition leaders has not reached Argentinian proportions in South Africa, uncontrolled vigilante activity remains a constant possibility that is feared for different reasons by the potential victims as well as the more sophisticated government planners.

It is difficult to discern how far the fear for personal safety has dampened political activity. As far as rank and file blacks are concerned, the repeated reports about systematic torture and thinly disguised suicides in police custody may well have inhibited risk taking. The sudden explosion of bottled up anger in unpredicted uprisings also reflects successful previous intimidation. In these instances, the isolation of atomized individuals has been overcome by identity granting organization. The social structure of a riot can lend extreme courage to the formerly fearful through immersion in an emotive powerful cause. Success of the rebellion appears then as a likely outcome, dependent only on subjective determination.

Such periodic experiences of spontaneous commitment have given rise to a long and agonizing debate among South African radicals and liberals about the need for patient organization versus the strategy of instigating mass uprisings at the right moment.

The latter course has been traditionally favored by the Pan Africanists who now identify themselves with the "Marxist-Leninist" label. This perspective places more emphasis on the revolutionary potential of the peasant sector and the Bantustan contradictions within the system. While the Black Consciousness Movement (BCM) insisted on organizational autonomy against the parental claims of both ANC and PAC, the latter's rejection of white sympathizers makes for greater ideological affinity to the Soweto-students. According to the "Marxist-Leninist" journal *Ikwezi:* "Taking Poqo a step further, the BCM strategy was to seize control of large African townships and Bantustans, from where a generalized assault on South African colonialism would be launched."[30]

30. *Ikwezi*, no. 8, (March 1978), 1.

Above all, the Moscow-Peking rivalry shapes the inter-
necine quarrels. For the adherents of "Marxist-Leninist-Mao
Tse Tung Thought," the "Soviet Union is the more aggressive
of the two superpowers in Africa today and wishes to recol-
onize Africa in the name of Socialism."[31] The most venomous
attacks are therefore directed against the so-called petty-
bourgeois, multiracialism of the ANC/SACP leadership. This
group is portrayed as pulling the strings in "direct service of
their masters, the social imperialists."[32] Since the ANC represents the more widely recognized movement, the constant
tenor of the PAC publications concentrates on "The bankruptcy of the ANC-CP and the cowardice of its leadership,
which, from the carpeted seclusion and comfort of offices in
London and elsewhere, have been sending romanticists on
suicide missions."[33] A former SASO president and subsequent PAC representative in New Zealand accuses the
ANC/SACP of deliberately "sacrificing patriots for the propaganda value of show political trials," since they "have converted our liberation struggle into a finance industry."[34] Vorster is said to be "quite prepared to assist the ANC/SACP" by
crediting the organization "with all the organized Black resistance in Azania" since the ANC "pose little if any threat to his
regime."[35]

It is impossible to reach an independent assessment of the
conflicting claims about revolutionary underground activity
in South Africa. Those arrested come from both organizations. But it is generally believed that "the PAC has been less
active than the ANC."[36] The Soweto events, however, have
given the exile movements for the first time a mass influx of
new recruits. According to South African sources: "About
75% of the 4,000 in training camps had been recruited by the

31. Ibid., no. 9 (June 1978), 21.
32. Ibid., no. 9 (June 1978), 55.
33. Ibid., no. 4 (December 1976).
34. Henry Isaacs, "ANC-SACP and the Politics of Fraud and Sterility,"
Ikwezi, no. 9 (June 1978), 7–13.
35. Ibid.
36. *Africa Confidential*, 19, no. 24 (December 1, 1978), 2.

ANC."[37] It can also be safely assumed that all exile organizations are heavily infiltrated by police informers. In this respect, the unorganized spontaneity of the Soweto students allowed them an undetected scope that the traditional methods of underground activity have still to overcome. With the possible exception of Bantustan institutions, there exists at present no organizational shelter, neither churches nor schools, in which opposition could foment for long without interference by the authorities.

Rather than on the battlefield of township streets or in Bantustans the fate of South Africa may well be determined in the factories of an integrated economy in which blacks have assumed an increasingly decisive role both as producers and consumers. A future accumulation of coordinated bargaining and strike threats under the direction of better organized unions, or substitutes, such as Inkatha, could achieve substantial economic improvements. In this respect, the Trotskyite line is a bit closer to the mark than peasant warfare.

The Trotskyite position advocates translation of "the hatred of apartheid shown during the black youth rebellion of 1976 into the struggle for power within the factories.[38] It loathes the so-called petty-bourgeois leadership of national liberation movements, such as ANC. Neither does it expect the fragmented peasantry with a limited vision to lead the revolution. Trotskyites dispute the Communist definition that South Africa does not yet represent a fully developed capitalist economy, as evidenced in the suppression of unions and the racist control of the labor force. They accuse Communists of neglect of working-class organization, whose interests should not be subordinated to an all-class, patriotic, common fight against a colonial power. Otherwise the revolution would easily be sold out to a reactionary black bourgeoisie, whose emergence

37. South African Security Police Chief C. F. Zietsman in *Rand Daily Mail*, June 3, 1978.

38. The most explicit recent elaboration of this position is found in Alex Callinicos and John Rogers, *Southern Africa after Soweto* (London: Pluto Press, 1977), p. 212.

the South African government is said to favor now. The Trotskyite analysis detects such a neocolonial sellout to imperialism among the front-line states, particularly in the persons of Kaunda and Nyerere but also in Angola and Mozambique, due to the economic integration of nationally perceived economies into the South African center. The answer, therefore, is seen in an international working-class struggle against capitalism rather than in the vain hope of national liberation. In this vein it is postulated "that the ultimate survival and success of a revolution in South Africa will depend on revolutions in the advanced capitalist countries."[39] A classical prescription as to how such a collapse of Western capitalism will come about is also provided: "It seems highly possible that growing numbers of workers, hard hit by unemployment, may realise the necessity of cementing an alliance with the independence movements of third world countries in general and Africa in particular to achieve the necessary structural changes to advance their own welfare."[40]

The outlined strategies may seem to the empirically inclined observer as unreal a flight of fantasy as the liberal belief in the power of reasoning. And yet in the absence of a discredited middle-ground, the allegiance to alternatives that may be radically different from both liberal as well as traditional Marxist solutions could grow rapidly indeed.

For all committed socialists it is basically irrelevant whether South Africa is ruled by Afrikaner Nationalists or liberal capitalists. Both represent but two faces of the same monster. In fact, any piecemeal reform, it is said, would cheat the subordinates out of their well-earned total victory. In the words of Immanuel Wallerstein: "Liberal interventionism stands forward today as the most dangerous enemy of African liberation movements in South Africa."[41] The advocates

39. Ibid.
40. Ann Seidman, "Southern African Contradictions: Part I," *Contemporary Crisis*, 1, no. 3 (July, 1977), 336.
41. Immanuel Wallerstein, "South Africa and Liberal Interventionism," *The Nation* (November 12, 1977), 489–92.

of further polarization always assume that the oppressed would inevitably win an escalation. Realists, on the other hand, point to many historical reversals of the Hegelian telos into much worse forms of misery, from outright fascism to the Gulag Archipelago. They welcome any improvement in the life of apartheid victims, even if it is undertaken for the wrong motives. Indeed, who can predict the unintended consequences of carefully planned designs?

FUNCTIONS OF LIBERALS

The functions of the liberal voice, regardless of its influence, remains to be assessed. Nationalists tolerate it because the liberal minority is no threat and has no power to initiate any change. In their powerlessness the liberal dissenters, albeit unintentionally, fulfill useful functions for the Nationalist design. They demonstrate the "civilized standards" of white democracy compared with totalitarian repression in many societies of South Africa's critics. Even more so, the liberals illustrate grievances and point to potential friction points in the system before they become explosive. Their visible deviance from official policy makes them a useful rallying point for internal nationalist cohesion. The existence of liberal outsiders allows the regimentation of internal dissenters by delineating boundaries of the permissible for the insider. To attack and scapegoat an out-group contributes to the solidarity of the Nationalist group.

From the interracial perspective, the presence of liberals has undoubtedly blunted black militancy and delayed the polarization and confrontation between two exclusive nationalisms. Alan Paton makes this point by emphasizing the decisive role of the liberal bridge-builders: "If Black power meets White power, and there are no Black liberals and White liberals around, then God help South Africa."[42] Until very recently liberals have succeeded in instilling hope among black activists that there is a chance of change from within,

42. Paton, *Knocking on the Door*, p. 258.

that what Leo Kuper calls the "policies of reconciliation"[43] might work after all and that the channels of peaceful reform are not yet exhausted. It is for this pacifying effect that the apostles of confrontation politics hate the liberals in between more than their outright opposite adversary.

Few liberals have illusions about their precarious role in the quicksand between extremes. Many have left the country, which amounts to effective withdrawal from South African politics, although few exiles would admit that they are cut off from the vital touch with the local scene. Those who have stayed and continued with reformist politics in the Progressive Party, the press, and some other English institutions have succeeded many times in ameliorating harsh measures and curbing excesses. Without the presence of a Helen Suzman and now her party colleagues, the government would not be held publicly accountable for many specific deeds.[44] In this respect, the white parliament might not be as irrelevant for the total South African scene as is often suggested. Such considerations apply even more to the liberal press with a sizeable black readership. By providing relatively uncensored information or articulating alternative visions of justice, the liberals keep a critical discourse alive. Who could say with certainty that the silence of the cemetery would be more advantageous to black liberation? Who could advocate that the liberals concern for better black education, the provision of shelter for evicted squatters, the legal aid for the politically prosecuted, or the advice centers for the victims of the passport laws and numerous other activities of morally motivated individuals working within the system should be abandoned? Their activities might indeed be palliatives that make the overall system more tolerable. And yet in the end the accumulation of such small-scale reforms at the microlevel may well account for more change than the advocates of an instant

43. Kuper, *Pity of it all*, p. 9.

44. A recent biography of Helen Suzman [Joanna Strangwayes-Booth, *Cricket in a Thorn Tree. Helen Suzman and the Progressive Party of South Africa.* (Bloomington: Indiana University Press, 1978)] bills her as "one of the bravest political figures in South Africa." As long as the Security Police can control

revolution will ever admit. In this respect, liberals have not failed.

The notion of "the failure of political liberalism" may suggest that there was an option of overall success not being realized due to the shortsightedness of politicians or sheer historical accidents. The slight Nationalist victory in 1948 (5 seats) is frequently cited, and speculations about a different course of South African history revolve around the liberal successor of Smuts in the person of Hofmeyr, had he lived longer. Indeed, Hofmeyr could have extended the Coloured franchise to women and redrawn the electoral boundaries (reverse gerrymandering) so as to preclude a Nationalist victory at the polls. Such speculations, however, remain academic, not to mention that the entrenched racism of the United Party majority would have severely constrained Hofmeyr's liberalism.

South Africa's turning point must be dated much earlier than 1948. The "parting of the ways," in Leonard Thompson's suggestive phrase, started in the nineteenth century with British policy in Natal, later confirmed in the South Africa Act of 1909, granting "responsible government" to the South African colonies. The provision that members of Parliament had to be of European descent and the acceptance of the constitutional color-bars of the Transvaal and the Orange Free State in the Union constitution, doomed the nonracial franchise of the Cape. The safeguards of a two-thirds majority of both houses for its removal, were finally circumvented in the 1950s. However, as has been argued in this analysis, constitutional liberalism failed for much deeper structural reasons in South Africa. The ethnic mobilization of backward and defeated people as a political class against both the colo-

---

its lunatic fringe, it probably needs much less bravery for a national figure, such as Suzman, to deliver well-tempered disdain to Nationalists benches than for an ordinary African worker to join a walkout or an African student at a tribal university to question his Afrikaner instructor. Nevertheless, Helen Suzman served as the lone ombudsman for African grievances in the absence of other legitimate channels.

nial capital and the African competitors in the labor market proved to be stronger in the specific circumstances than the liberal notions of color-blind individual advancement in the capitalistic market place. Whether in such an illiberal tradition liberal notions of federalism or consociationalism have any chance of institutionalized conflict resolution in the future polarization or whether radical geopolitical partition and mindless violent escalation will eventually constitute the "solution" in South Africa remains to be seen.

10   Political Alternatives
Heribert Adam

There is no turning back for South Africa on the road it has taken. As many as possible of the Black areas within our geographical entity will have to exercise the option of co-existence on an ethnic basis, for this is the only guarantee of peace in a plural society.

A recipe along those lines also opens the possibility of negotiations round a table in which South Africa with its White, Coloured and Indian components and the residue of urban Blacks (included through a future network of regional councils); the homelands, independent and non-independent; plus other neighbouring countries which are or will be part of the Southern African common market, could take decisions of overriding importance on a future constitutional association.—Beeld, November 17, 1977

*Constitutional developments in Southern Africa are going to be a by-product of bullets and power—*Gatsha Buthelezi

Among the more far-sighted politicians and intellectuals, solutions to conflict regulation in divided societies are now discussed in the framework of consociational democracy. This, they argue, could be a more feasible model, compared with unitary systems, partition, or a confederal solution. However, crucial preconditions for consociationalism do not exist in South Africa.

According to Arend Lijphart the consociational model consists of (1) a grand coalition of the political leaders of all population groups, (2) mutual veto power, (3) proportionality,

286

particularly in the allocation of resources and civil service appointments, based on (4) a high degree of internal autonomy for each segment.[1] In theory, there seems nothing objectionable to the principle of *communal* representation as compared to *individual* participation in the political process, independent of communal or ethnic affiliations. Such a normative judgement is based on the empirical evidence of likely worse alternatives. Indeed, as Lijphart writes: "And since in a plural society true brotherhood is not a realistic short-term objective, democratic peaceful co-existence is a perfectly honourable goal in itself: It is vastly preferable both to non-democratic peace and to strife-torn democracy."[2] There is no reason to assume that the liberal Westminster model of the winner taking it all should be considered the only just, let alone effective, democratic mode of conflict settlement under all historical circumstances. The slavish export of the British model into the former colonies has (perhaps with the exception of India) proved highly unsuitable for democratic nation-building, because the formula disregarded the deep persistence of communal loyalties. It is also conceivable that a mutually agreed upon partition may sometimes be preferable to a strife-torn undemocratic national unity.

However, quite unlike all other plural European or Third World societies, the present South Africa distinguishes itself by the presence of three related decisive obstacles to consociationalism. These are: (1) imposed group membership instead of voluntary association, (2) enforced restriction of segmental leadership, (3) unequal distribution of power and resources among competing groups.[3]

1. Arend Lijphart, *Democracy in Plural Societies. A Comparative Exploration* (New Haven: Yale University Press, 1977).

2. Arend Lijphart, "Majority Rule versus Democracy in Deeply Divided Societies," *Politikon*, 4, no. 2 (Decmber 1977), 123.

3. For an incisive analysis that emphasizes different and additional obstacles to consociationalism in South Africa see Lawrence Schlemmer, *Social Preconditions For, and Consequences of, the Adoption of Alternative Constitutions in South Africa*, manuscript 1978. Schlemmer rightly warns of approaching mere constitutional change as a sufficient basis for solving South Africa's problems.

(1) In all plural or divided societies, with the sole exception of South Africa, members of subgroups voluntarily identify with their ethnic unit. It is indeed their *self*-concept. They do so primarily in order to lay claims for an equal share at the power center, or alternatively for secession from an existing domination if they feel they cannot find redress for their grievances within the existing political structure (as in Quebec and Biafra). This ethnic identification is facilitated by historical disadvantages of culturally different subgroups that desire to seek redress for past inequities. In other instances, the subgroups resist state expansion into their domain. If, for example, one language in a multilingual state becomes the official and dominant medium of business and government, those raised in any other language find themselves decisively disadvantaged in the competition for jobs and status. Such was the situation of Afrikanerdom at the beginning of the century before it mobilized linguistically, economically, and politically to capture exclusive state power in South Africa.

In order to preserve this political monopoly, despite their being a numerical minority, the successful ethnics in South Africa disenfranchised black political competitors at the national level. They restricted the opportunities of mobilization and competition for the excluded majority. In order to cement this power, the dominant minority now wishes to institutionalize its own fragmentation of challengers in the name of preserving group identities as the "most important dimension of human rights."[4] However, these "cultural identities, life-styles and basic social institutions of historically established groups" as far as blacks are concerned exist in South Africa mainly by definition of the ruling group. For example, there are no enthusiastic Coloureds in the self-perceptions of those classified as Coloureds, were it not for the imposed labeling as such by those in power. The putative separate life-styles that they supposedly wish to maintain are those of poverty and anomie, resulting from exclusion. The

4. Nic Rhoodie, "Instead of Crude Apartheid," *Daily Telegraph*, September 1, 1977.

unique cultural identities that they do desire to preserve are (or at least, were, prior to Black Consciousness) identical with those of white Afrikanerdom from which the ruling group excludes them. Now brown people do indeed constitute a "historically differentiated community"[5] but only as an out-come of racial discrimination. Why then should it amount to a "normalisation of inter-group relations"[6] to provide separate parliaments for what is an artificial invidious category of as-sociation in the eyes of its members in the first place? South Africa displays the revealing paradox that the more its govern-ment asserts voluntary ethnic identification as the basis of its policy, the more it has to enforce the divisions by legislation.

Similar questions apply to the blueprints for African home-lands as far as the urban blacks are concerned. The Xhosa (or Tswana) speaking inhabitants of Soweto have, so far, not been given a choice as to whether they wished to become Transkeian citizens or remain South Africans. Had they been given the choice, the concept of *self*-determination would have been credible. If the definition of the groups to be ac-commodated does not correspond to their self-concept of identity, then no well-intended constitutional design based on such imposed definitions can satisfy "social, economic and political aspirations".[7] The assertion may be ventured that ethnicity will always be considered a form of racialism by those affected, as long as it is imposed and does not corre-spond with the self-concept of ethnic group members. Iden-tity is a subjective concept and genuine identity is bound to the individual's free choice. This presupposes that ultimately no restrictions on boundary crossing exist apart from indi-

5. Ibid.
6. Ibid.

7. It has been empirically proved again and again that the great majority of urban Africans with Section 10 rights do not wish to be associated with homelands. The 5 percent participation in respective elections in Soweto underlines this fact. The high turnout at urban rallies of a homeland leader, such as Buthelezi, is no disproof. On the contrary, the overwhelming popu-larity of Buthelezi, whom 44 percent of a sample of urban Africans in the Hanf study named as their preferred leader, results to a large extent from his very rejection of homeland independence.

vidual intent. Only when the segments are allowed to define themselves through individual voluntary group affiliation can the liberal notion of individual political rights be reconciled with the consociational concept of participation through communal units.

(2) The outstanding characteristic of a consociational democracy is the grand coalition of elites. This elite cartel presupposes representative leaders who "retain the support and loyalty of their followers."[8] In South Africa this precondition clearly exists for the Afrikaners. There is also still widespread respect for the traditional positions of the leadership in Zulu society and some other rural areas. However, the support that Coloured, Indian, or urban black leaders receive is not due to communal attachments. They are "leaders" because they articulate grievances. As mouthpieces of interest groups, they merely represent spokesmen in the literal sense. However, they can hardly guarantee loyal, unquestioned support if they would enter into a controversial elite cartel. This could only be achieved by group representatives with wide legitimacy. The only way to establish such legitimacy in nontraditional societies is through an open test in free elections. This means democratic competition of all leaders who claim a following. However, such black intrasegmental democracy is absent, as evidenced in the restriction of politicians who advocate alternative policies. In this situation, existing "leaders" face the permanent danger of illegitimacy. They are considered stooges and collaborators. In order to avoid being outradicalized, those officially tolerated elites have two choices: (1) to acquiesce in the restriction of their intragroup competitors and rationalize their own role, or (2) to move themselves continually in the direction of the radical demands. Both versions necessarily undermine essential preconditions of elite cooperation, namely legitimacy in the first and moderation in the second instance.

So far, the government has not even allowed a representa-

8. Lijphart, *Democracy*, p. 53. See on this crucial point also Eric Nordlinger, *Conflict Regulation in Divided Societies* (Cambridge, Mass.: Harvard University, 1972), chap. 5.

tive and authentic urban African leadership to emerge, let alone has it initiated accommodation. Proposals by the opposition that future negotiations would undoubtedly have to include political prisoners or exiles, if elected, have struck no official response. Informal consultations between leading Nationalists and formerly imprisoned Soweto leaders, such as Motlana, have taken place, but without a mandate. However, the more farsighted section of Afrikaner Nationalists has come to realize that continued suppression of urban African political dissent proves counterproductive. As *Beeld* has put it:

Since the Government envisages the wider objective of finding political solutions for our problems, it is unwise constantly to go on cutting off the leadership cadres among the urban blacks as soon as they say things which sound dangerous to whites. The black middle class is with us in the urban areas and its voice will become more and more audible. There must be room in the system for that voice to be heard, otherwise the pressures will build up so strongly that precautionary safety devices will no longer suffice to prevent a pressure burst.[9]

Such pragmatic tolerance bases its hope on the capacity of an as yet weak African middle class to act as a buffer. The history of black politics, however, raises doubts about this assumption. Rather than pacifying militancy, relatively privileged professionals have led the black resistance in ways similar to how Afrikaner intellectuals fanned cultural mobilization.[10] Under conditions of ethnic exclusion, the subordinate middle class too is included among the victims of

9. *Beeld*, October 25, 1978.
10. According to Gerhart, among the 28 top rank leaders (National Executives) of the ANC and PAC between 1957–60, all but 5 came from the "professional elite" and "other middle class," none from the working class. The five exceptions are listed as three university students and two trade unionists. See Gail M. Gerhart, *Black Power in South Africa* (Berkeley: University of California Press, 1978), p. 319.

institutionalized inequality. This applies particularly to the realm of status-humiliation, as many scholars of race relations have described with the concept of "status inconsistency." Mere economic amelioration, even equal salaries for black and white academics as now instituted in South Africa, does not necessarily guarantee compromising attitudes if other discrimination persists. For one, the compromising stance exists under the permanent challenge to justify its position against appealing utopian demands. Already the banned movements, afraid to be left out of an internal elite cartel, discredit "sell-outs" with notions to "seize power." "We are not aiming at compelling the Nationalists to negotiate with us," declares the ANC journal *Sechaba*. [11] Its equivalent, *The African Communist*, reiterates a common theme of desired polarization: "Those who propose compromise when the strength and resolve of the people are growing must be swept aside." [12] The easy dismissal of such rhetoric, however, would be justified only if the "moderates" could show tangible benefits, which percolate through to their constituency. Again, these would have to extend but cannot be restricted to the psychological realm. It is one of the widespread misconceptions among English progressives and Afrikaner pragmatists alike that under conditions of racial exlusion (1) a subordinate elite can be bought off, (2) that co-optation can be confined to the elite, and (3) that this can be achieved without much change in the traditional symbolic interaction. Abolishing exclusion in terms of statutory laws will hardly pacify militancy without also abolishing racial exclusiveness. In short: only a genuine attitudinal deracialization—in addition to legal equality—can realistically expect African acceptance.

What would this entail concretely for those who now preach that "the Afrikaner must stop trying to protect his identity in a way which hurts non-Afrikaners"? [13] In the view of the subordinated, mobilized Afrikaner identity remains offen-

11. *Sechaba*, 12: 3rd q. (1978), 59.
12. *The African Communist*, no. 74 (1978), 94–99.
13. *Die Transvaler*, August 23, 1978.

sive because it is associated with their own conquest and exclusion. However, it is never Afrikaner culture as such that is objectionable. Therefore, the task would be to extricate the oppressive features of Afrikaner mobilization from its earlier antiimperial and humanistic content. Because both aspects were historically so closely intertwined, such purification presents a predicament. However, if the Afrikaner claim of truly African roots is to be taken seriously, Afrikaner identity ought to be expected to come to terms with its history more easily than can temporary European colonizers.

Such conscious Afrikaner reorientation toward Africanization could begin, for example, with the school curriculum. Along the same lines as the reeducation program in post-war Germany, a glorified group history would be rewritten in order to enlighten the new *volk* about its real identity. This would imply a reinterpretation of the mobilized advance through the restriction and exclusion of the majority. Such ideological confrontation may even harden the racial obsession in sections for whom putative racial purity has indeed become "the ultimate taboo."[14] Since Afrikaner hegemony, as has been argued in this study, does not primarily result from a "racial neurosis,"[15] a demystification of Afrikaner identity, an internationalization of Afrikaner culture, would not encounter insurmountable emotional obstacles. Already many Afrikaner students speak African languages. Unlike most colonial traditions, Afrikaner culture is characterized by an absence of cultural imperialism, the initial insistence on Afrikaans-medium instruction in Soweto's schools notwithstanding.

The consociational grand coalition presupposes such mutual understanding. Basic trust of rival groups would have to replace collective antagonism. And even in the ultimate Afrikaner vision of a partitioned state, in which Afrikaners exercise just sovereignty as a majority, they would still need

14. Ian Robertson and Phillip Whitten, eds., *Race and Politics in South Africa* (New Brunswick, N.J.: Transaction Books, 1978) p. xii.

15. Ibid.

the goodwill and cooperation of other ethnics. Only in such an atmosphere of changed perceptions could the prognosis of Munger come true: "The Afrikaner need not dominate to survive and thus need not fight to the last man for what he now possesses."[16]

This discussion has stressed that restitution in the symbolic realm, while never sufficient on its own, may nevertheless be almost as decisive as real equality in achieving the goal of reconciled coexistence. However, the consociational model is based on a depoliticized public. As Lijphart writes: "Both in Africa and elsewhere in the Third World segmental isolation entails a strengthening of the political inertness of the non-elite public and of their deferential attitudes to the segmental leaders."[17] In South Africa, the very opposite trend can be noted. The processes of rapid urbanization and geographical mobility in an industrial economy have not only abolished mutual group isolation but weakened deferential attitudes toward political elites. The urbanized blacks comprise an atomized and increasingly politicized mass of independently acting individuals. Since these trends cannot be reversed, they can either be (1) repressed or (2) channeled into legitimate institutions of intergroup bargaining.

Coercive stability and enforced immobility in a modern economy cannot prevent further political earthquakes. In fact, the very prohibition of representative institutional channels for airing grievances compounds the devastating impact of unregulated tremors. However, the mere airing of misery and despair—the government concept of consultation, or the workers council or liaison committees at the industrial level—remain token palliatives without two essential preconditions: (1) the subordinate spokesmen must be perceived as truly representative, (2) they must have the constitutional power and factual weaponry (such as legal strikes) to effectively bargain for their demands.

16. Edwin S. Munger, "Prognosis: The United States of South Africa," in *Race and Politics in South Africa*, p. 265.

17. Lijphart, *Democracy*, p. 169.

(3) The gross imbalance of power must be considered the third decisive obstacle for consociationalism in South Africa. The historical inequality between the segments has never been rectified by effective group bargaining. South Africa "suffers from the kind of illegitimacy characteristic of systems in which ethnic and class divisions completely or nearly coincide."[18] A redistribution of wealth, education, and other resources from white to black would have to precede a workable consociationalism. Although gradual progress in this respect has been made, it is too slow and erratic. A good example is the irrelevant debate about the pace of so-called homeland consolidation according to the 1936 formula. The issue is no longer whether a few farms should be bought out and added to a scattered Kwa Zulu, but whether the establishment of a future multiracial Natal can accommodate wider black claims.[19]

The discussion about consociationalism in South Africa does not address itself to the central problem of redistributive mechanisms. This applies particularly to the constitutional proposals, incorporating Coloured and Indian representatives into the white system. In fact, it can be shown that the constitutional engineering, which is mainly concerned with minority rights, prevents precisely a majority from attaining its proportional share.

As is well known, the official constitutional proposals of the Nationalist Party so far explicitly exclude black Africans from political representation in the reorganized legislative process. They allocate to the Nationalist Party, by virtue of its majority among whites, an in-built numerical dominance

18. Ibid., p. 173.

19. Examples of the debate are: John A. Benyon (ed.), *Constitutional Change in South Africa* (Pietermaritzburg: University of Natal Press, 1978). Similar papers given at the Forty-Eighth Annual Council Meeting of the South African Institute of Race Relations, January 1978, Cape Town, particularly the contributions by Nic Rhoodie, M. I. Hirsch, Robert Schrire, and Gibson Thula. Selected papers of a similar conference appear in Nic Rhoodie, ed., *Intergroup Accommodation in Plural Societies* (London: Macmillan, 1979). A detailed speculation about future alternatives is Wolfgang H. Thomas, *Plural Democracy: Political Change and Strategies for Evolution in South Africa* (Johannesburg: SAIRR, 1978).

over the other group delegates. A potential successful alliance between the liberal-progressive elements among the whites and the so-called Coloured and Indian representatives could never emerge, since the majority Nationalists alone represent the white camp. The blueprint makes the Coloured and Indians accomplices in depriving Africans of their citizenship rights. It installs the middle groups as custodians for upholding their own ethnic separation by administering their underdeveloped group areas. Little wonder that most Coloured and Indian spokesmen, including conservative politicians, have rejected the plan.

However, the proposals for the first time publicly recognize the political equality of formerly excluded out-groups. To be sure, this does not indicate an attitude change but, above all, more sophisticated co-optation tactics. Nevertheless, the rhetorical acceptance of power-sharing with the Coloured and Indian minorities breaks with the rigid past apartheid doctrine and may have unintended ideological repercussions in the future. For example, the question frequently heard is, why are there no separate parliaments for Afrikaner and English-speaking whites if the system claims to be based on ethnic pluralism instead of racialism.

In the new terms of a more sophisticated rhetoric, the traditional system of white domination is now described as: "co-operative self-determination for the white, Coloured and Indian national communities in their common homeland; and, for the urban blacks, local autonomy and an improved quality of life, as members of self-determining nations centered in their separate homeland-states."[20] All official South African proposals rest on the suggested principle of "consensual decision-making."[21] The seeming advantage that no group can overrule the other mystifies the disadvan-

20. SABC, *Current Affairs*, September 15, 1977.

21. See the official constitutional proposals as well as the "Swiss model" outlined by P. G. J. Koornhof in a speech in 1977: "I believe that South Africa is moving in the direction of developing through consensual political negotiation a system not unlike that of Switzerland, which will have built-in guarantees."

tage for those who desire change. The system obviously favors the status quo since one group can forestall change at its expense that runs counter to what the others presumably want foremost. The ensuing paralysis works in the interest of existing conditions that remain under the legalized control of the segment most benefiting from this state of affairs. The entrenched minority veto, in other than cultural and educational matters, amounts to a conservative device rather than a liberal protection from majority dominance. In political reality, the blockage of the legislative process will increase further the power of the executive, in which the forces of the status quo dominate.

A dynamic notion of democracy that stresses the aspect of permanent group bargaining contrasts with such a static concept of self-determination. In this perspective, there are no permanent solutions to an ongoing conflict. There can only be different expressions of conflicting interests, dependent on the strength of those forces that determine their relationship. Any participation in political decision-making by formerly excluded groups becomes meaningful only if it allows for actual or at least potential impacts on the existing distributive mechanisms of a state apparatus. Meaningful democratic participation aims at influencing the stakes in scarce resources according to institutionalized trials of strength. Where interest groups are cheated out of such negotiated power relations, genuine democracy does not exist. The South African blueprints of impoverished independent Bantustans or even future black city states merely freeze constitutionally an utterly unequal distribution of commonly produced wealth. They cement an existing class relationship without giving the poorer section a legal way to lay claims for restitution from the richer parts, accumulated largely from black labor. So long as constitutional designs do not address themselves to this fundamental problem of agreed upon mechanisms for redistribution, they remain futile exercises. Only a freely negotiated (not imposed) formula between representative leaders of all interest groups could truly substitute the game of unilateral constitutional engineering. The few buyers among those whom the blueprints were supposed to pacify are mostly discredited. Their support only helps to deceive the manipulators that their paternalistic schemes would work out. The awakening in the face of a different reality is likely to be the costlier, the longer the charade of a pseudo-democratic solution is upheld.

Similar considerations apply to the fashionable game of devising new maps for partition of the country. The grand apartheid policy amounts to one form of partition whose success, however, is no longer trusted as ever more new "radical" designs indicate. Historical precedents of geopolitical partition in other parts of the world all occurred in basically agricultural societies. Alternatively, partition was imposed along the frozen battlelines of exhaustive wars. Political partition in an interdependent industrial economy runs counter to the economic necessities of larger markets, free trade, and unrestricted mobility of a free labor force. If the authorities in one area succeed in monopolizing the political control over its richer resources by depriving groups from poorer territories of their share in the commonly produced heritage, a subsequent economic confederation of sovereign units will hardly rectify the newly cemented inequities. It only creates new dependencies. The boundaries that mainly regulate the social costs of labor (education, health, old age care) become themselves controversial and meaningless as long as one area has to rely on the other for the exchange of labor and other resources.

This false separation of political and economic issues also characterizes much of the more realistic and pragmatic Afrikaner thinking. In this vein an influential Afrikaner academic with close ties to the Nationalist hierarchy put the predicament of the white oligarchy:

> Of one thing I am very sure and that is that the National Party power establishment regard a simple one-man one-vote majoritarian system in a unitarian state system as the inner non-negotiable core of their "case." Therefore, the Whites will be compelled to introduce federalist and/or con-

federalist devices in order to create a pluralist accommodation—that is, as long as they retain sufficient power
to initiate major structural changes in South Africa's sociopolitical system. Should the Westminster system be extended to all South Africans, simple political arithmetic
tells me that only one outcome is possible: the substitution
of Zulu hegemony for Afrikaner hegemony. After all, the
Afrikaners exploited one-man one-vote to grab power; I
have not seen any proof that the Zulus would be greater
gentlemen and be more magnanimous than the Afrikaners.
This all boils down to what I call the critical dimension of
the South African problem namely the White-Black power
struggle. This is the primary problem, White-Coloured and
White-Indian relations constitute a secondary problem.
From this analysis I infer that the first logical step towards
conflict resolution would be to demarcate the geo-political
(territorial) spheres of hegemony of the White dominated
South Africa and the Black dominated South Africa respectively. This demarcation delimits *political* jurisdiction and
not basic universalistic human rights pertaining to employment, movement across boundaries, equal access to public
facilities, etc. (Personal correspondence, March 12, 1978)

A division of political hegemony, however, even in the
hypothetical case that it was still possible on a mutually
agreed upon formula, does not solve the problem of an inextricably intertwined economy. Racially separate political
jurisdiction will inevitably be superceded by continuous conflict over labor and productive resources. Effective political
control rests on access to the crucial economic sources of
power that render artificial boundaries meaningless.

In such a situation of historical unevenness between rich
metropolitan areas and impoverished hinterlands—largely
coinciding with ethnic cleavages—a negotiated federalism
may indeed be the most feasible constitutional formula to
reduce conflict and alleviate anxieties among minorities.
Widely decentralized autonomous decision-making in a federal state, however, would have to be paralleled by a built-in

just and proportional exchange of revenue at the central level. The *"Länderausgleich"* in the Federal Republic of Germany or the considerable payments by the richer provinces in Canada to Quebec and the poorer Maritime areas could be an example for a workable formula. In South Africa, such a radical equalization arrangement would seem particularly important since the federal units would likely have a high degree of ethnic homogeneity, coinciding with gross inequalities. Suffice to say that federalism, in whatever number of new autonomous units, will only be credible if the new administrative entities are not unilaterally set up to perpetuate central Afrikaner power in a new guise (gerrymandering). More important, they would have to avoid any reference to race or ethnicity as their constituent rationale. Linguistic and ethnic settlement patterns as well as historical, geographic, and economic conditions would of course have to be taken into account in devising the precise boundaries and optimal size of the entities. A crucial provision would not allow for any mobility restrictions between the units. This would abolish the present influx control. Together with affirmative action in an expanding economy in a country with substantial natural resources, beauty, and human talent, there is no reason why all of South Africa's people could not benefit from such a gradual change of policy. The present collision course will allow hardly any other choice. Prolonged mutual misery for both rulers and ruled is the alternative.

This study has attempted to show how an ethnic oligarchy, as presently mobilized, hardly anticipates the rising costs to its rule but instead mostly reacts to pressure only. The benefits of a slightly modified apartheid scheme still far outweigh its costs for the dominant group at present. However, the dynamics of the conflict permanently change this ratio one way or the other. The internal dynamics of pressure still appear to be the decisive factor. But they also develop in conjunction with outside events over which Afrikanerdom has no control. Rapid developments on the international scene have not been the major focus of this study. It is readily apparent, however, that they have a direct bearing on South Africa. Foremost among those changes would be a closer alignment of key African states with communist bloc countries, including calls for military assistance against white-controlled Southern Africa. Together with the rise of Nigeria and other Third World nations as important trading partners for Western countries, the traditional silent alliance between white South Africa and the West may indeed crack under the threat of increased Soviet involvement and African belligerence for its own reasons. John Marcum has aptly described this U.S. predicament: "And if it [the United States] does not join in international sanctions to induce peaceful change, the political, military and economic realignment of a very large part of the African continent will take place despite and against the United States. Africa's front-line states are forcing the pace of a major test of American will and purpose."[22]

Foreign threats are said to impress the need for unity and solidarity on elites in divided societies.[23] This is the case as long as the outside threats are directed against the society as a whole and not a specific segment. In the case of South Africa, however, the outside interference does exacerbate the domestic cleavages. Foreign threats are rightly perceived as a danger by the ruling minority, but are construed as beneficial by the majority of subordinates.

Although there are few signs of fissure among Afrikanerdom at present, the latent cleavages lend themselves to various possibilities of splits. Contrary to conventional wisdom, increased pressure does not necessarily mean a threatened group will close ranks in intransigent defiance. Because various sections are affected differently by the costs and benefits of pressures, they respond accordingly. Thus far the talks about boycotts and sanctions against South Africa's oligarchy have remained abstract and general. However, this situation could rapidly change with escalating regional instability and

22. John Marcum, "African Front-Line States: Forcing the Pace," *The Nation*, November 12, 1977, pp. 492–95.

23. Lijphart, *Democracy*, p. 67.

emerging alternatives to Western hegemony. In this case, serious diplomatic initiatives, similar to the involvement of five Western nations in the negotiations about Namibia, can be expected. If such moves were precisely geared to the domestic South African interest constellation, the alleged stubborn defiance of all Afrikaners would be severely tested. Particularly if a compromising attitude would hold out the realistic prospect of carrots as well as credible sticks, further erosion of a divided oligarchy, rather than a Massada mentality, can be expected. In the short run, it will be at this juncture of Afrikaner fissure that South Africa's alternative future will be decided. South Africa can change without destroying itself when the past ethnic mobilization of Afrikanerdom has finally faded into pragmatic survival calculations of its heterogeneous constituencies. It is only then that the ethnic mobilization of Afrikanerdom has matured and reached fruition by demobilizing itself in a new, nonracial and just South Africa.

Index

Union; South African Student Organization
Suzman, Helen, 283

Tambo, Oliver, 277n
Theron commission, 225–26, 246
Thompson, Leonard, 284
Thula, Gibson, 295n
Tomlinson commission, 245
Transkei, 10
Treurnicht, Andries, 74
Trust Bank, 169, 188
Trotskyite strategy, 280–81
Turner, Rick, 277–78

Unions: white, 49, 109, 158; garment workers, 159; loss of power of, 181–82; suppression of African, 183. *See also* Labor
United Party, 104, 161
United States: policy toward South Africa, 59–60, 133, 263–64, 301–02
Urban Foundation, 227–28; code of employment, 57n

Van den Bergh, Hendrik, 28, 73, 75, 77
Verligte-verkrampte differences, 217–18
Verwoerd, H. F., 42, 67, 118, 124, 155, 201–02, 215, 222, 241, 245–46
Viljoen, Gerrit, 120, 137, 139, 234, 243
Vorster, B. J., 27, 211, 215, 252; visit to Israel by, 141; decision-making style of, 202

Wassenaar, Andries, 169, 188
Western policy: in the event of escalation, 9, 57–60; South African views of, 137, 139, 140, 301. *See also* Imperialism; United States
Wiechers, Marinus, 212, 222
Wiehahn commission, 182, 183

Zimbabwe, 15, 51
Zulu: consolidation of Kwa, 295; projected behavior of, 299

About the Authors

Heribert Adam, born on July 1, 1936, in Offenbach, West Germany, has been a professor of sociology at Simon Fraser University in Vancouver, British Columbia, since 1968. He was educated at the Frankfurt School where he worked at the Institute of Social Research from 1961 to 1965. Subsequently he held visiting appointments at other universities in Germany, Egypt, and the United States. Adam's interest in South Africa dates back to a six-month research visit in 1966, followed by a year's teaching at the University of Natal in Durban, the home of his wife.

Previous books include: (in German) *South Africa: Sociology of a Race Society* (Frankfurt: Suhrkamp, 1969; 4th edition, 1977); *Modernizing Racial Domination* (Berkeley: University of California Press, 1971); and, as editor, *South Africa: Sociological Perspectives* (London: Oxford University Press, 1971).

Hermann Giliomee, born on April 4, 1938, in Sterkstroom, South Africa, grew up in the small Afrikaans town of Porterville in the Western Cape. He studied at the University of Stellenbosch where he presently teaches South African history. In 1973 and 1977/78 he worked as a research fellow at Yale University with Leonard Thompson.

Giliomee is the author of a study of the British occupation of the Cape Colony, *Die Kaap tydens die Eerste Britse Bewind* (Cape Town, 1974) and co-editor of *"The Shaping of South African Society, 1652–1820* (Cape Town, 1979). Together with André du Toit, he is working on a study of Afrikaner political thought since 1778.